Raise Your Soul

ALSO BY YANIS VAROUFAKIS

Technofeudalism: What Killed Capitalism
Another Now: Dispatches from an Alternative Present
Talking to My Daughter: A Brief History of Capitalism
Adults in the Room: My Battle with Europe's Deep Establishment
And the Weak Suffer What They Must?: Europe, Austerity and the Threat to Global Stability
The Global Minotaur: America, Europe and the Future of the Global Economy

Raise Your Soul

A Personal History of Resistance

YANIS VAROUFAKIS

THE BODLEY HEAD
LONDON

1 3 5 7 9 10 8 6 4 2

The Bodley Head, an imprint of Vintage, is part of the
Penguin Random House group of companies

Vintage, Penguin Random House UK, One Embassy Gardens,
8 Viaduct Gardens, London SW11 7BW

penguin.co.uk/vintage
global.penguinrandomhouse.com

First published by The Bodley Head in 2025

Copyright © Yanis Varoufakis 2025

The moral right of the author has been asserted

Photographs courtesy of the author and Danaë Stratou

Penguin Random House values and supports copyright. Copyright fuels creativity, encourages diverse voices, promotes freedom of expression and supports a vibrant culture. Thank you for purchasing an authorised edition of this book and for respecting intellectual property laws by not reproducing, scanning or distributing any part of it by any means without permission. You are supporting authors and enabling Penguin Random House to continue to publish books for everyone. No part of this book may be used or reproduced in any manner for the purpose of training artificial intelligence technologies or systems. In accordance with Article 4(3) of the DSM Directive 2019/790, Penguin Random House expressly reserves this work from the text and data mining exception.

Typeset in 11.7/16pt Calluna by Six Red Marbles UK, Thetford, Norfolk
Printed and bound in Great Britain by Clays Ltd, Elcograf S.p.A.

The authorised representative in the EEA is Penguin Random House Ireland,
Morrison Chambers, 32 Nassau Street, Dublin D02 YH68

A CIP catalogue record for this book is available from the British Library

HB ISBN 9781847929068
TPB ISBN 9781847929075

Penguin Random House is committed to a sustainable future
for our business, our readers and our planet. This book is made
from Forest Stewardship Council® certified paper.

For the fearless women who turn whispers into soul-raising roars

Contents

Prologue   1

Eleni

1. Hotel Pefkakia — 7
2. Roof with a view — 10
3. Dawn of ghosts — 13
4. Like an owl before an earthquake — 18
5. A healing fever — 21
6. Sultanas, partisans and traitors — 27
7. Bad chemistry — 32
8. Hypatia — 36

Anna

9. Praying to the moon — 41
10. One day we shall not have to hide, sister — 48
11. Strategic debt — 53
12. Bitterly cold comfort — 56
13. A friend is born — 58
14. Hiatus — 62
15. Through a porthole darkly — 67
16. At daggers drawn — 72
17. In war's shadow — 76

18	Athens calling	82
19	For a mere signature	92
20	The final plea	98
21	Double exile	103
22	And the ship sailed on	108
23	We have much to do	113

Trisevgeni

24	Run with it	119
25	What if the bastard exists?	121
26	To keep you in lipstick	124
27	You might as well summon *Sputnik* back from space!	128
28	Sacred snakes	133
29	TWA Flight 800	137
30	Anna's wake	141
31	Fireplace marvels, interrupted	144
32	Get out of my home, mongrels!	147
33	Murder in Los Angeles, slow train to Munich	152
34	Like vermin in a zoo	155
35	My own special Miss Havisham	158
36	Riveting darkness, nauseating light	163
37	You two, pack a bag and run	168
38	Off to Blighty	174
39	The blacks of Europe	179
40	Fiona	183
41	To Serbice!	188
42	To Australia	192

Georgia

43	To the serpent's lair	197
44	The white angel	201
45	A red flag is raised, another lowered	206
46	Red widow	210
47	One of seven	214
48	Double jeopardy	218
49	Demonic women	223
50	Endless requiem	228
51	From Kyparissia to Kabul	236

Danaë

52	Into the wind	241
53	Define her in one word	244
54	Stepping out	247
55	The fence, the mirror, the river	249
56	In the fences' long shadow	254
57	*The Globalising Wall*	258
58	Art as politics by other means	262
59	Eleni's verdict	265
60	Midnight missive	268
61	In the eye of the storm	271
62	Holding on	275
63	The incomplete purge	279
64	Hypatia's daughters	282
	Epilogue	285

Prologue

The year 2024 was marked by an unrelenting personal slump. The darkness didn't just loom – it *consumed*. It stretched endlessly across my horizon, not a gentle twilight that comes with the setting sun, but a deeper, more insidious gloom that seeped into the very fabric of existence.

Fascism was in the air – a sour, metallic taste that clung to the back of my throat. Somewhere to the north of our island home, the killing fields of Ukraine devoured lives with a ruthless, mechanical precision. Woman, Life, Freedom, the campaign by Kurdish heroines, had been trampled by the manosphere's unyielding juggernaut, lost, as though the three little words had never been whispered at all. And from Palestine, the acrid stench of genocide drifted on the wind across the eastern Mediterranean, which grimly confirmed to me the fragility of humanity's most solemn promises to itself.

Authoritarianism was entrenching itself as the new world order. My political struggles against it had met with three consecutive electoral defeats in the space of one year, making me feel like a doomed character in some twisted simulation.

And then came the violence, the thugs who broke my face in front of my wife and friends. It was the anguish in their eyes that haunted me, their expressions of pained helplessness that cut far deeper than the ringleader's iron fist ever could.

For the first time, I felt my age, the gravity of my sixty-plus years a remorseless force that weighed me down like a stone, cold, heavy and inevitable. I was in injury time now and, all around, the world seemed to shudder, the grapes of wrath swelling, heavy and black, ready for yet another cruel harvest.

It was then that I turned to the five women who had shaped me, whose incredible stories I carried like a secret flame. I would write them down, I decided, not to escape the darkness but to confront it, to let their strength, their love, lift me as my mother used to. She had always known how to find the light even in the deepest dark. And so, I would save their stories from oblivion, not for glory or for gain, but for the simple, stubborn hope of rising again.

It proved one of my better decisions. Recording their lives opened a portal to something far greater: it revealed the origins of our current predicament, and it linked Europe and America to north Africa and the Near East. Every word I wrote raised my soul a little.

This book belongs to the tradition of fictionalised history, an earnest attempt to bridge the gaps between the available facts and what I remember, while keeping at bay the urge to colonise the past with my myths. In writing it, I had an advantage: unlike historians studying distant subjects, I was deeply involved in the lives of the protagonists. Besides my vivid memories of them, I was also aided by the sources that had been lying around the house I was born and raised in: letters, diaries, photo albums, one of them dating to 1920s Egypt, as well as thirty-seven 8mm home movies made by my father, which I keep in an orange box by my desk.

Throughout, every time I put words into someone's mouth, it is because I've been told it is something they said, or because it is something they could plausibly have said, judging by conversations I witnessed over the years. And whenever there is dialogue, I have tried to capture the essence of the person I knew – their voice, their spirit.

PROLOGUE

Two younger women appear fleetingly in these pages – my sister and my daughter – yet it is for them too that I wrote this book, hoping that they will see themselves in its marrow, that they too will recognise their heritage. It is also my solemn hope that in immersing yourself in the worlds of Eleni, Anna, Trisevgeni, Georgia and Danaë, you too, dear reader, might rediscover your resolve to resist authoritarianism, fascism and chauvinism, and feel your soul growing lighter, even if just a little.

Yanis Varoufakis, April 2025

PART ONE
Eleni

1. Hotel Pefkakia

Eleni's lips stiffened as the taxi set us down at the entrance of the boutique hotel in Drosia, a leafy northern suburb of Athens. Before we got out, she put her arm around me and whispered, 'Raise your soul, my son,' into my ear. The shuttered windows and lifeless facade were the first signal that something was amiss. The second was the two fierce men standing on the pavement, adorned in military police uniforms emblazoned with the logo of ESA, our version of the Gestapo.

It was early September 1969. Hotel Pefkakia had been commandeered by ESA and converted into a temporary holding gaol for the regime's most embarrassing political prisoners. One of them was Panayis – Eleni's older brother, my favourite uncle, whom we had come to visit. Heavily pregnant with my sister, Eleni struggled out of the taxi and swayed unsteadily towards the entrance. I still treasure the memory of her leaning on me for support.

Sat down in front of what used to be the quaint reception, we waited, dread and expectation drawn on Eleni's face. Before long, a rigid man in a dusty brown suit arrived with a gang of uniformed henchmen in tow. As he passed us, he stopped and expressionlessly peered down, first at me, then at Eleni. Furious that she would not make eye contact, he grabbed her jaw violently, forcing her gaze, and slapped her across the face yelling: 'When I look at you, you look at me. Got it, whore?' Satisfied, he turned towards me, grinned widely and, with the same hand, patted my head saying, 'That's a good boy,' before receding into the hotel's interior. Eleni looked at me. 'Remember what I said?' she said, squeezing my left hand. 'Keep your soul up high, let it soar above the filth.'

I cannot remember how long we waited before we were eventually ushered by one of the guards into the room in which Panayis was being held. Even though it was morning, the closed shutters kept the room dark, concealing his state after weeks of relentless interrogation and torture. Long before my eyes had adjusted to make out his features, I heard his distinctive voice, and felt his gentle embrace. He showered me with questions about school, jokes about Eleni and lashes of almost grotesque exuberance which, nonetheless, made me giggle. Eleni looked on while her brother and her son pretended to be somewhere else.

Panayis then said: 'I've got something for you, to make amends for being such a terrible godfather.' He reached under his bed and pulled out a model aeroplane, which, thanks to his considerable engineering skills, he had fashioned out of matchsticks, cigarette paper and carton. As Eleni and Panayis chatted in muted voices, I sat on the bed, mesmerised by the plane which, courtesy of the countless war movies I had watched, I recognised instantly. It was a Stuka, a Junkers Ju 87 to be precise, with black iron crosses and swastikas that Panayis had somehow painted on its wings and tail, eerily resembling the infamous Luftwaffe dive bomber that had terrorised populations across Europe and north Africa.

When the guard terminated our brief reunion, Panayis hugged us and made sure I did not leave my gift behind. 'A Nazi plane? Really?' Eleni asked disapprovingly. 'Of course, *this* they may let him keep – as good Nazis, they ought to appreciate it,' he replied, smiling mischievously. He was not wrong. Once we were out in the corridor, a passing petty officer spotted my Stuka and smirked with approval. At the reception, where Eleni was frisked before collecting her identity card, a couple of ESA nasties spotted my plane. 'What's this?' the taller of the two asked in a menacing voice feigning intrigue. 'He made you a Stuka, did he now? Let me see. Does it fly?' Before I could protest, he snatched it from me and launched it violently against the wall. It was his way of provoking Eleni, seeking a confrontation. But Eleni did not bite. She quietly picked up the broken Stuka from the carpeted floor, took my hand and, looking straight ahead, led me to the fresh air outside.

We walked for what felt like ages, never looking back, until Eleni hailed a taxi. Despite its crash, my Stuka was in relatively good nick. Nothing a little glue couldn't fix. I could not wait to show my dad, Yorgo, my new toy at home.

It all looked promising, at first. Yorgo welcomed us at the front door with a generous smile and the three of us strolled into the kitchen. Eleni took my Stuka and gave it to Yorgo, who placed it on the kitchen table, without either of them exchanging a word, leading me to believe that they had telepathically communicated with one another about how to fix it. But to my horror, instead of mending it, they cut its fuselage in half, and carefully retrieved a tiny piece of paper, on which Panayis had written a message to his comrades on how to coordinate their testimonies during their forthcoming court martial.

My model plane was a ruse. Nevertheless, once lovingly repaired, it remained a prized possession, until sometime in the late 1990s when its fragile materials succumbed to the sands of time. To this day, when I think of my little Stuka, my heart fills with unalloyed delight.

2. Roof with a view

Eleni liberated my childhood from any sense of shame by keeping me in the know. With a simple, proud and steady narrative that a young boy could grasp, I was never left in any doubt that we were in history's good books. The idea that, as a nine-year-old, I had smuggled out a message from a prisoner to his accomplices was intoxicating. Months later, once my sister was born, I would do so again, this time knowingly. I smuggled a message into the notorious Averof prison complex, on Alexandras Avenue, where Panayis had been transferred after the court martial convicted him for 'sedition and acts of armed subversion'.

While Eleni ensured that I regarded prison sentences as a badge of honour, she did not hesitate to expose her loved one's darker side. Several years later, in 1979, catching a glimpse of the Stuka in our summer house, she sighed with her characteristic honesty: 'It was not just a ploy to get it out. Love at first sight came first.' Puzzled, I asked her to elaborate.

She began in 1941, on the sixth day of that cruel April. The sun had hardly risen over Mount Hymettus when fourteen-year-old Panayis woke Eleni up and breathlessly dragged her up the narrow spiral metal staircase to their house's rooftop. As she ascended, she was overwhelmed by the roar of engines. Never having seen or heard an aeroplane before, Eleni was terrified by the rumble of two waves of low-flying Luftwaffe bombers, eleven of them emanating from the outskirts of Vienna and twenty from Catania, heading for Piraeus, Athens' ancient port city.

Holding back tears, she was appalled by Panayis' delight. Jumping up and down, he was waving frantically at the planes overhead, cheering them on – not even pausing when the bombs started dropping and the sound reached their ears. Later that evening, gathered around the wireless, they listened to the news of Greece's Pearl Harbor. The British merchant ship *Clan Fraser* and another six Allied vessels, which had brought munitions and troops to Piraeus in anticipation of the Nazi invasion of Greece, had been sunk. A good number of Greek navy and merchant ships were lost too. Hundreds had been killed or maimed. But that was not the worst news. As the Luftwaffe was destroying Piraeus, Hitler's troops had invaded Greece from Yugoslavia, in coordination with Bulgarian troops that were descending towards the Aegean coast through Thrace.

Eleni was not coy about it. When the two of them were alone again, she confronted her brother. 'How dare you cheer them on?' she demanded. Panayis did not defer to his twelve-year-old sister. He defended his earlier enthusiasm with a thesis about Greece's chronic backwardness, its need to industrialise-or-perish, Germany's magnificent engineering feats and, lastly, how only by being occupied by a superior industrial power would our country be forced to join advanced, civilised Europe. Eleni, though two years younger, looked the brother she adored up and down, screwed up her face and called him a 'disgusting cad'.

A fortnight later, on Easter Sunday, the Battle of Athens unfolded over Attica's blue skies, pitting the ageing Royal Air Force Hurricanes against almost two hundred of the Luftwaffe's Stukas and Messerschmitts. Eleni and Panayis watched from their rooftop as nine British and more than twenty German planes fell out of the sky, with only a handful of pilots managing to bail out in time. 'This time he did not cheer but, from the corner of my eye, I could see him smiling when a Stuka would hit a British plane. Now you know why I hate this,' she said, pointing to the model Stuka from Hotel Pefkakia.

Eleni recounted that at the time of the battle, 'Tsolakoglou had already begun his long act of treachery,' naming the Greek general who, without authorisation from the government, had ordered our troops to surrender to the Wehrmacht. A few days later, he would become Greece's Quisling – the Nazis' first appointed 'prime minister'.

On the following Sunday, the sky was a leaden grey. As German troops entered Athens' northern suburbs, Penelope Delta, the author whose books have nourished generations of Greek girls and boys, myself included, drank her version of the poison hemlock, unwilling to live to see the Nazis waltzing past her home on their way to the city centre. Soon after, Radio Athens would transmit its final message:

> Brothers and sisters, a few minutes from now, our radio station will no longer be Greek. Do not tune in. Brothers and sisters, keep your souls up.

Less than an hour later, Eleni and Panayis watched from their rooftop as the swastika was raised over the Acropolis.

3. Dawn of ghosts

Eleni and Panayis grew up in Gouva – an unbearably poor Athenian neighbourhood which literally translates as 'The Depression'. The first four decades of the twentieth century in Greece were marked by continuous war and military dictatorships. This created a society steeped in sadness, discord and mistrust. Greece was, geopolitically, in the British sphere of influence, but its fledgling modern industry had largely been funded by German capital and supplied with German machinery. Determined from the age of eight to become an engineer, Panayis saw German flying machines as harbingers of the future he craved.

'Thankfully,' Eleni contended, 'the stench of the Occupation put paid to his illusions. Soon, he grew to loathe the Nazis as much as I did.' I believed her. But, nevertheless, my mind raced to our fridge, the washing machine in our bathroom and the telephone resting on a stool next to the settee in our living room, all displaying proudly the Siemens logo – everyday reminders of discounts Panayis secured as managing director of Siemens Hellas, a job he retained even as he was crafting my Stuka at Hotel Pefkakia, locked up and ritually abused by dyed-in-the-wool Greek Nazi sympathisers. Eleni explained: 'Germany's de-Nazification drive enabled my brother to have his cake and eat it – to wire himself into German tech without the guilt that weighed him down that bleak Sunday on our rooftop.'

Did he mean it, I asked, when he branded his guards Nazis? Eleni replied that unlike those left-wingers who recklessly brand any right-wingers they dislike Nazis or Fascists, Panayis chose his words carefully. He, himself, had been a recalcitrant rightist who would never have called the ESA Nazis before they staged the putsch that brought them to power. He would have dismissed them as, at most, uncouth nationalists. This is exactly, Eleni suggested, why they loathed Panayis with perhaps greater passion than they did the communists: they expected him to defer to them, to keep quiet and carry on making a fortune at Siemens. That someone like Panayis would turn against them had not been on their radar. It was their sadistic reaction to his resistance that convinced Panayis they were Nazis.

Thinking back, the choice of Hotel Pefkakia to detain Panayis was deliciously suggestive of the military government's bewilderment. Rounding up leftists by the thousands into a network of dingy prisons, black sites and barren island concentration camps was second nature to the thugs who had staged their *coup d'état* in the early hours of 21 April 1967. They had been doing it since the 1930s under successive Greek governments that relied on them to harass, torture and intern communists, socialists, student organisers, anarchists and trades unionists. Except now, emboldened by the full backing of the CIA and the tacit support of the United States government, they were also forming a government themselves. Within days, they had swapped their drab uniforms for shiny suits which, they hoped, would make them look the part as ministers of state.

In their warped minds, Eleni explained, they were killing democracy to save it. Not so much from the dastardly leftists but from the woolly centrists, wet conservatives and assorted degenerates whom they blamed for the nation's moral decline and political paralysis. What they had never expected, however, was armed resistance from establishment figures like Panayis, whose suits were considerably sharper than theirs.

The military government were baffled by this new breed of respectable insurgents. It included royalist navy officers, intellectuals with impeccable conservative credentials, reputable law professors, even the army general who had recruited Panayis – himself a powerful figure in his capacity as de facto ambassador of German industrial capital. Stunned at first, they soon recovered their poise and captured the improbable rebels. For Eleni, Hotel Pefkakia symbolised the regime's descent into confounded absurdity. Though they tortured them, occasionally up to the thin boundary separating life from death, they felt a strange duty to keep them separate from the usual leftist riff-raff.

During their court martial, a classic show trial that took place in March 1970, the defendants looked like ministers, a 'cabinet in waiting' as the *Guardian* reported at the time. This image was grossly at odds with that of dangerous subversives the regime aimed to paint. In the midst of her anguish, sitting on the hard benches, listening to the prosecutor wax lyrical about the state's duty to seek the death penalty, Eleni could not help but admire her brother's imposing presence – his greying black hair, the striking architecture of his profile and his air of superiority that weighed heavily on the little men who struggled to pretend they were passing legitimate judgement.

The question that baffled the military government also troubled Eleni: what had got into these bourgeois insurrectionaries? What had made Panayis, her dear, affluent, conservative businessman of a brother, fill up a Samsonite briefcase with explosives one fine morning with the intent to blow up the Ministry of Industry?

Whenever I asked her, her answer was always the same, fluent and unforced: my uncle was a brilliant but cavalier young man who saw himself as a potential captain of the universe. In 1945 Panayis gained admission to Greece's top engineering school, the

National Technical University of Athens – known as the *Polytechneio*. By the time he graduated, in 1950, his cohort was in great demand due to the mini industrial revolution spearheaded by the Marshall Plan – and Panayis was top of his class. After a year or so of additional training in West Germany, he was snapped up by Siemens. Two years later he was top dog at Siemens Hellas, a post he held until 1977.

Panayis' career path would have been inconsequential had it not embodied the three-way marriage of qualities that make men like him stand out: ambition, ability and authoritarianism. Siemens Hellas was more than a company. It was a state-within-the-state, the wholesale supplier of the machinery and know-how that built, almost from scratch, Greece's electricity and telephone systems. Every time Panayis visited the Ministry of Industry, he would be greeted by the minister himself, with the fanfare normally reserved for visiting foreign dignitaries. He loved every minute of it, Eleni recalled. His devotion to the established order was absolute because he considered it to be his very own realm.

When Eleni would broach the small matter of the state executions of leftists throughout the 1950s, including women, or the 1963 state-sponsored brutal murder of Grigoris Lambrakis, a left-wing member of parliament, or the massive electoral fraud in 1961 organised by the palace, Panayis would spring to their defence with an argument not too dissimilar to the attitudes of the current generation of hard-nosed American or northern European liberals: Sometimes, he would retort, we must deploy authoritarian means to save democracy from authoritarianism. Sometimes, to safeguard the constitution and the rule of law from its greatest foes – communists and their fellow travellers – we must bend it to our will.

Echoing Franklin D. Roosevelt's famous dictum that Rafael Trujillo, the dictator of the Dominican Republic, 'may be a bastard but he is our bastard', Panayis considered the ruffians who ended up torturing him in 1969 'his' bastards – louts who kept troubled Greece a democracy, albeit an imperfect one. They were, he thought, the steep insurance premia democracy must pay. But that was before the Dawn of Ghosts, as Eleni liked to refer to the early hours of 21 April 1967. For it was then that, as Athens slept, Panayis' boorish guardians of democracy, led by George Papadopoulos, a boorish colonel, dissolved parliament, imposed martial law, trashed the constitution and broke down our front door to drag Eleni's husband, my father, to a football stadium along with thousands of others on their list of potential 'enemies of the state'. That morning, Panayis flipped.

For more than a year he ran on empty. He continued to drive to work in his scrumptious white Alfa Romeo GTV coupé and carried on, in an *au fait* style, representing Siemens' business interests in regular meetings with the stooges the military had appointed to ministerial posts. To outsiders, he seemed unabashed, as if nothing had changed. But it was all a show. Inside, he was broken.

Life acquired meaning again in November 1968, as he told me years later, when a retired general recruited him to Democratic Defence, the hodgepodge of incensed bourgeois men determined to plant small bombs, whose blasts would, in the words the general used in his defence during their court martial, 'express the cry of the nation'.

4. Like an owl before an earthquake

Eleni had her own theory of why Panayis flipped. When the axioms sustaining our worldview dissolve in the harsh light of brutality, she believed, our true character comes to the fore. The timid recoil. The wise are humbled. The cunning seek scapegoats. Women try to find fault in themselves. But men accustomed to power reach for its most masculine version to restore the shattered equilibrium in a world they consider their estate. 'Panayis', she pronounced, 'was a cad on our rooftop, he was a cad when he championed our nasty post-war pseudo-democracy, and he was a cad when he decided to plant bombs against those other cads who overthrew it. Only when in custody, stripped of his dignity, did I see in him the decent boy I knew he was.'

Eleni trod a fine line between censuring and praising Panayis. I knew she adored the ground he walked on. I had experienced her grief during his incarceration. I sensed her intense pride that, unlike other men of influence, Panayis never bowed to our tyrants, choosing to risk his life and fortune to resist them. And yet, like an owl before an earthquake, Eleni was alive to good men's vulnerability to the corrupting influence of power. Observing her relationship with her brother was, thinking back, an effective inoculation against today's descent into incendiary identity politics that began with the George W. Bush doctrine: 'If you are not with us, you are against us.' She knew how to love and to loathe him without allowing the contradiction to destabilise her, to make her lose her moral poise.

I once asked her how she felt about his decision to join a group espousing violence, which I knew she abhorred. 'I never succumbed to the enormous pressure from friends and foes to condemn his stupid bombs,' she replied. 'Violence has its uses against beasts like Theofiloyiannakos who are always ready and willing to use it indiscriminately,' a reference to the man who had slapped her at Hotel Pefkakia and who, I learned later, had personally tortured Panayis. I was more intrigued than ever. 'Why then call his bombs stupid?' I asked. 'Don't you dare,' she snapped back with a venomous look usually reserved for her brother during one of their tense exchanges.

Eleni gave no quarter to anyone who dared dismiss her as meek. Though I had not meant it that way, my question awakened in her a memory of when Panayis had dismissed her objections to his group's bombs as the reaction of a 'jumpy female'. As a chemist who had spent years on the floor of a fertiliser factory mixing deadly chemicals, she was not afraid of explosions. But to her mind, his readiness to resort to bombs came from the same place as his earlier deference to violent thugs – perhaps even the same place as his rooftop speech in 1941. 'Once you look for solutions in the abyss that is violence,' she concluded, 'the abyss swallows you whole and, before you know it, you can't even begin to imagine non-violent resolutions.'

That conversation left me feeling self-conscious. How different was my boyish excitement at having smuggled messages in and out of Panayis' prison? Eleni's magnetic words threw off course an inner compass which, as in most boys raised in patriarchal societies, was calibrated to point to the celebration of brute force. Eleni made me appreciate a softer type of power.

That Eleni's power was silkier did not, however, guarantee us a quiet life. When Panayis debated with other men, their waltz was well rehearsed. But with Eleni in the room, his fury was impulsive, authentic. The trigger was invariably her capacity to move swiftly from empathy that his illusions were dashed, to scorn for his assumption that society owed him the realisation of those illusions. In nanoseconds, as he realised that her understanding did not procure approval, the backlash was on. From those thunderous clashes I remember Eleni always emerging shaken but with her wings unclipped.

Soon after the collapse of the military regime in the summer of 1974, with Panayis free and back in his stride, Eleni entered municipal politics where she was to flourish for three decades. She stormed into an arena where packs of men were eager to throw tantrums every time she challenged their entitlement or questioned their status.

Employing a blend of tender mockery, plain speaking and genuine compassion, Eleni held her own. Today, almost two decades after her passing, I wonder how she would have reacted to the upsurge of Donald Trump, J. D. Vance, Elon Musk, Nigel Farage, Viktor Orbán and a host of copycats. Probably with a few cutting words and a telling smile of the sort I first saw at Hotel Pefkakia under the nose of that man in the dusty brown suit.

5. A healing fever

The daughter of loving parents, both of whom had been orphaned at a young age and thus were eager to envelop their four children in love, Eleni's childhood was modest but happy. Her father, Konstantinos, was a talented cobbler with a loyal albeit impecunious clientele, and her mother, Trisevgeni, who had grown up on the land, knew how to transform the very little they bought, and what she grew in their garden, into a feast.

Eleni grew up on the north-eastern fringes of the poorest suburb in Athens. But their home was a haven, not far from the nearby woods that extended all the way up to Mount Hymettus. Built haphazardly like a small quad, complete with tall external walls keeping prying eyes at bay, it had an inner garden dominated by a lone apple tree, a main house with three rooms, a tiny rooftop laundry, an outdoor kitchen and a loo that had been exiled to the garden's western end, furthest away from the living quarters.

As Eleni grew older and ran errands around the city centre with Panayis, she began to get a sense of their neighbourhood's lowly status. Unlike other suburbs, most of Gouva's roads were unpaved, turning into a bog at the first sign of rain. Not a fancy shop in sight. No bus service. No post office. A no man's land where people had a fierce look in their eyes. But the smells of freshly baked bread wafting from ramshackle houses, spiced with the scents of lemon trees and rosebushes lovingly nurtured in back gardens, reminded Eleni that she was among her people.

Squeezing pleasure out of misery was a skill hardwired into Eleni and her friends. As kids, they played football with a mass of fabric that mysteriously retained its spherical shape, courtesy of Trisevgeni's elaborate stitching. And when their football frayed, they invented games such as *toka*, Eleni's favourite until Trisevgeni spoiled it for her when, one day, she melodramatically likened herself to the game's cornerstone: the upright slab of stone, the *toka*, that the kids manically threw rocks at to see who could topple it first.

The only time Eleni complained about Gouva was when her father gave her a pair of brand-new white leather shoes that he had crafted especially for her birthday. That day, to keep them shiny and dust-free, her journey home took three times longer as she strove to stay on as many paved streets as possible. But even that inconvenience caused her heart to grow fonder of their place 'out there', her term for their slice of Gouva.

'Out there, before the Germans came,' she told me once, 'love burnt like a healing fever, our laughter and our games giving us a thrill that not even the devil could snatch from us. Out there, before the Germans came, whenever grief clawed its way into us, we didn't run, we turned towards it, we defeated it. And when it lay defeated, on the dirt, we got to live our way.'

Then came the Occupation. As the German army confiscated entire crop fields at gunpoint to export back to Germany, the Great Famine descended upon Greece's urban centres. An unusually frosty winter followed that made the hunger harder to endure. 'Remember the "Bring out your dead" scene?' Eleni asked me one night after watching *Monty Python and the Holy Grail* at the cinema. 'I saw you noticed I wasn't laughing.' For her that scene was too like the mule-driven cart which, every morning through January and February of 1942, traversed Gouva to collect the bodies of those who had expired overnight, many of them children with whom she had once played *toka*.

The first sign of the disaster the Occupation had wrought, Eleni recalled, was the sudden disappearance of the smell of fresh bread from Gouva's muddy streets. Then she noticed that stray dogs were beginning to grow scarce. Then cats. Only rats remained, but even they were getting thinner. When people dropped in, she noticed that her father would turn the valve of their stove canister just a little, releasing a small amount of gas to mask the stench of hunger.

And when the first swallows of spring returned, Konstantinos told them off: Greece was now occupied, a place unfit for their free spirits. He urged them to keep flying north and return only when they could truly symbolise the merciless winter's end. A few days later when Eleni smelled a neighbour's flowering jasmine, she too felt a surge of anger, unwilling to accept Nature recycling life so soon after the loss of so many. That night she felt closer to her father than ever before.

That Eleni's family suffered no deaths during the Occupation was wholly due to Trisevgeni's resourcefulness, and her knack for catching and breeding pigeons in a makeshift loft she had assembled in their tiny rooftop laundry. Besides being a rare source of protein, the pigeons' cooing soothed Eleni as she lay in bed at night, struggling to block out the chilling sound of Nazi boots pounding the dirt.

Trisevgeni would also patrol the nearby woods for days in search of wild olives and carob, which she would then pulverise into a flour substitute to bake something resembling bread. One day, her youngest daughter, Eleni's little sister, was struck down with acute appendicitis and had to be operated upon. A starving surgeon agreed to carry out the operation. His fee? Half a loaf of Trisevgeni's bread substitute and some olives thrown in for good measure.

Eleni could hardly chide my exhilaration at being at the centre of a court martial drama when her most sentimental memories were of the Occupation years, in particular the never-ending procession of hungry people that entered her home to be fed by Trisevgeni. Everything they had was shared. In return, visitors shared stories.

After wolfing down Trisevgeni's 'hunger recipes', their yarns would unfold and stretch deep into the night. Not one night went by when Eleni's tummy did not rumble. Yet not one night was she not glad to swap her food for tales, especially those of Panos and Pantelis.

Panos lived alone in a nearby squat whose roof had caved in under the snow that the skies spewed during that first winter under the Nazis. Aged beyond his years, it took all of Trisevgeni's powers of persuasion to coax him round for the first time. But after a few visits, and once she had plied him with retsina, which could only be procured as the Germans disliked it intensely, stories redolent of Federico García Lorca spilled out about his three years in Catalunya, where he had joined the International Brigades in 1936 to resist Franco's fascists.

Night after night, the Catalan, as they called him, exposed Eleni to an unfamiliar land and history. She would often speak of one character decades later: a partisan, a free spirit, a former prostitute, a communist whom the fascists executed. 'Without trying,' Eleni said, 'Panos made me believe the world would be even less forgivable if I allowed her name to be forgotten. So, I kept her name etched in my thoughts. Bianca.'

Pantelis, a cousin of her father's, was the odd one out in his long brown robes and expansive greying beard. At the tender age of eleven he had entered the ascetic order at Arcadi, the ancient Cretan monastery famous for having harboured the armed resistance to the Ottoman occupation of Crete. The family paid a steep price for losing their male heir to otherworldly realms: as a condition for taking him on, the Arcadi abbot demanded that Pantelis hand over the title deeds to what land Konstantinos' family owned. Flabbergasted, landless and, understandably, outraged, they turned their backs on him.

But then the Germans came. Providence, Pantelis insisted, stranded him in Athens where he had been sent by the abbot to commission an iconographer to paint a fresco of the Madonna and Child on their refurbished dome, which had been burnt down decades earlier by irate Ottomans. Penniless, with the mainland church refusing to extend him the care afforded to its own priests, he threw himself at Trisevgeni's mercy. One more mouth to feed, one more source of mystical stories for Eleni to devour.

Pantelis seized upon Eleni's incomprehension of why anyone would want to be a monk like a man who discovered a waterhole in a desert. Had he been visited by the divine? He hadn't. How could he then be sure there was a god at all? He wasn't, was his disarming answer. Then, why on earth be a monk? For the hell of it, he replied defiantly. Eleni insisted: Surely there was a reason to sacrifice not just his chance of having a family, but his land? No, he countered, he did it for no tangible reason. A puzzled silence descended upon the room. Before Konstantinos could challenge him, Pantelis calmly elaborated.

Whenever you do something for a reason, any reason, he said, you are acting selfishly. Even when you are being charitable to others, you want to be regarded as a good Samaritan. To be genuinely selfless, to enact authentic good, you must be acting for no reason. Freedom, he concluded, is to do extraordinary things, things that make no sense to most, just because they feel right. At every other time, when you do stuff for a reason, you are nothing but the plaything, the instrument, of forces beyond your control. That's what faith with no reason means to me, he concluded.

Though Eleni disagreed passionately, something in his words struck a chord – and motivated her to do difficult things gladly even when reason advised against them. Pantelis' rationale for having a faith, any faith, empowered her to develop, and stay true to, her own.

Eighteen months into the Occupation, a German patrol passed by Panos' squat, on whose wall a single word, painted in large blue letters, offended them: *Eleftheria*, Freedom. Eleni never found out whether it was Panos or some stray kids who had painted it. It didn't matter. A single bullet cut Panos down, undoing all Trisevgeni's efforts to keep him alive.

6. Sultanas, partisans and traitors

Trisevgeni's hunger recipes were not Eleni's only saviour. There was also the stash of Mr Kimon – the local black marketeer who snitched on his neighbours in exchange for favours from the Nazi-run police precinct. He became Gouva's oligarch. A determined Panayis, with Eleni in tow, followed Kimon discreetly for days until they discovered his secret warehouse, where he kept the sultanas, olives, almonds and mouldy flour which netted him everything from pianos from starving bourgeois families to, by war's end, a large swathe of land and dwellings across Athens.

Behind the warehouse was a wild, overgrown plot where the siblings could hide. It took them days, using no more than a spoon, to dig a small hole beneath the warehouse's brittle wall that was wide enough to squeeze an arm in, pierce a sack of sultanas and extract a sweet handful. Scared to pieces of getting caught, Eleni and Panayis practised moderation to the extreme. But when, a couple of weeks later, the sack had become noticeably emptier, they upped the ante. They dug out the hole enough for Eleni to sneak in to rearrange the sacks so that, from Kimon's vantage point, they looked undisturbed. They would then cover the hole with a fake gypsum wall that Panayis had cut out. Remarkably, the brutal winter passed with no sign that Kimon had got whiff of their 'tax scheme', as they called it.

The Nazis printed mountains of the national currency, the

drachma, which they used to 'buy' whatever emerged from the ravaged land, for their own use in Greece or to export to the rest of Occupied Europe. The German high command knowingly created hyperinflation that rendered all wages a joke. With nothing left even to barter, nothing resembling an economy remained. Instinctively, Athenians sought innovative ways of taking back some of what was plundered from them, while desperately seeking to reconnect with cousins, nieces and uncles in the countryside where the hunger was less severe.

Trisevgeni had grown up on a smallholding in Rododafni, a village close to the northern Peloponnesian coast, and she pleaded with her extended family there to take her children in. She could not read or write, so Konstantinos transcribed her grovelling letters. He only vetoed one: Trisevgeni wanted to write to the most powerful man she knew, her uncle Thomas. 'Over my dead body,' Konstantinos snapped.

Uncle Thomas worked for the Nazis, heading their hated security corps in Patra, Greece's third-largest city. He drove expensive cars, lived luxuriously and commanded hundreds of men to eradicate partisans in north-western Peloponnese, flushing them out by terrorising their villages. Starvation was preferable to contacting the family collaborator, Konstantinos decreed.

Luckily, one of Trisevgeni's missives resulted in an invitation to Rododafni. But for only two of the children – that was all the extra mouths they could feed. Trisevgeni chose to dispatch Panayis and Eleni, keeping their eldest and their youngest daughters, Marika and Georgia, with her.

That summer in Rododafni was a magical time for Eleni. The great-aunt who hosted them had access to a shack on a nearby beach where they stayed during July's heat. It was there, one moonlit evening, that Eleni realised Panayis was a sleepwalker.

She watched him get up in the middle of the night, walk across the sand, swim in the sea for a while and then return to bed, never to remember any of it in the morning. But the magic dissolved a few days later, when Panayis began to cough blood. Despite the pigeons, the sultanas and the escape to the Peloponnese, the previous winter had caught up with him, infecting his lungs, like countless others', with tuberculosis. It was time to return to Athens, where a semblance of medical care was available.

In the absence of antibiotics, the surgeon removed his infected right lung and filled the cavity with an inert liquid. 'Get him out of Athens, preferably to a place up on a mountain where the crisp, clean air may save him,' was the advice. And so it was that in the autumn of 1943, Trisevgeni and her four children made their way to the top of Mount Penteli, having rented a cottage belonging to a monastery with the help of Pantelis. Only Konstantinos stayed behind in Gouva to eke out an income by cobbling increasingly dilapidated shoes.

Penteli also proved too good to hold them for long. By early 1944, Trisevgeni had to gather her kids and return to Gouva because Konstantinos was faring badly, malnourished and with a weakened heart. Athens, they discovered, was buzzing with hope, despite the famine. The news from afar gave them heart. The partisans of EAM (Greece's National Liberation Front) controlled most of the countryside. The Red Army had crossed the old Russian border with Poland, heading for Berlin, while American, Canadian and British forces were on course to enter Rome. Liberation was in the air. It was simply a matter of time.

But when the time came in October 1944 for the Germans to pack up and retreat, the joy evaporated. Greece went straight from a hideous occupation to a gruesome civil war. On one side were the British forces, the pre-war bourgeois establishment and, yes, former Nazi collaborators – who counted their blessings that, instead of being sentenced for high treason, they had become the backbone of the new security forces. On the other were the partisans of EAM, the Communist Party which held sway within EAM, and a majority of the poor for whom EAM had promised a fairer post-war deal.

On 3 December 1944, the brewing tensions erupted into a fully fledged war after British and Greek government troops opened fire from the rooftop of Parliament House into a crowd of peaceful, leftist demonstrators assembled in the adjacent Syntagma Square, killing thirty-three of them. The four-week-long Battle for Athens commenced, complete with RAF aeroplanes bombarding working-class suburbs and door-to-door street fighting. No Greek family lacks, to this day, a horror story involving atrocities perpetrated by one side or the other.

Midway through the Battle for Athens, a week before Christmas, Eleni was walking back from school, which she had found closed until further notice. A group of teenage partisans, two of whom she had seen around Gouva, held her at gunpoint. Then, for a good two hours, they marched her up Mount Hymettus where, they told her, she would receive a fair trial. 'They had put two and two together,' she explained to me, 'or so they thought.' Unlike all the other emaciated children in their neighbourhood, Eleni's cheeks were rosy, and her body was not as shrunken from malnutrition. Then there were the long absences from the neighbourhood. And, crucially, they had recently heard about her great-uncle Thomas, the Nazi collaborator. To those boy partisans, it was an open-and-shut case. She was the daughter of secret collaborators.

When, eventually, they arrived at the partisans' Hymettus campsite, a lieutenant whom Trisevgeni had once fed and hidden from a Nazi patrol recognised Eleni, scolded the youngsters for taking her prisoner and escorted the fifteen-year-old girl back home. From that day, despite the lieutenant's kindness, Eleni harboured, often despite herself, an antipathy towards communists.

7. Bad chemistry

Forced into illiteracy by her father's early death – which caused her to drop out of primary school, after only one year, to work the land and care for her younger siblings – Trisevgeni was adamant that her kids would go to university. All four of them. The older ones, Marika and Panayis, got there just before the civil war had fully taken hold. But Eleni had another three years at Gouva's state secondary school, with its broken windows and bullet-ridden blackboards, not to mention teachers too starved to teach. Lacking even two pennies to rub together, Trisevgeni nonetheless decided to put Eleni through private school.

No one knows how she convinced the Ursulines, Catholic nuns who ran a selective school for well-to-do pupils in central Athens, to take her in. All Eleni knew was that every second day, Trisevgeni would fill a cloth bag with carefully wrapped pigeon eggs, some greens and a little goat's cheese, for her to deliver to the headteacher. This lasted no more than six months, a touch longer than a semester. Eventually, the Catholic hierarchy stamped out such barter deals, forcing the Ursulines to let Eleni go. Nevertheless, Eleni was grateful, convinced that these months had made all the difference – the blessed nuns, as she lovingly called them, had taught her how to learn. After that, even though she hardly attended the dilapidated neighbourhood school, she knew how to sail through exams.

In the autumn of 1948, with excellent grades, she could enrol in any department at the University of Athens. Her mind was set on the School of Medicine, but her heart was urging her to study literature. However, in the end, under the influence of Panayis, she chose neither. A year earlier, in 1947, Greece had begun to receive Marshall Aid to the tune of 25 per cent of its national income annually. While that was a lot of dollars, the civil war had another two long years to rage, and so it did little to ameliorate poverty or prop up the drachma. However, they did fund the industrialisation of Elefsis, ancient Greece's holiest of places, a short distance south of Piraeus. Panayis, already in his third year of a five-year electrical engineering degree, had a plan for the two of them, together, to tap into the Elefsis industrial miracle.

Eleni would study chemistry, which, together with engineering, was the bedrock of heavy industry. He would be the engineering genius and she the chemical virtuoso. Once they learned the ropes working side by side for one of the fledgling industrial complexes, they would eventually go into business for themselves. 'Why, before you know it,' he told Eleni excitedly, 'we will become Greece's Krupp family.'

He was hard to resist when at his most exuberant, Eleni confessed. She often lamented missing out on being a doctor or a philologist. Instead, lured by the idea of the two of them building a factory on nothing more than a wing and a prayer, she enrolled in the School of Chemistry to read perhaps her least favourite subject.

The University of Athens School of Chemistry was located in the city centre, on Solonos Street, named after Solon, ancient Athens' philosopher-legislator. Eleni had to climb a well-worn and slippery marble staircase to reach the elevated and impressive main gate. She was one of the first female students, which made her climb all the more symbolic.

Once inside, a sea of male students and professors looked at her as they would an exotic animal. Clenching her teeth, she made her way into the amphitheatre where first-years gathered to be welcomed by the rector. Sticking out like a sore thumb, not only as a woman, but on account of her tattered attire, she was not sure whether to fret more about her gender or about her shabby clothes.

Soon, the rector made her forget her dilemma. 'If, my dear, you plan to rear children,' he asked piercingly, 'why in the good Lord's name enrol here in the first place? And if you plan not to, do you seriously expect us to waste our teaching talents on a woman who refuses to play her part in the nation's reproduction?' His outpouring on the audacity of a woman taking a university place from a future breadwinner continued. Eleni bit her tongue but she made a point of not breaking eye contact with him, not even for a heartbeat. Moments later she almost faltered as the amphitheatre erupted in derision, when the rector invited the men to welcome 'this wayward female equipped with the arrogance of a stray dog to join us here today'.

Twenty-six years later, upon returning from school one day in 1974, I had a question for her as a practising scientist. Earlier that day, a fellow pupil, a boy, had put my thirteen-year-old self in a tight spot with a difficult question: 'I bet you can't name *one* woman in Antiquity who was an accomplished mathematician, physicist, astronomer or something useful like that. Do you know why you can't? Because women just don't have it in them to be a Pythagoras, a Euclid, an Archimedes.' The truth was that I could not answer him. Thus, I ran to Eleni.

'Hypatia,' Eleni said without a second thought, smiling broadly while sipping a camomile tea at our kitchen table. 'Never heard of her,' I replied unhappily. 'I had not heard of her either,' she said. 'Until I did my research to discover a good answer to precisely that question. You see, son, for me, your friend's question posed an existential threat not just for the four long years I spent at university but for as long as I remember breathing.'

8. Hypatia

Hypatia, I came to learn, was the foremost philosopher and mathematician between 380 AD and 415 AD. Like Cleopatra, she was of Greek descent but lived and flourished in Alexandria, Egypt. The daughter of a famous astronomer, known for her civic duty and religious tolerance; rich young men would sail, ride and walk from all corners of the known world to be educated by Hypatia in the high arts of geometry, physics, astronomy and engineering. An acknowledged beauty, she had chosen a life of celibacy to prevent any husband from confining her in a household, and she allegedly quelled the advances of her students by calming them with music.

Hypatia was a brilliant communicator of science, the utmost authority on the mathematical properties of cones and the inventor of two critical scientific instruments: the astrolabe, which tracks celestial movements and predicts events such as eclipses; and the hydrometer, which measures the density of liquids. She even invented the long-division method that every child still learns in Greek schools to this day. And, yet, none of us had heard of her. Or of her brutal murder at the hands of a Christian mob who seized her on the street not far from the Great Library of Alexandria, dragged her to a nearby church, tore the clothes off her back and beat her to death before skinning her with sharpened shells.

'Once I discovered Hypatia's story,' Eleni reminisced, 'it became my special mental shield, fending off the abuse hurled at me by the overgrown boys on Solonos Street.' It must have been the most perilous of times, I suggested, what with the civil war at its zenith in 1948. Eleni didn't agree. Quite the opposite, she said. Life was but a fragile flower, so she felt she could take on the bigots. 'In any case,' she added playfully, 'the loveliest times, and the heartiest laughter, were intertwined with all the ugliness.'

In 1949, Eleni was still enduring the professors who would only give her a lowly pass grade if she outscored the boys. It was also the year the civil war officially ended. After the Greek National Army defeated the partisans, courtesy of the Truman Doctrine that mobilised the United States' military and economic might in their favour, the rabid right dominated. Leftists continued to disappear in the middle of the night to reappear in damp cells, to be convicted in kangaroo court martials, often to end up on barren islands where they were incarcerated for years. Nevertheless, the civil war's ending also marked the family's exit from Gouva and their move to a smaller house but in the far more desirable seaside suburb of Paleo Phaliro. Marika landed a job as a teacher of ancient Greek, married and moved into her new home. Not long afterwards, Panayis graduated from the Polytechneio. All Eleni had to do was to keep her head and graduate too.

As her second year progressed, she began to realise that not all the boys were irredeemable bigots. Most merely felt the need to toe the line in front of a powerful chauvinist minority. Once they worked together in small groups in the laboratories, she discovered that most boys were, quietly, on the political left and thus lived in greater terror than she did. Though she still harboured her lingering antipathy towards communists, the sense of dread she shared with her peers at the School of Chemistry began to change her.

It was in the same large amphitheatre as her initial humiliation that one day, at the beginning of her third year, the men from the X Group approached her. Apologetic and reassuring, the X Group were clearly trying to recruit her. Eleni knew of the organisation's sordid notoriety – of their collaboration with the Nazi occupiers, of their reputation as the nearest Greece ever had to the Ku Klux Klan, targeting not blacks, which Greece lacked, but leftists. Still, she decided to humour them, to see what they wanted.

They had got wind of her 'communist allergy', as they put it, and so had a proposition: in exchange for their protection and support inside the department, she would do some little, easy jobs for them. 'Like what?' she asked, looking them directly in the eye. 'Jotting down the things that specific individuals, whom we shall point out to you, say and do. What do you say? We are not asking much.' To get them off her back, and buy time, she nodded.

Satisfied, they gave her the first target – a young man she had never seen before, sitting alone on the far side of the amphitheatre, looking like death warmed up having spent several years in prison camps. 'He will be in your inorganic lab group this afternoon, just keep an eye on him. We think he may try to organise students. We need no more than a page of notes on him every week. Think you can do that?' 'Yes, I think I can,' Eleni replied. Little did they know what they had just done.

PART TWO

Anna

9. Praying to the moon

Anna barely noticed as the searing khamsin filled her nostrils and covered her clothes with fine sand. Usually, the desert gale would have driven her to seek shelter in the Armenian café she was passing. But on that hot June afternoon in 1923, her mind was too exercised to care about her appearance. Minutes earlier, she had left the Collège du Bon Pasteur, the boarding school in the working-class district of Shubra that she had called home for the past four years. Sisters Marie and Colette, the Ursuline nuns Anna had looked up to as surrogate mothers, had kissed her goodbye and wished her well. The heavy burden of her newfound freedom, and the even heavier prospect of losing it, was no match for the fierce khamsin as she headed to Cairo's Ramses Station to meet her cousin Nina for afternoon tea.

Nina was the daughter of her father's brother, Argyris. Nina was the only family Anna felt she had after her mother's early death, her father's almost immediate remarriage and her twelve-year internment in Cairo's prestigious French girls' boarding schools – first the Collège de La Mère de Dieu, near the splendid Garden City, then the Collège du Bon Pasteur. Anna appreciated her sweet cousin, but she also knew she could not risk sharing with anyone her ambition to enrol at the recently established American University of Cairo. Nina, Anna was convinced, would consider her mad for wanting to go to university, rather than marry quickly and start the family she never had.

As she approached the art nouveau railway café, walking

alongside the railway line on which the express from Alexandria was slowly approaching, she allowed her mind to wander. She imagined the Nile's tributaries on which the feluccas and the dahabeeyahs let their sails catch the wind, the fellahas balancing clay water jugs on their heads as they passed under tall date trees, the Pyramids casting their shadows. Suddenly, a wave of anxiety jolted her. What if the extended family had already laid down plans to marry her off?

The café hummed with the clatter of silver and the low murmur of well-heeled European commuters, its high ceilings gilded in the lazy afternoon light. Thick with the aroma of cardamom and French perfume, the air carried the distant whistle of stressed steam engines. Sitting alone at a small round marble table, Anna waited for Nina. Increasingly self-conscious of her dusty attire, she looked intently around at women in dropped-waist dresses, not a speck of dust on them, sipping from porcelain cups. Suddenly she saw it for the first time: the high society she was about to join. A jewel-box world spinning just beyond the bounds of the khamsin-lashed, sun-scorched streets outside.

Nina's gentle presence calmed her. As they took their sweet tea, Anna was reassured that Nina's parents did not have a groom waiting in the wings. Not yet, at least. Instead, Anna could have a bedroom in their home, as well as a long list of social events to usher her into society – alongside the Greeks, Brits, French, Italians, Jews and a few American expats who were Egypt's de facto ruling class. 'Time is of the essence,' Anna wrote in her diary that night, adding in bolder letters: 'I must buy time!' For Anna, finding a palatable man, to avoid a brutish one imposed upon her, felt like an escape route leading through a sewer. 'If an evil is necessary,' she wrote, 'it better be a lesser one.'

Days later, a woman called Huda Sha'arawi scandalised Egyptian society by ceremoniously removing her veil in public almost at the very spot where Anna and Nina had met for tea. Anna immediately sought out Huda, and learned that she was the inaugural president, indeed the founder, of the Egyptian Feminist Union. After further digging, she found that the union met every Thursday afternoon in an inconspicuous city-centre apartment. For the first time Anna realised that she was not one of a kind, that there was a word for what she was: feminist.

At the first meeting she attended, ironically wearing a veil to shield herself from the wandering eyes of other European expats, she found herself surrounded by dozens of fearless, veil-free Egyptian women. That afternoon, Anna's loneliness was both shattered and sealed.

A month later, in between her underground union meetings and high-society soirées, Nina invited Anna to her tennis club in Mataria, close to Chelmia, a half-hour train ride away. It was there that Anna spotted Yango, an enigmatic twenty-three-year-old Greek sporting a white linen suit, a Panama hat and a pair of pince-nez glasses which he took off only when trying to impress with his tennis skills. Anna then discovered two things about him that intrigued her.

One, he was an alumnus of the American University of Beirut, perhaps the eastern Mediterranean's finest higher education establishment. And two, unlike her family, he had no roots in Egypt: he had only recently arrived from Leros, a small Dodecanese island, first in Alexandria, then Cairo.

Though they both came from ethnic Greek families, like everyone in the Cairo tennis club scene, they conversed in French, switching to English only when some British dignitary joined, and, of course, never in Arabic, a language the expatriate community felt no need to learn. Anna had in fact secretly taught herself the poetic language of her country, with the help of the collège's cook and night cleaner.

The more she spoke to the suave Yango, the more he surprised her. Besides having studied law and politics in Beirut – a privilege that made Anna green with envy – he had landed a dream job days after arriving on the steamship. Unlike the other young men she had met in the preceding weeks, who worked for their fathers in dull banks, accounting firms and family businesses, Yango ran Thomas Cook's Egypt operation, organising Nile cruises for, predominantly, British aristocrats – unhurried voyages to Sudan and back that inspired the likes of Agatha Christie.

On only their second rendezvous, Yango confessed that his passage to Egypt had not been exactly voluntary. In fact, it was the culmination of a long walk of shame. Yango's father was, apparently, something of a bigwig on Leros, a small island north of Rhodes no more than seventeen miles off the Turkish coast. The owner of several fishing vessels, Yango's father employed a few dozen fishermen, sat on the island's elders' council and lived in a two-storey villa in a piazza named after him.

After Yango graduated in Beirut, his father had ambitions to see him with a 'proper' American law degree under his belt. He therefore decided to send his firstborn son to Los Angeles to read for a Master of Laws, an LLM, at UCLA no less. In the autumn of 1921, after a lengthy voyage involving three ships and a railway journey, Yango arrived in the booming city.

Los Angeles agreed with Yango a little too much. He was in his element. His deep pockets, oriental gentlemanly look and Italian passport (courtesy of Italy's opportunistic occupation of the Dodecanese at the outset of the Great War), along with his impressive English, good French and passable Italian, made him something of a hit. The cosmopolitan city afforded him endless opportunities to mix not only with white Protestants but also with Jews, Italians, Armenians, the odd German, even a few

Chinese and Japanese newcomers, with whom he forged long-lasting friendships.

Life was so good that he found new excuses every day to postpone his enrolment at UCLA just a little longer. But as the months passed, and the anxious missives from Leros accumulated, he knew the moment of reckoning was nigh. In June 1922, a letter arrived with an ultimatum: 'Return with your degree by September or don't bother coming back at all.'

It took Yango more than three weeks to locate a gifted forger to produce an exact replica of a UCLA LLM certificate and a trustworthy photographer to stage the award ceremony – complete with extras who looked the part as president, dean, professors, jubilant fellow graduands and beaming parents. Although Anna was repulsed by Yango's dishonesty, she was also secretly fascinated by his nonchalance as he recounted the staging of his subterfuge like a Hollywood director.

On 5 September 1922, when he sailed into Porto Lago, Leros' main harbour, he received the red-carpet treatment as the proud island's first American lawyer. When Anna asked him how he could live with himself knowing that, back in Leros, impressionable people would rely on legal skills he never actually acquired, he responded coolly, as a true utilitarian: 'I was the best lawyer they would ever have access to with or without an LLM. Would they be served better if I stayed away? I don't think so.'

'My timing was diabolical,' Yango explained. Indeed, on the very same day he returned to Leros, unbeknownst to the crowd that had gathered to greet him, the Greek army had been, finally, defeated by the Turkish troops of Mustafa Kemal on the other side of the water separating Leros from Asia Minor, today's Turkey. On that day, the Greek army began fleeing to the mainland on navy vessels, leaving behind almost three million Greeks, whose subsequent ethnic cleansing is remembered, at least in Greece, as the Asia Minor Catastrophe. In the days and weeks that followed, Leros, a stone's throw from the slaughter of so many, was to receive boatload after boatload of heartbroken refugees, whose grief cast a long shadow over the locals. It was not a good moment for Yango's father to discover his son's fraud.

Two months after his return, in December 1922, Yango's father summoned a naval carpenter from Piraeus to help repair a leak in one of his fishing boats. As fate would have it, the carpenter had just returned from New Jersey on a steamship carrying another passenger who had spent time in Los Angeles, and had heard of Yango's exploits. One thing led to another, and soon, the whole of Leros knew. There was no family meeting, no opportunity to explain, no negotiation. Yango's incensed father ordered his son to pack and board the first boat leaving Leros. As Yango put it to Anna, he received a textbook tar-and-feathers treatment. Indeed, within a few hours, Yango was cut off, disowned and exiled – never to return to Leros or to speak with his father again.

The small fishing boat that he was bundled into was bound for Rhodes. From there, having spent his last lira on a third-class ticket, Yango boarded a passenger ship to Alexandria. Within two days he had landed a job as an insurance salesman working for a Lloyd's of London broker. Three weeks later he quit to join the head office of Thomas Cook in Cairo. 'My escape from the drudgery of my father's small-town ways and expectations was complete,' he told Anna proudly. Years later, she would scribble in her diary: 'I never fully worked out whether Yango was rationalising his disgrace or genuinely celebrating his freedom.'

In the end, despite the alarm bells, what tilted the scales for Anna was Yango's escape from another man's expectations. Every other man she had met, married or unmarried, younger or older, eschewed any deviation from patriarchal norms. Were such men to find out what swirled around in her head, they would run a mile. It's why she willed herself to imagine him as someone with whom she could share her concealed world. So when in February 1924 Yango proposed, she said yes.

Anna suggested that they wed not at home, as was customary in Cairo's Greek community, but in St Constantine's Orthodox church. The ease with which Yango agreed, despite knowing that it would create a minor scandal, gave Anna heart. In April, which, unlike T. S. Eliot, Egypt's poets considered the gentlest month, Anna wed Yango. By autumn that year, she was pregnant.

The day she found out she rushed to her old boarding school in Shubra to bring the news to Sisters Marie and Colette. The long walk to the *collège* cleared her mind as she traversed neighbourhoods as chaotic as the anxieties within her soul. By the time she returned to the city centre, where she and Yango had rented a smart, third-floor apartment, night had fallen and an immense full moon was above the Pyramids. Instinctively, she prayed to the moon for a boy. She would have loved a girl, but what mattered more was that her child should have no limitations. In the coming months, every time a full moon ascended over Cairo's night sky, Anna repeated her prayer. On 12 June 1925 the moon heeded her prayers and her first son was born: Yorgo.

10. One day we shall not have to hide, sister

Salma, Anna's closest comrade in the Egyptian Feminist Union, paid her regular visits to keep her company throughout her pregnancy. Almost twice Anna's age, Salma filled the living room with a dynamism that those four walls had probably never seen before. Speaking no French, Salma delighted Anna with her loud proclamations, hilarious stories and poetic exuberance, all in Arabic. A former factory worker, she was the union's chief underground organiser for women labouring for a pittance in the textile factories owned largely by expats in Anna and Yango's social circle. When, one day, the wife of one such industrialist dropped by for tea unannounced, Salma broke the silence by pretending she was Anna's seamstress. Afterwards, they laughed it off, but Salma counselled Anna: 'One day we shall not have to hide, sister.'

Anna's isolation was exacerbated by Yango. He went out of his way to hire Nadeen, the wife of the neighbourhood's grocer, to help with domestic chores. He purchased a mahogany cabinet containing a top-of-the-range electric gramophone, complete with a dozen hard vinyl records of her favourite music – from Verdi's *Nabucco*, Beethoven's *Eroica* and Schubert's melancholy eighth in B minor, to Vivaldi's *Four Seasons* and Strauss's waltzes. On weekends, they would go to the cinema, the theatre, the opera or on excursions by first-class train to the delightful

Delta Barrage, riding riverboats and camels to some cool oasis. Anna did appreciate Yango's efforts to provide her with a life of luxury; but with every act of kindness, he inadvertently added another brick to the wall between them. This barrier kept her from sharing with him her politics, her friendship with Salma, her joy in speaking Arabic and her dreams of an Egypt liberated from people like themselves.

Yango differed from other European expats. Being on the run, and having parachuted into Egypt accidentally, he did not feel he was one of Egypt's owners. But, like all European settlers, he believed Egypt was lucky to have them. After all, no sentiment grows faster or stronger in the mind of the privileged than the belief that they deserve their privileges. If it were not for Europeans, Yango thought, who would have built the textile factories, the railways, the dams, the bridges, the splendid Cairo Zoo, the museums and public buildings? It was an attitude that made Anna's blood boil.

Anna never ceased to be astonished by the expats' ignorance of Egypt's long and proud history between the Hellenistic period and their own arrival. They dismissed the idea that Egypt had modernised on its own, without its colonisers' assistance. Anna, by contrast, talked to the cooks and the cleaners at her school, and caught wind that she lived in an occupied country ruled by settlers who exploited the indigenous people while erasing their history. In homage to them and the land she treasured, she did her best to dig up the history that the French nuns had never taught her.

Piece by piece, she established a picture that challenged the orientalism of Yango and his mates. Anna's Egypt had a rich industrial history, with roots in the reign of Muhammad Ali, from 1805 to 1848. Determined to make Egypt independent of Constantinople, and transform it into a global power, Ali emulated the British industrial miracle by combining Mumbai, Manchester and Liverpool: growing cotton in plantations nourished by the Nile, turning it into fine textiles in factories nearby, then exporting them to every corner of the world through the port of Alexandria. But what was to stop the sultan of the fragmented Ottoman Empire, Egypt's overlord ensconced in faraway Constantinople, from skimming Egypt's riches? A formidable army and navy, of course.

Munitions plants thus began to pop up across Cairo, producing muskets and cannons in their thousands every month. Extensive shipyards opened in Alexandria. Before long, Egypt's defence industry was capable of arming a vast army and constructing warships with more than a hundred cannons each. 'Loathsome as any war machine may be,' Anna told Yango over dinner one night, 'surely the fact that Egypt had an advanced one in the early nineteenth century is clear evidence that a technologically advanced, independent Egypt pre-dated the European colonialists.' 'I suppose so,' he murmured.

Anna's research into Egypt's industrial and military past, which Yango seemed so uninterested in, instructed her in the different political and ethical conclusions people could derive from exactly the same facts. For her, Muhammad Ali's legacy was of home-grown modernity. But among the Greeks in her circle the mere mention of Muhammad Ali's name triggered hostility. They had good reasons. In 1821 the Greeks, back in the old country, had raised arms against the Ottoman Empire. This bloody and desperate national liberation struggle started in the Peloponnese and later spread further north. Sultan Mahmud II tried to suppress the revolution from Constantinople, throwing one huge army after another at the rebels, but to no avail. So he turned to Egypt's Muhammad Ali for help, making him an offer he could not refuse: if he crushed the Greeks in the Peloponnese, he could have Crete, and full autonomy for Egypt.

And so it was that Egypt's ruler dispatched sixteen thousand soldiers in one hundred ships, accompanied by sixty ancillary vessels, under the command of his son, Ibrahim Pasha. After disembarking in the south of the Peloponnese, the Egyptian troops defeated the exhausted Greek rebels in battle after battle, taking no prisoners and burning down any village that stood in their way. Had it not been for the Great Powers – England, France and Russia – who sent a joint fleet to burn down Ibrahim's ships at Navarino on 20 October 1827, and thus force the Egyptians into a hasty retreat, the modern Greek state would be nothing but a sad footnote in the annals of modern history.

Naturally, Cairo's Greek community celebrated the British and French empires (less so the Russians, who had almost no presence in Egypt) as their saviours. Not Anna. While she celebrated Greece's independence, she could see that the English, the French and the Russians sided with the Greeks only by an historical accident, and would have abandoned them in a jiffy, or even subjugated them themselves, had it been in their strategic interests to do so.

In 1832, Muhammad Ali did something extraordinary. He enabled Antoine Clot, a French doctor locally known as Clot Bey, to found a school of medicine in Cairo exclusively for women. Before long, doctoresses, or *hakimas*, began graduating from a school that would have been unthinkable in Paris or London, let alone post-independence Athens. The school resonated with French and other European proto-feminists, who began descending upon Cairo in the mid-1830s to study medicine and social care. And it was not just a flash in the pan. The progression of women continued, in parallel to further economic development, during the reign of Muhammad Ali's grandson Ismail Pasha, who ruled from 1863 to 1879.

It made Anna wonder what had gone wrong. Why, from a proud society producing *hakimas* nine decades earlier, had Egypt regressed to the point where women like Salma had to pretend to be a white woman's seamstress?

11. Strategic debt

With guidance from Salma, Huda and her other Egyptian sisters, Anna discovered that Egypt's decline and subsequent fall had its roots in the Suez Canal, built by the French in 1869.

The British saw the Suez Canal as an existential threat to their near monopoly on overland trade routes. But, gradually, they found a way to seize control by leveraging the hidden powers of the City of London. Egypt's woes began when she tumbled into the trap of British bankers. In a pattern that has been repeated several times since, including in curtailing the dream of sovereign development in Africa, Latin America and much of Asia in the 1970s, it all began with a financial crisis in the United States.

The end of the American Civil War in 1865 had triggered a railway construction frenzy financed through loans made of thin air. When that bubble burst, in what became known as the Panic of 1873, the banking dominoes began to fall across the Western world, plunging Europe and North America into the Long Depression which lasted until 1879. Nations that had borrowed to invest in their modernisation, including Egypt, suddenly faced either ruinous interest rate hikes or demands from panicking bankers for immediate repayment of the loans.

By 1875, Ismail's government owed £4 million and was forced to sell its 44 per cent stake in the Suez Canal to the British government. Thinking he had no alternative to tax rises and austerity, Ismail's hold on power slipped and social unrest ensued. Ostensibly to restore peace, but in reality to take over, now was

Britain's cue to invade. In 1882, London declared Egypt a British protectorate and proceeded to bombard Alexandria, while deploying troops near the Suez Canal. 'That's how the British colonised us,' wrote Anna in her diary a little less than a month before she had Yorgo.

Egypt became a new India, a new Kenya, a new Rhodesia: yet another colony where British and European expatriates sought their fortunes at the expense of the indigenous population's living standards, freedoms and dignity. 'The British rejoice that they can walk from Cape Town, through our lands, all the way to Rangoon without ever leaving British territory,' Huda had once remarked during a union meeting. 'They wanted us to celebrate that they are free to walk all over us – well, we didn't oblige them.'

Colonialism had dealt Egyptian women a double blow: subjugation to their new European masters as well as resurgent Islamist fundamentalism, the reliable upshot of the sudden death of sovereignty and economic growth. Colonisation wiped out most of the rights women had gained since the 1830s, from the right to equal pay in the textile industry to the opportunity to become doctors. Still, women refused to abandon the tradition of feminist activism and public service rooted in the 1830s.

In 1919, as empires tumbled in the dark shadow of the Great War, the underground women's movement incited a magnificent revolution against British rule. Huda had been a central figure in that rebellion, leading mass protests of working-class women in the cities, while the fellahas (women who work the land) supported them with food packages and by providing sanctuary both from the British and from irate husbands. In fact, it was said that one of the reasons the colonial government backed down was that troops and officers were overwhelmed by the crowds of determined women who were encouraging and shielding their male comrades in the streets of Cairo, Alexandria and Port Said.

STRATEGIC DEBT

By 1923, the British were forced to concede. They promised a constitution and the nominal transfer of powers to Fuad I, the local sultan now anointed King of Egypt. But, as Huda and Salma explained, it was a retreat in name only. True power remained in the hands of the British, the king proving a pathetic figurehead. As for the economy, it remained fully in the hands of European expats, with Egyptians enduring quasi-bondage in their own country.

'I always knew that Huda Sha'arawi had not suddenly succumbed to a spontaneous urge to remove her veil at that Ramses railway station café in 1923,' Anna wrote in her diary.

12. Bitterly cold comfort

How should Anna break the news to Yango that she believed Egypt's fall into the clasps of the British Empire was a massive setback for modernisation? Could he stomach the clash between her new perspective and their comfortable life funded by Thomas Cook, a company deeply enmeshed in the fabric of empire? Could he handle the cognitive dissonance? Would he even care for her analysis of Egypt's great leap backwards? Could he accept that Ismail Pasha was removed from power in 1879 by British functionaries for whom an independent, proud, modern Egypt was merely an impediment to their control of the Suez Canal? Would she ever be able to make her case that the colonisers' weapon of choice was strategic indebtedness? With these unspoken questions polluting her mind, every trip she took down the Nile, every visit to some museum, amounted to cold comfort.

Yango had no idea, of course. Caught between her gratitude for his *joie de vivre* and her guilt for having a secret life, she lacked the words to let him in. She feared his reaction were he to find out about Salma and Huda. She hoped he would notice her glow while on their building's ground floor mixing with the labourers, handymen, seamstresses and janitors who lived there. And how her glow dissipated as she climbed to the upper floors where they lived alongside other Europeans. But Yango never noticed, confusing her delight for kindness.

Eventually, she learned not to care. It was enough that Ahmed, their building's *bawaab*, or doorman, noticed. One morning, after

Anna had spent almost two hours chatting and laughing with his wife, Ahmed gave her a concerned look and whispered: '*Sayenta* Anna, be careful!'

In 1920s Cairo, locals addressed European ladies as *hawaga*, which meant 'one whom the air (*ha-wa*) had blown in the direction of their land' – like sand the khamsin blew into the cities. But Ahmed called Anna *sayenta*, from '*santa*' or 'saint', his words of warning springing from his heartfelt concern for the risks she took in mixing with them and, in particular, with women like Salma, whom Ahmed had seen sneaking up the stairs.

That night, Anna wrote in her diary: 'Not even the great university that I attend in my dreams could bestow a greater honour upon me than the one word Ahmed whispered this morning.'

13. A friend is born

Yorgo's arrival changed everything. Suddenly, Anna could imagine a real person on this planet who was both her flesh and blood and her trusted friend. Yango was also excited to have a boy to mould.

During the day, Anna sang him Sappho's poetry. She introduced him to the sounds of different creatures through Saint-Saëns' *The Carnival of the Animals*, a record that she had bought from an Austrian tennis instructor who dreamt of a career as a violinist. Before Yorgo could even crawl, she prepared a catalogue of all the French Enlightenment texts the Ursuline nuns had kept away from her. Thus, Yorgo grew up believing that the world was bathed in critical thought, with a divine soundtrack to match.

Over the years, Anna taught him how to think as a refugee as well as a foreigner. She enlisted Montesquieu's *Persian Letters*, in which two enlightened Persian notables describe French society to their family and friends in Isfahan. Through Voltaire's *Candide*, she tried to arm him against the Panglossian faith that we live in the best of all possible worlds. To highlight the mighty chasm between Christianity's founder and the practices of established churches, she introduced him to Jesus through Buddhist parables. She went to great lengths to familiarise him with Ibn Khaldun, the late-fourteenth-century Cairo-based scholar, who had written incisively on how, as cooperation takes hold, civilisations rise, and how the resulting economic success is pregnant with the discord that brings them down. She read to him tales of love and loneliness from Marguerite de Navarre's

Heptaméron, the first book to be published by a French woman in her own name. And to complete Yorgo's introduction to the modern French canon, she read to him Rousseau's *The Social Contract*.

Of all the Greeks she could have introduced him to, Anna chose two, both expats, both from Alexandria. One was Constantine Cavafy, a contemporary whose poems she worshiped, especially 'Waiting for the Barbarians' with its deliciously subversive last verse: 'Those people were a kind of solution.' The other, of course, was Hypatia.

Anna also landed on another 'soaring owl' – her phrase for her female idols. This was the greatest scientist of their own time, and perhaps ever: Marie Skłodowska-Curie. She was the first woman to win a Nobel Prize in Physics, and also the only person to claim a second Nobel Prize in a different field, chemistry. Moreover, she was a pioneer, a revolutionary, a patriot, a humanist and a decidedly freethinking spirit.

Then Yango would get his turn. At five o'clock, Yorgo shifted from his mother's French to his father's Greek, to keep him grounded in their common heritage. However, the shift was not so much linguistic as philosophical.

Yango's father had escaped to Leros from Crete in 1869 at the tender age of fourteen. The teenage refugee was escaping certain execution for his participation, alongside his father and older brothers, in an attempted revolution against the Ottoman Empire, which had maintained its grip on the island following the Greek Revolution of 1821. Yango's relationship with his father might not have been the best, but, nonetheless, he named his son after him, Yorgo, and regaled that son with his father's tales from the failed uprising.

There were also stories of Eleutherios Venizelos, Crete's best-known political son, whose father, like Yango's, had taken up arms in the late 1860s and fled following defeat. Venizelos, however, returned to Crete after studying law at the University of Athens, to pick up the struggle where he had left off.

History remembers Venizelos as the politician who led the ultimately successful Cretan Revolution of 1899 which turned Crete into an autonomous state. In 1910, Venizelos returned to Athens. He was lionised by young patriotic army officers on the verge of storming the palace, and intensely popular among the masses, and the King of Greece was strong-armed into anointing him Prime Minister of Greece. Though never averse to taking up arms, Venizelos' success at claiming Thessaloniki and pushing Greece's borders all the way to Thrace was due to exquisite diplomatic skills and, crucially, to a gigantic wager which could have gone disastrously wrong. He dragged Greece into the Great War on the side of the Allies, and against the will of the Danish-born King whose sympathies lay with Germany, having served in the German imperial guard and studied politics and business in Heidelberg and Leipzig.

For twenty years, Venizelos, a renowned anglophile, struggled to keep Greece closely aligned with London. A pragmatist's pragmatist, he never doubted London's readiness to sacrifice Greece, but he considered the British Empire to be the most agreeable of the Great Powers and, importantly, Greece's preferred ally against the Ottomans. Venizelos' mindset suited Yango perfectly. And in order to prepare his son to inherit this good life, Yango read him two books.

For Yango, *Robinson Crusoe* epitomised the apotheosis of the industrious Englishman. In explaining his choice, Yango confided in Anna that, when the Mediterranean's currents spewed him out onto the shores of Alexandria, he had felt like Daniel Defoe's protagonist: rummaging in the wreckage of his life for raw materials that might help him build a new one. In his eyes, *Robinson Crusoe* was a suspenseful and didactic tale about sin and repentance and, also, about the loneliness of the human condition.

Gulliver's Travels was Yango's second choice. Gulliver was a quirkier version of Crusoe, a peripatetic Englishman gathering tall tales from far and wide with which to impress his friends back at home. Anna joked that Yango, like Gulliver, had a predilection for embellishing his own exploits in faraway places.

Young Yorgo loved both books, reading them again and again. Anna nudged him towards a more incisive reading of both. Isn't it splendid, she asked, how Defoe created a story of Robinson being taken out of England to demonstrate the impossibility of taking England out of Robinson? In Anna's mind, Defoe's story was extraordinary for the way it plants Mr Crusoe among tropical fauna and sandy beaches to have him discover there, in a state of extreme solitude, the Protestant ethic and the spirit of capitalism.

Crusoe tames Nature by means of the technology retrieved from the shipwreck – fishing rods, assorted tools, a gun, etc. Friday and Xury symbolised the heavily racialised domination that Anna yearned for Yorgo to be aware of. Pointing out how Crusoe's world was bereft of women, or indeed of any significant relationships, she highlighted what was missing in the world Defoe had created as a tribute to rational economic men.

And whereas Yango emphasised Gulliver's spirit of exploration, Anna steered Yorgo back to Jonathan Swift's original intention: to warn readers against identifying imperialism with progress. Gulliver, she pointed out, visits neither desolate islands nor barbaric societies but sophisticated cultures. In fact, Anna suggested, were Yorgo to delve deeper, he would detect that the Yahoos – the miniature humanoids Gulliver encounters – exhibit the obnoxious materialism and elitism of the English ruling class.

14. Hiatus

Yorgo's early years were Anna and Yango's happiest. 'For three years now the child has been bringing us closer together,' Anna merrily reported in 1928. The twenties were still roaring. The ensuing Great Depression remained inconceivable. The next world war was beyond the horizon.

Before Yorgo's first birthday, Yango had insisted it was time to move from the congested city to a house with a garden in affluent Pont de Coubah. During the mild Cairo winter, the three of them would cycle down the acacia-lined boulevard, past Abdeen Square and into the gardens of the king's summer palace where the guards, who knew them, waved them on. On Tuesday evenings, they would receive friends and nosy relatives curious to meet Yorgo. Wednesday and Thursday evenings were reserved for the cinema, occasionally the theatre, followed by dinner in Ezbekiyya – a central, cosmopolitan district with an array of restaurants, music venues and cabarets.

Anna loved how the streets of Ezbekiyya pulsed with decadence, and the warm night air of jasmine and petrol fumes. Neon signs flickered above crowded cafés, their glow washing over men in sharp linen suits and women in bias-cut dresses. Italian and English cars slid past, their headlights cutting through the haze, tyres whispering over wet cobbles. Laughter spilled from open doorways, jostling with the wail of brass bands and the distant clatter of streetcars. Somewhere, a glass would shatter, a reveller would sing, the whole district throbbing – alive, reckless, drunk.

HIATUS

Almost every weekend, Anna, Yango and Yorgo would go on excursions that wealthy Europeans only experienced maybe once in their lifetimes. One glorious Saturday night in May 1930, Yango got them tickets for an outdoor staging of Verdi's *Aida* right in front of the Pyramids. When the orchestra and choir started on the second act, 'Gloria all' Egitto', the crowd joined in, singing at the top of their voices what had become Egypt's de facto national anthem. The single tear rolling down his mother's cheek was to become one of Yorgo's enduring memories.

Anna lovingly documented their outings and pasted her photos on the dark brown pages of a photo album, penning captions of inviting place names in calligraphic white ink. Aswan, Barrage, Badrashin, Petrified Forest, Wadi Koff, Fayum. A century later, today, Anna's album sits on my desk, captivating anyone who wishes to look inside.

Next to her album sits a pile of her diaries brimming with opposition to the ideology of Thomas Cook or P&O – the empire's great companies whose imprints are emblazoned on their covers. Her beautiful French prose was my introduction to her inner conflict. Whereas the beautiful photos evoke an orientalist bliss, her diaries reveal a darker side. They speak of her growing premonition that the happier those days were, the greater the price she would pay when her facade inevitably cracked.

For while they lived the European oriental dream, the disenfranchised people that she considered her sisters and brothers often went to bed hungry a stone's throw away. When they got sick, the shabby hospitals that they could afford were more likely to kill than to cure them. Could Yango not see this? What allowed him to sleep like a baby when she could not? Anna understood the stark reality: the white man's deep-seated belief that unsatiated hunger and untreated disease befall brown people independently of the systems that uphold white wealth and health.

Even more insidious was the conviction that any political effort to redress the inequity would only serve to harm the disadvantaged further.

In one of the Egyptian Feminist Union meetings, which Anna began attending again after six months of breastfeeding, she put forward her theory. Her comrades found it hard to agree that white men genuinely doubted that wealth could be redistributed in favour of the poor – that, in today's parlance, altruism could be effective. 'Come on, Anna, surely they know it can be done but they will be damned if they let it happen.' Anna did not share their view. She knew Yango. He was not merely callous – he slept with an easy conscience because he sincerely believed that the road to hell is paved with good intentions.

To make her case, she brought along to one of their meetings Yango's copy of Adam Smith's *The Wealth of Nations*, in which her husband had twice underlined: 'I have never known much good done by those who affected to trade for the public good.' When the other women heard that line being read out in Anna's steady voice, they fell silent. To break the eerie silence one of them came up with a teasing suggestion: 'Next time, sister, why don't you bring your camera along to photograph our subversive lot?' They all laughed raucously at the thought of that particular snapshot appearing in Anna's album next to the images of plush riverboats.

Anna's decision to bring a book to their meetings started a trend. Other women who had already been translating important texts into Arabic began bringing their manuscripts along to discuss with the group. Many were lost poetry or novels. Some were revolutionary texts, such as Mary Wollstonecraft's *A Vindication of the Rights of Woman* or Karl Marx's *Das Kapital*. Anna devoured them all but found one particularly insightful: Thorstein Veblen's *The Theory of the Leisure Class,* in which the quirky

Norwegian-American hypothesised that, under capitalism, the new ruling class used conspicuous consumption, like male peacocks use their feathers, to project and replicate power.

She was intrigued by Veblen's assertion that it was the function of the social power of a bourgeois husband to have a non-working wife whom he encourages to indulge in 'conspicuous leisure'. She chuckled thinking that, subconsciously, she was part of Yango's game.

When Wall Street crashed in the autumn of 1929, the shockwave travelled swiftly across the Atlantic. After taking its toll on the moneyed men of London, Edinburgh and the Home Counties, it immediately hit Thomas Cook's business in Egypt, casting a shadow over Yango's hitherto sunny disposition. Anna felt him growing grumpier by the day.

It wasn't just Yango. The entire expatriate community was getting nervous. With nervousness comes suspicion, especially of dissent. And with suspicion, prejudice. And prejudice easily becomes paranoia. Throughout the 1930s, as fascism was rising in Europe, Anna felt her peers taking a keener interest in her out-of-turn phrases, her demeanour, her occasional slips. Yango intuited it too. With every nasty look from an aunt or socialite, Yango's ability to overlook Anna's subversive side diminished. The grapes of discontent were growing heavy for the bitter harvest.

During the summer of 1930, Yango and Anna were debating which nursery to enrol Yorgo in. Yango insisted on an English-speaking one. English was already overtaking French as the lingua franca. Moreover, English was a language the boy never spoke at home. Anna could see Yango's point and relented, despite her strong preference for a French education. So, in late September, Yorgo arrived at the gates of what was to become, a few years later, Cairo's English Mission College. There, he mixed with Jewish, Armenian, Italian and, of course, British kids. Within weeks, his English began to dominate his French and his Greek. One afternoon, three months later, he announced to Anna: 'You know, Mum, I have decided I am English.'

'Imagine what he will be like in twenty years,' Anna told Yango in a fit of rage, 'if it only took three months for him to swallow the empire's bait hook, line and sinker! What next? We draw up his application for a place at Eton?' Such was her fury that Yango did not put up much of a fight when she announced she was pulling Yorgo out of the English nursery. Even though he thought she was overreacting, Yango was placated by her suggestion that he attend a Greek nursery instead. While still keen for Yorgo to get a British education, his heart warmed to the idea of giving his son the education that had shaped himself, back on Leros.

Greek nursery meant a direct path to Greek primary school and, then, some Greek *gymnasium*, or secondary school. Of the many available in Cairo, the obvious choice was the renowned Ampeteios, the 'Greek Eton' to many. Established in 1861 with a large endowment from two ethnic Greek Syrian businessmen, and run by a committee presided over by the Patriarch of Alexandria, the school attracted enlightened teachers, often migrants from the old country, but could neither pay them decent salaries nor provide them with high-calibre pupils.

Soon, Yorgo was in his element in Ampeteios' majestic building on Fuad Street, surrounded by new friends, teachers and challenges.

15. Through a porthole darkly

Yorgo's schooling threw into sharp relief the fact that neither he nor Anna had ever set foot on Greek soil. So, in the summer of 1932, it was decided that mother and son would board the good ship *Attiki*, bound for Piraeus. Strange as it may now seem, diaspora Greeks thought of Greece as a forlorn subset of the Greek world – a feeling they shared with Jewish friends, for whom Thessaloniki, Berlin and Vienna were more vibrantly Jewish than Jerusalem. After all, the best Greek schools were not in Athens or Patras but in Cairo, Constantinople, Venice, Smyrna and Odessa. Similarly, the best Greek publishers and record labels were in Firenze and New York City. Greece was to them an emotionally important but still unproven experiment in nation building.

Yango used work as an excuse to join them in Athens a few weeks later. In his absence, mother and son spent time on the island of Poros and, from there, took a trip to Mycenae where Anna claimed in her diary to have summoned the spirits of Clytemnestra and her daughters, Iphigenia and Electra, 'to exchange notes'. Then, in Athens, once Yango had joined them, they took in the sights, visited the museums, attended a performance of Aeschylus' *Persians* and visited distant relatives. Years later, Yorgo would reminisce that 'Mother found Greece intoxicating and the Greeks uncouth.'

It was a terrible year to visit Greece. The twin shocks of the crash of 1929 and Britain's abandonment of the gold standard in 1931 had forced London bankers to call in Greece's loans. In May, despite persistent efforts by Venizelos and his ministers to contain the shock, Greece had declared bankruptcy. Every expense in foreign currency had to be cancelled overnight. Even the artists that had been dispatched days earlier to represent Greece in that year's Venice Biennale had to rely on the kindness of foreign friends for their keep and return fare.

By the time Yango, Anna and Yorgo boarded the steamship to Alexandria, the machinery of Greece's state was paralysed, the depression was ravaging the already brittle social fabric, and the scene was set for Venizelos' defeat in the general election scheduled for November. On board *Attiki*, Yango was inconsolable that his political idol was about to be defeated when his country, in a state of advanced disrepair, needed him most. But Anna had greater worries. While in Poros, the seat of Greece's naval academy, she had made the acquaintance of high-ranking navy officers who were talking openly about Italy's fascist government planning something big in the Aegean.

After a long delay, *Attiki* sailed out of Piraeus just before midnight on 4 September 1932. After clearing the port, opposite Salamis, its engine slowed down and its propeller stayed idle. While Yango slept in their cabin, Anna and Yorgo were glued to the porthole struggling to make out what was happening in the misty darkness. For what seemed like hours, there was nothing. Just the hum of *Attiki*'s idling engine and occasional shouts from crew members. Then they saw it. Like an ascending whale, a French-built submarine surfaced next to *Attiki*, before heading out to the open sea beyond the eastern edge of Aegina, where Anna imagined the goddess Afea looking on. Were they witnessing a dress rehearsal for when Mussolini would dispatch a fleet? Anna wanted to believe that she had been too easily impressed by the rumours she heard on Poros. The Italian passports in her bag, the only passports they possessed, felt like a practical joke only a vengeful deity would play on them.

Back in Cairo, Anna detected a change in the air. The British made less of an effort to conceal their stranglehold over the government or their contempt for King Fuad. Their instructions from London were to protect, come what may, British investments in Egyptian cotton, the Suez Canal and, of course, debt owed to the City by Egypt's government and privateers. Salma confirmed that the police were under orders to crack down on organised labour in the textile factories. Their union meetings thus had to take place in a different location every week.

With Yorgo at school, Anna's ability to stay under the radar diminished. When his headmaster summoned her to bring Yorgo to church one Sunday morning for a special mass in honour of Greeks who had been slain by the Turkish army during the 1922 Asia Minor Catastrophe, she rushed to the school and demanded to see him. 'Are you telling me, Headmaster, that I am obliged to help your school instil nationalist hatred for the Turks into my son's soul? What about the Bulgarians? The Italians? The English colonisers of this land? Wasn't it the French, the British and the Italian governments who helped engineer the Asia Minor Catastrophe? Should I make my son hate them too? Or would you rather I teach him Christian love for the peoples of the world? You tell me!'

The poor headmaster, whose politics happened to be close to hers, tried to make amends. Their meeting ended amicably but it was not the end of the story. Because Yorgo was let off by the headmaster, a reactionary teacher made sure to inform the chieftains of the Greek community of the incident. Within days, the headmaster was transferred to a school in Sudan and Yango was sternly told to rein Anna in. 'It is one thing', he yelled that evening at the top of his voice, 'for me to tolerate putting Yorgo to sleep at night with the story of Antigone's disobedience to men's law. But it is quite another to risk my social standing with your public displays – that I shall not permit.'

Yango's liberalism, it turned out, was conditional: it did not extend to his wife's acts 'out there', acts that showed him up and jeopardised his authority.

Holding on to what hope remained of salvaging their relationship, she bit her tongue and reluctantly let the storm pass. To feel like less of a sell-out, she spent the next couple of years building, with the union's abundant help, a rudimentary health service for locals, especially women living in Cairo's city centre. It was the kind of thing that could pass as philanthropy, as opposed to activism. But even in this, Anna took precautions to stay out of the limelight as much as possible.

A year later, in 1933, days after Hitler had become Germany's chancellor, Yango agreed to move the family back to the city centre, where they rented a lovely fourth-floor apartment close to the Ezbekiyya Gardens. There, Anna found it easier to meet her colleagues and work on their health network. During 1934, Thomas Cook's business started picking up again, and so did Yango's spirits. For a fleeting moment, it seemed as if their bubble could be reinflated. The news that Anna was pregnant again, almost a decade after Yorgo's birth, added to the illusion.

Unfortunately, by the time their second boy arrived, whom they named Stavro after Anna's father, the dark clouds were gathering again. On the third day of October 1935, Mussolini ordered the invasion of Ethiopia – the only African country never to have been colonised by Europeans. Two long years before the Nazis tried out their Luftwaffe on the Spanish republicans resisting Franco's fascism, Mussolini's fascists did even worse to the Ethiopians: devastating aerial bombardments, mustard gas and flame-throwers, and concentration camps for those they didn't kill. It was a dress rehearsal for the atrocities they would soon inflict on other European peoples.

For Anna, the Ethiopian tragedy appeared to be the fulfilment of the prophetic image of the ascending evil that she had witnessed three years earlier through their cabin's porthole, just outside the port of Piraeus. Every cell in her body told her it had to be resisted. With whatever it took.

16. At daggers drawn

Cairo's polite society was shocked by what Italy was up to in Egypt's underbelly. However, the British discouraged any serious animosity towards Mussolini's thugs. It was 1935, after all – a time when London considered fascism an ill-mannered ally against communism. They discouraged public discussion of the Ethiopian crisis and placed under surveillance societies, organisations or unions mobilising against the fascist surge. With Yango keeping his head below the parapet, anxious to toe the British party line as any director of Thomas Cook had to do, Anna was suffocating.

A year later, in July 1936, the Spanish Civil War erupted when a fascist coup failed to overthrow the Republican government but, nevertheless, triggered a long, bloody and ultimately successful military campaign to do so three years later – with the full, material support of Mussolini and Hitler. The British government's de facto support of Spain's fascists solidified Anna's understanding of her husband's world. A month later, on 4 August, another fascist coup, this time in Greece, succeeded outright in installing a ruthless dictatorship, hammering the last nail into the coffin of Venizelist liberalism – Yango's ideological refuge.

By the time fascism had swallowed up Spain and Greece, it took no great intellect to recognise that it was becoming a pandemic. Japan's version had already spread to China, with its 1931 invasion of Manchuria and the creation, a year later, of the puppet state of Manchukuo. Across Europe, fascist regimes sprouted in Hungary, Romania, Bulgaria and Slovakia – with the Croat and Serb fascists waiting in the wings. Even in Britain, after months of terrorising Jews across England, Oswald Mosley triggered the Battle of Cable Street on 4 October 1936. During that pogrom, the Metropolitan Police sided with fascists in vicious street fighting across London's East End targeting Jews, leftists, trades unionists and Irish workers.

Financially, life continued to be easy. In his later years, Yorgo's memories of those pre-war times included his mother teaching him how to waltz to Johann Strauss' *Blue Danube*, their summer holidays in Alexandria, and playing tennis or swimming at the Cairo Sporting Club's Olympic-sized pool. But, under the surface, nerves were tense, daggers were drawn and a most peculiar civil war was in the offing.

One afternoon in late 1938, Yango returned home and, for the first time, ordered Yorgo to go to his room – he wanted a word with Anna. The secret police had come to see him that morning at the office with shattering information: his wife had been seen in subversive meetings where industrial strikes and other seditious acts were being planned. Yango protested, telling them that they must be mistaken, unable to believe it. Except that the police had evidence, testimony, eyewitnesses. They gave him a roll-call of campaigns she had been involved in, from proselytising dock workers in Alexandria to refuse to load cargo bound for fascist-held Spanish ports to organising strikes by textile workers in Cairo and pro-democracy groups in Port Said. They told him about Huda and Salma. They helped him connect the dots between her unexplained absences and the texts in Arabic that Yango would occasionally find in the apartment – which, though he could not read, filled him with unease.

Upon hearing his father screaming at his mother, Yorgo

rushed into the living room to intervene: 'Stop harassing my mum,' he said in a steady voice. Older in mind than his thirteen years, he was determined to stand by 'the light of his life', as he called his mother until the day he died. Though Anna had never told him about her activism, Yorgo sensed what was going down. At Ampeteios, he was friends with a couple of older Syrian boys who were active in the anti-fascist youth movement. As the only Greek pupil to have opted for the Arabic-language courses, he could read the rousing literature produced by Egyptian progressives against the British colonialists' toleration of the fascists in Ethiopia and across Europe.

Incensed, Yango ordered him to return to his room. In the same breath he barked at Anna: 'Are you happy now? Was this your game all along? To turn him into a mindless follower of your ridiculous rebellion?' Before Anna got a chance to calm him down, Yorgo interjected: 'I am neither mindless nor anyone's follower. Just because I do not think or act like you would like me to, Dad, gives you no right to blame it on Mum.' Ignoring him, Yango snapped at Anna: 'Do you realise what you have done? You have pushed him on a path to certain ruin. Don't you understand that rootless people like us, like him, need to stay on the straight and narrow? That our prosperity, our very survival, rests on being able to be like chameleons who blend in, not bulls in a china shop?'

'Deep in my heart,' she told Yango calmly, 'I always knew you would stay on the fence even when the jackals arrived. It's the price one pays for believing that matters are too complicated to justify picking sides, even when the barbarians are at the door: one ends up as either the beasts' prey or their handmaiden.' 'I see no jackals Anna, except your agitator friends,' Yango replied angrily. Alert to how sensitive Yorgo was to their quarrels, Anna chose her words carefully:

> There is a time and a place to resemble chameleons, Yango. But there is also a time and a place to take a stand. When you actually see the fascists, they will be breaking down our door. At that point, you won't be able to blend in – unless you join them. But, then, you will be a jackal not a chameleon.

Anna's composed rejoinder enraged Yango further. 'You have no concept of the depth of your folly, woman. Me? Be my guest. Destroy me. My job? My reputation? Wreck it at will. But your own son? Making him think it is OK to punch a naked blade with his bare fist is going to come back and bite you – mark my words. And you,' he added, turning to Yorgo, 'you get out of my sight. Now!' Anna turned down, calmly but steadfastly, Yango's repeated demands that she give up the union, her comrades and their campaigns. That night, for the first time, Yorgo witnessed scenes that imbued him with a lifelong aversion to his father.

Life would never be the same again. From that night, Anna and Yango embarked on separate lives under the same roof, addressing each other politely but sparsely, keeping up appearances in public for the benefit of Yango's career and to keep relatives in their place. Yango never properly tried to reach out to Yorgo again, an attitude the teenager reciprocated. Meanwhile, as Anna and Yorgo grew closer, Yango turned his attentions to Stavro, their second son.

17. In war's shadow

At six in the evening on 10 June 1940, a few hours after Norway had surrendered to Hitler, Benito Mussolini climbed onto the balcony of the Palazzo Venezia to announce that Italy was declaring war against Britain and France. Anna was amused. Not with the theatrics, nor with the deepening calamity to have befallen Europe and the world, but with the speed at which the expat ruling class of Egypt, who had been lambasting her and her comrades as madwomen, suddenly became fascism's greatest foes!

On the orders of Sir Miles Lampson, Britain's Ambassador to Egypt, Cairo's British high command declared enemy aliens all adult male Italian passport holders who had lived in Egypt for less than twenty years. Within twelve hours, they had to report to specific locations from where they would be dispatched to internment camps in Mansura, Tantah, Fayed and Moascar. Anna learned the news while in Alexandria, where she had only just arrived to spend the summer with her sons. Unable to contact Yango, and convinced that he would have not lost a second to surrender to the British authorities, she and the boys rushed back to Cairo.

The train sighed into life, its carriages carrying Anna past the ochre sprawl of Alexandria, where the sea breeze still clung to the windows. Her first-class compartment was a cocoon of velvet and mahogany, the air spiced with Turkish coffee and the faint musk of cigars. A steward moved stealthily, serving chilled lemonade, the distant laughter of ladies in silk dresses mingling with the clink of ice in crystal. But Anna could hardly breathe, struggling even to swallow her lemonade. Outside, the delta slowly unfurled – emerald fields, mud-brick villages, the Nile a silver thread in the distance. Time stretched, languid and lustrous, offering her a chance to plan her strategy.

In a letter she sent Yorgo late that night, she described the state she had found his incarcerated father in when she arrived in Cairo: 'I was expecting Buster Keaton surviving a house falling about him, but I found Richard the Third begging for a horse.' Yango, ashen-faced and panicky, was locked up in a classroom of the Italian school Giuseppe Garibaldi, which had been turned into a holding cell. Anna reassured him: 'Leave it to me. I am getting you out of here.' She soon managed to get the brigadier-general in charge of the internees to meet with her. Deploying her signature combination of charm and firmness, and addressing him in old-school French, she impressed upon him that Yango's internment constituted a double injustice. As a casualty of Italy's brutal occupation of his native Leros, her husband – she explained – had been an early victim of Italian proto-fascism. His Italian passport had been imposed on him as Leros and the rest of the Dodecanese had been taken by force. Detecting sympathy on the brigadier-general's face, and switching to English for effect, she continued:

> In this light, my husband's Italian passport, sir, rather than evidence of potential connivance with the fascist enemy, is proof that he, more so than most British subjects, will be your steadiest ally against Mussolini's stooges here in Cairo. Consider too, if you please, two other facts: for seventeen long years he has worked loyally for Thomas Cook, an iconic British company. Secondly, he speaks Italian terribly,

in contrast to his Chaucerian English, not to mention that he has never set foot in the Italian Consulate, let alone Italy itself.

The brigadier-general smiled broadly but needed another prod in the right direction: 'Furthermore, as your people will confirm if you care to ask them to look into my record, I have been a person of interest for a number of years courtesy of defying your authorities' attempt to discourage people like me from organising demonstrations and actions against Italian fascism – from the day they invaded Ethiopia to today. Do you think I would be able to get away with this if my husband sympathised with Mussolini?' Half an hour later Yango was released and the whole family received police clearances.

For the next three years, the very real possibility that Cairo would fall to the advancing Axis armies produced a new détente, and even warmth, within their family. A couple of days after Yango's release, the British army crossed into Italian-held Libya but were soon defeated, the Italian army pushing them back and capturing Sidi Barrani, a coastal Egyptian town. On 22 June, France surrendered and the Vichy collaborationist regime was formed. This meant that, to all intents and purposes, French Morocco and French Algeria were handed over to Hitler. On 15 August, on the orders of Mussolini, an Italian submarine torpedoed, and sank, the Greek navy's light cruiser *Elli* in Tinos harbour – a warning shot foreshadowing the wholesale invasion of Greece by the full might of Italy's army and air force on 28 October.

In December 1940, the British army in Egypt managed to regroup, defeat the Italians at Sidi Barrani and chase them back into Libya. In February 1941, to prevent the Italians' surrender, Hitler dispatched the famed Afrika Korps to north Africa under the command of General Erwin Rommel. But that was not all. The Greek army's unexpected successes against Italy's crack troops on the Greek–Albanian border had forced the Italians to retreat deep into Albania. Hitler had no choice but to bail out Mussolini in the Balkans too – a move that involved nothing less than invading Yugoslavia to reach Greece, defeat the Greeks and, in so doing, create a Balkan–Mediterranean corridor through which Rommel's troops in north Africa might be resupplied.

In April 1941, as Eleni and Panayis were watching from their rooftop, Piraeus was bombed to smithereens and Athens was swarmed by Nazis. German cargo ships supplying Rommel would soon set sail from Greek waters. Around that time, unbeknownst to Anna, sixteen-year-old Yorgo, furious at the news coming from Greece and the north African front, joined the Antifascist Vanguard – an underground organisation established by Greek, Arab and Jewish youths. The expat community in Egypt were on tenterhooks. If Rommel managed to break through the British army defences west of the Nile, nothing could stop Hitler from taking over the whole of Egypt and, arguably, the Middle East. The local population were less fazed. Many professed indifference, refusing to care deeply about which European power would suck them dry. In that environment, the Egyptian Feminist Union played a crucial role.

Initially, the women were inclined to a neutral stance, echoing Turkey's neutrality and influenced by the pro-Ankara position of their ageing founder Huda Sha'arawi. After prolonged debates, however, the point of view put forward by Salma and Anna prevailed: a fascist victory would set back the struggle for Egyptian women's emancipation by decades. The union worked tirelessly to spread the anti-fascist message in the factories, the poor neighbourhoods, their health network, the mosques and the Coptic churches, in every nook and cranny of Egyptian society.

The union also published articles, essays and pamphlets arguing for anti-fascist unity within society's upper echelons. So, when the French wife of Egypt's minister of culture announced an essay competition on the general theme 'Egyptian Woman', Anna decided to enter. Under the title 'The Fellaha of 2000', she described a utopia of emancipated rural women in the year 2000, when colonialism, patriarchy, fascism and systematic exploitation of humanity and Nature had become extinct. Yorgo volunteered to take the manuscript to the minister's wife in person, pedalling his bicycle with immense pride. They both laughed when the results were announced. Anna's essay was the runner-up behind one submitted by the British Ambassador's Italian wife.

After two and a half years of shifting front lines in the north African campaign, in October 1942 the Second Battle of El Alamein changed the mood. As Winston Churchill would say: 'Before Alamein we never had a victory. After Alamein we never had a defeat.' Nevertheless, Cairo never really regained its pre-war feel. The cafeterias and the restaurants were busy but most of the clientele were in uniform – many of them Greek soldiers who had been transported to support the British troops.

Anna and Yorgo would take tea with them to gauge the mood back in Greece, only to discover deep divisions running across their ranks. Very few supported the Greek government in exile in Egypt. Incredibly, some were sympathetic to the fascists. Most, however, leaned towards the leftist partisans in occupied Greece who were putting up the only serious resistance to the Nazis. On one occasion, Anna was horrified by a brutal fist fight that broke out when Cypriot Greeks, fully enmeshed into Britain's army due to Cyprus' status as a formal British colony, picked on Greek soldiers calling them losers and hangers-on. That was not their Cairo, she told Yorgo.

In May 1943, six months after Anglo-American landings in

north-west Africa, two hundred and fifty thousand German and Italian troops surrendered. The spectre of the swastika flying over Cairo had evaporated. A month later, Yorgo graduated from Ampeteios. Almost immediately, he landed a decent job at the Bank of Athens, a Greek-owned bank whose managing director moved in Yango's circles. Unable to think of an alternative, at a time when the war was entering its ugliest phase in Europe and the Far East, Yorgo kept his head down and saved his wages for the moment he could fly the coop.

18. Athens calling

Anna's admiration of Marie Curie had rubbed off on Yorgo. Curie was a woman doing things women were not supposed to, just like his mother. He was also inspired by Curie's courageous – and for some outrageous – rejection of Democritus' belief that the atom is indivisible, which led her to discover radiation and X-rays, thus paving the way for nuclear physics. And then he marvelled that Marie's husband, unlike his mother's, was ready and willing to support her feminism-at-work. Pierre Curie was a loyal partner and collaborator, with whom she shared the 1903 Nobel Prize – thus proving, in Yorgo's mind, that patriarchy is not ingrained in men's genotype.

Yorgo had known what he wanted to do with his life ever since Anna told him the story of Lord Kelvin visiting the Curies' laboratory. Upon seeing radium glow in the dark, the legendary physicist had remarked: 'I have now seen the impossible.' Yorgo, too, wanted to come face to face with the impossible. After hours, telling no one but Anna, he attended advanced science classes at Cairo's Lycée Français, an institution preparing students for science degrees in French universities. One evening, as the war was ending, he dropped his well-rehearsed bombshell over dinner: he intended to resign from the bank and go to read physics and chemistry at the University of Athens.

Yango was aghast. Resign a cushy, well-paying job? For what? To study in, of all places, a devastated Athens where the soil on the graves from the previous December's civil war was still moist?

A city in ruins ruled over by armed men, hunger and want? Yes, answered Yorgo. To begin with, he preferred a quick death to a slow withering of his soul behind a desk at some bank. Why Athens and not Paris or London? Because it was time to connect with his Greek side, he replied. Moreover, Greece's poverty had a silver lining: the small stash of English pounds he had saved would probably suffice to see him through a four-year degree.

Anna was equally unhappy with Yorgo's decision. Unlike her husband, she wanted Yorgo to go to university. But Greece sounded like a nightmare. Would the armistice hold? No one really knew. But Yorgo had made up his mind. Anna knew that he had taken after her and it was futile to oppose him. So, she backed him up against Yango's livid objections. Seven years had passed since he had given up on controlling Anna or influencing his elder son. Yorgo's decision to move to Athens was the final straw. 'His blood is on your hands,' were Yango's last words on the matter.

On the mild January day when Yorgo boarded *Korinthia*, the steamship that would transport him to Piraeus, Anna was grief-stricken. 'An inner voice is urging me to stop you,' she told him on the quay. 'But I did not raise you an independent spirit only to boss you around now. So, I shall grit my teeth and wave you farewell.' Two nights and a day later, Yorgo arrived in a bitterly cold Athens that was nothing like the city he remembered from their 1932 summer holiday. During the day, emaciated, shabby folks rushed by, occasionally glancing at him with empty eyes. Buildings loomed over him, forcing his eyes to focus on the bullet holes that scarred them. Unkempt streets summoned his attention to the lack of cars, save for some tattered military Willys Jeeps and a few dilapidated buses struggling not to come to a permanent halt. As evening fell and the curfew approached, stragglers frantically darted in the shadows to avoid the numerous checkpoints.

Within forty-eight hours of his arrival, he had enrolled at the School of Chemistry and, having paid a year's fees up front, probably one of very few students to have been able to do so, he was welcomed with wide smiles by the clerk at the Students Office. But his acceptance felt like a trophy on the mantelpiece that one knows one never won fair and square. Everything made him feel guilty: knowing that he could afford to buy as much bread as he needed, or that, if needs arose, he had a way out – the next ship to Alexandria was only a forty-minute cab ride away. Most embarrassing, at least at first, was the realisation that his heavy new coat and his foreign passport made the stone-faced policemen slavishly wave him through their checkpoints.

One freezing February night, after a late physics class, he chose to walk around a little to get some fresh air. Having left the chemistry building on Solonos Street, he ended up on Eolou Street, in the heart of the old shopping precinct. The shops brimmed with merchandise but only one or two people were inside – and they were chatting, not shopping. Suddenly, a young man walking in front of him collapsed. Yorgo and a few other passers-by rushed to help. 'What's wrong with him?' Yorgo asked anxiously. His question was met with contemptuous frowns. 'What do you think?' said one of them. 'He is famished.' Yorgo dashed to a nearby bakery where he bought several tyropitas – cheese pies. 'You can't give him these, they won't go down,' a man shouted at him. A woman who seemed in the know split one of the cheese pies in half, scooped out a small amount of melted cheese with her forefinger, opened the young man's mouth and spread it on his tongue. Soon, he came around. Meanwhile, the others helped themselves to the cheese pies and disappeared. Yorgo stuffed a few banknotes in the young man's pocket and, trying to hide his mortification, walked on.

That night he sat down to write to Anna about his indignation that, outside shops laden with luxuries, starving people dropped like flies. 'What kind of an evil city Athens has become!' he exclaimed. Anna's answer put him in his place.

My dearest Yorgo,

I read your letter and was disturbed, as you wanted me to be. But, make no mistake: I was disturbed not so much by the incident you described but by the fact you found it so disturbing – and by your conclusion that Athens is evil, in a way that our Cairo is not. Have you forgotten, my sweet boy, how, as we used to exit the plush restaurants in Ezbekiyya, or cinemas like the Rex, the Royal or the Dianna, a swarm of malnourished Egyptian children would approach us begging for something to eat? That they would ransack our rubbish bins? That children your age would go to bed hungry on our very street? And all that in a rich city lucky enough, unlike Athens, to escape Nazi occupation? Shame on you, my dearest boy. I thought I had taught you better.

I am looking forward to your next, more nuanced, letter – please write soon. In the meantime, just know I can't sleep at night worrying over the explosive mix of destitution, injustice and authoritarianism the Nazis bequeathed our Athens. I live in terror that it will blow up near you.

Take good care of yourself. Your adoring mother.

Anna

Anna's caustic letter stiffened Yorgo's lip.

Besides science, Yorgo tried to educate himself as much as possible on his new country's byzantine politics. The School of Chemistry was an excellent microcosm from which to glean the bigger picture, helped by the first friend he made there, Kostas Kouloufakos. Also a first-year chemistry student, Kostas hailed from a staunchly conservative family in Mani, the southernmost part of the Peloponnese known for its ruggedness and ultra-right politics. During the Occupation, he had been arrested for participating in a rightist resistance group's botched attempt to bomb an Italian unit near his village. His peers were all executed but, as he was only fourteen, he was spared and sent to a prison in Milan, where, because he was literate, he was put to work in the prison's library. There, he explained to Yorgo, he read incessantly, beginning with Victor Hugo's *Les Misérables*. It would be the beginning of his left-wing conversion. By the time he returned to Greece, after the war's end, he had been inducted into EPON, the vast communist youth movement that had played a major role in the recent civil war. Upon meeting him, and spending time together, Yorgo recognised a kindred spirit.

During their very first conversation, Kouloufakos admitted that EPON had been informed by Cairo's Antifascist Vanguard of Yorgo's impending arrival. 'You can be very useful to us, without putting yourself in danger,' he said. Yorgo did not have to wonder for long about what he meant. Days later, Kouloufakos and another student, Taki, approached him outside the lab. Seeing them together was a shock. Taki belonged to the X Group, EPON's mortal enemies. What were Kouloufakos and Taki up to? They had come with an astonishing proposition: Yorgo should run, with their full support, in the upcoming election for president of the student union representing the Faculty of Mathematics, Physics and Chemistry.

EPON and the X Group fielding a common candidate? It made no sense, until the two of them explained that this stemmed from 'high up' – orders by the Communist Party to EPON and by the British-supported government to X's paramilitaries. Apparently, they wanted to extend the official armistice deal into student unions of note. 'But why me?' asked Yorgo. He needn't have asked. Quite obviously, he was the closest thing to the man who fell to Earth – the very definition of the non-aligned outsider that both sides could support without losing face. For good measure, Taki added jokingly: 'If you turn us down you will have to endure sequential beatings, one day by my boys, the next by his. Choose wisely!'

Within two weeks, Yorgo was president of their union. Even though he knew his election was due to the lottery of birth, it was hard to contain his glee. When Anna got word of her son's meteoric advancement, she too brimmed with delight. Through his letters, her son had, from his first day in Athens, endeavoured to share university life with her, imperfectly trying to make amends for her shattered dreams of higher education. Their correspondence was thus more of an intellectual exchange than a conversation between a mother and her son. In a letter written soon after his election, Yorgo combined his angst over the new role with his field of study:

> I was petrified by the thought that I had to be two people at once; a committed anti-fascist but also a union rep tolerated by the X Group fascists. Can anyone be two violently opposed things at once? It was then that Einstein came to my rescue. Did he not prove that light is two incompatible things at once – a stream of particles and a wave? Particles are nothing like waves. Particles are like a speeding train that must always be located at only one point at every moment in time. They have momentum. They change their behaviour only when something pushes them. And they stop moving only when something, or some force, gets in their way. Waves, in contrast, wiggle of their own accord. They bend around

corners. And they transport energy in many different directions at once. Well, if Einstein could prove that light can be two different things at once, particles and a wave, maybe I can also be the two people they demand of me at once.

Anna's response was typical: 'In encountering Einstein, my boy, you too have encountered, like Lord Kelvin at the Curies' laboratory, the impossible. But remember that, unlike light, you *are* mortal. And, unlike Lord Kelvin, if the impossible turns against you, you will not have the panoply of the British state behind you.' Yorgo replied cheekily that his belief in a cosmic script guaranteeing him a long life rested on a close reading of Georges Lemaître, the Belgian physicist who in 1927 utilised Einsteinian principles to show that history is nothing more than the continuous expansion of the universe. To which Anna responded with a scolding:

My dearest Yorgo,

Your facetious response kept me up last night. So that you know: as you were being born, nothing was there, near or far, to promise you safe passage in this life. When, as Lemaître showed, the original singularity put in motion everything that is feasible in this universe today, it did so with no guarantees of good outcomes – for anyone! Yes, some miracle we cannot fathom has turned us into molecules with mindfulness, each of us a breathing improbability carved out of disorder and stardust. Broods of contingency, we make our own way in the world as best we can. All we can know is that we are beasts striving to escape burden and to take advantage of a miraculous capacity to recognise beauty in cow dung or to luxuriate in the loveliness of a cloud drifting across the sky. But make no mistake my son: we are the same creatures who have a well-documented capacity for massacres and mass rape – as well as the ability to rationalise any level of cruelty, even to call it divine providence.

Always yours.

Anna

A few days later, the university's administration announced they would be doubling tuition fees, effective immediately. With so many students malnourished, and paid work next to impossible to find, it was a blow to the student body – leftists and rightists. Yorgo immediately went to the rector's office, accompanied by Kouloufakos, Taki and a few other student reps. The rector, embarrassed and unwilling to defend the decision bearing his signature, blamed it on the US army command, to which the British army had transferred operational and geostrategic authority over Greece – the result of Britain's post-war bankruptcy that prompted President Truman to take control of the countries, from Greece to Palestine, where British power was receding. It was apparently the Americans who, from day one of their new role in Greece, demanded a new policy of 'user pays' in health and higher education. Undeterred, Yorgo had a suggestion: 'Mr Rector, in that case, it would be brilliant if you agreed to lead a delegation of students to the US army command to explain to them why, at the present juncture, the increase in fees is counterproductive.' The rector was furious. Turning to Taki, he said: 'What are you doing listening to this man? I expected more from you.'

A few hours later, Yorgo led a bipartisan demonstration of eight hundred of his fellow students down Metropolis Street to the Ministry of Education. Predictably, the minister – probably shaking in his boots – refused to see them. But it didn't matter. Passers-by were astonished at the sight of a student demonstration, smack in the centre of Athens, with members of EPON and the X Group walking side by side. Nothing like it had ever happened before. The powers-that-be resolved it would never happen again.

A couple of days later, in early 1946, an EPON functionary briefed Yorgo that the X Group had been ordered to withdraw from their arrangement. 'With X now gunning against us, the gendarmes will also be unleashed. We are no longer safe, my friend, especially not you,' he said in a low voice as they entered the classroom. 'What do you suggest?' replied Yorgo. The answer troubled him. EPON offered to organise a 'mountain run', code for a planned escape to the mountainous region outside Athens where, ever since the Resistance years, the leftist partisans had remained dominant. 'There is no way, after the other day's demonstration, they would let you be,' his interlocutor insisted. Yorgo thought he was exaggerating. Yorgo still had his foreign passport, and, surely, his zeal to represent students, including regime supporters, posed no threat.

That evening, Yorgo planned to visit a distant cousin from his father's side in Peristeri, a working-class suburb of western Athens. To get there on time, he chose to skip the afternoon's last lecture. As he descended the School of Chemistry's marble stairs onto Solonos Street, two fellow students approached him. 'We are from state security,' they said while grabbing him. They pushed him down the stairs and straight into a waiting car. No one witnessed the scene, Yorgo thought to himself as the two men cuffed and blindfolded him.

The first punches were thrown while he was still blindfolded. When the uniformed gendarme removed his blindfold, Yorgo could only utter one word: 'Why?' The gendarme mimicked him: 'Why? Because you are a dangerous bloody commie, that's why.' He laughed while continuing to beat him casually, joyfully. Once he got tired, two underlings threw Yorgo into a cold dark cell and left him there to stew for a few hours. Eventually, he was taken upstairs to the police inspector's office. When the inspector walked in, he reproached the two policemen in the room for having Yorgo in cuffs and called for ice to apply to his bruised face. Then, turning to his prisoner, he became apologetic:

> You know how it is these days. It is so hard to find civilised men to serve. The brutes that hit you don't know better – they come from rural parts where life is cheap. You have my apologies. I have read your file and it is obvious that you are a good boy, from a good family in Cairo. This is no place for you. I shall organise a car to take you home. No bad feelings, I hope.

Yorgo was relieved. It had been a mistake. 'No hard feelings,' he replied. As he was getting up to leave, the inspector raised his hand. 'Just one more thing before you go. A formality. Sign here,' he said, pushing a typewritten page his way. Yorgo read it hungrily. It was a denunciation of 'communism, communists and their fellow travellers'.

'Sir,' said Yorgo, trying to regain his composure, 'I am not a communist, I am not a Buddhist or a Muslim. However, just as I would not denounce Buddhists or Muslims, especially at the orders of the state, I must now refuse to sign this.' The inspector gave no word in reply. His face said it all. With a wave of his hand, the two gendarmes grabbed Yorgo and dragged him back to his underground cell. He would not be released for four years.

19. For a mere signature

Anna gasped when Nina, her loving cousin, and now also Yorgo's godmother, brought the news to their Cairo apartment. The thought of her son wasting in a police cell because he would not sign a stupid piece of paper was unbearable. The conviction that it was her fault was unendurable. Anna beseeched Nina to take the first boat to Piraeus and use her connections to get him out. For during the north African campaign, Nina had met and married Costa, a Greek army officer stationed in Cairo. By now Costa had risen to the rank of colonel and was the right-hand man of General Papagos, the nationalist army's top officer for more than a decade, a man destined also to become Greece's prime minister from 1952 till his death in 1955. If anyone could free Yorgo, it would be Costa.

Meanwhile, Yorgo was receiving a magnificent education in the mysteries of the human organism. Starved, frozen to the bone, enduring beatings day and night, unable to contact the outside world, he nevertheless discovered that his resolve not to satisfy his torturers grew as his body weakened. In the first few days he had come very close to signing the damned thing. Initially, he just wanted to hold out for a few hours. But with every minute he resisted the urge to sign, he felt able to resist one more blow. Over time, his resolve hardened like old bone. The thought of stepping from that cell a signee daunted him more than the prospect of another night of beatings and hunger. Besides, his body, wearing thin as threadbare linen, now granted him small mercies – long stretches of blissful unconsciousness when the world fell away.

A month into his ordeal, probably due to the overcrowding from a spree of arrests, they moved Yorgo to a large holding cell. He found himself sharing the cell with thirty other political prisoners, as well as common criminals. One evening an altercation broke out when a pickpocket claimed he was missing money and pointed an accusatory finger at a burglar, who protested: 'The cell is full of people and you are choosing to blame it on me?' A pimp interjected, telling the burglar: 'You fool! Those guys are here for a mere signature. You think they would steal from creeps like us?'

Later that week, Yorgo was summoned again to the inspector's office. There, to his surprise, he was greeted by a tearful Nina, her husband Costa clad in his resplendent uniform, and another colonel who had, in the meantime, apparently married Nina's sister. Yorgo was thrilled to see his godmother and encouraged by the presence of two of the army's top brass, hoping they were there to lean on the inspector. Alas, they were there to lean on him.

Costa grimly explained that, unless he signed, he would be exiled to some godforsaken island. Since his arrest, the civil war was back with a vengeance. Yorgo had suspected that the X Group's curtailment of its tacit alliance with EPON foreshadowed an all-out purge of leftists. Within weeks of the 'mountain run' he had turned down, they had joined other harassed former partisans in the countryside to form the communist-led Democratic Army of Greece, at war with the US-backed National Army in which Costa served.

When Nina's turn came, she concentrated on Anna: 'Your mother is not bearing up,' she said. 'She keeps fainting on us and the doctors say that high blood pressure has weakened her heart inordinately. She begged me to implore you to sign what is, after all, a worthless piece of paper. The inspector promised that, if you do, we can leave straight away for Piraeus. Think of Anna. Who will know if you sign? Who will care? Who will blame you?'

'I am very sorry you have had to come all the way here, Auntie Nina, dear Costa, to tell me that which I already knew,' replied Yorgo. 'The inspector offered me freedom from the first day in exchange for that signature. But freedom to do what? To live in humiliation under the permanent shadow of knowing that I have signed away my dignity? Today they want me to denounce communists and their fellow travellers. Tomorrow they will ask me to denounce Jews or maybe Buddhists. The day after, who knows, they may ask me to denounce impressionist painters, jazz musicians, maybe you and your husband. As for my mother, if anyone can understand what I am now telling you, she can.'

Less than a week later, chained and hooded, Yorgo was led to an open truck packed with dozens of other prisoners, and driven to Piraeus, to board not a passenger steamship to Alexandria but a navy vessel bound for the island of Ikaria. The sailing took fifteen hours, of which they spent the first four in chains, forced to urinate in their pants. Before the ship sailed into Eudelos harbour, on Ikaria's north coast, they were cuffed and hooded, before being led, in small groups, to the villages where they would be isolated from the local population.

Yorgo's group of fifteen prisoners, forming a chain gang, were taken to a stone house on the outskirts of Lampsachades, an inland village. The first rule of their new life was clear: if they dared approach any villager, for food or even conversation, they were promised five days in an underground hole punctuated only by regular beatings. The second rule was that every morning they would have to walk to the gendarmerie, located forty-five minutes' walk away, to report. Failure to do so could mean execution. The third rule was that they had to fend for themselves, scavenging in the forest for food. Hunger was to become a constant companion in their open prison.

They all slept on the floor around the fireplace in the living room of a picturesque house close to a lush forest, with springs and waterfalls. The setting was straight out of a travel agent's brochure. This was the sickening irony: a group of men were condemned to waste away slowly in a romantic setting. The resourcefulness of Yorgo's comrades, some of whom had grown up in the countryside, kept them alive – barely. They knew which wild fungi could be eaten safely, which weeds contained some protein, which leaves could alleviate infected wounds. But all they could do was slow down the men's decline.

Malnutrition spawned moral dilemmas. Grigori, a partisan who had been captured in battle, was the first man to start coughing up blood. Tuberculosis had invaded their household, forcing them to choose between solidarity with the infected comrade and the logic of quarantine. As the men were wrestling with their decision, an act of humanism gave them heart. Upon opening their front door to begin their morning walk to the gendarmerie, carrying their sick on stretchers, they stumbled upon a bottle of olive oil and a jar of fresh sheep's milk that was still warm. On another occasion, they found a misspelt note giving them directions to fig trees they could harvest unseen. At other times, bread and cheese would appear out of nowhere. Anonymous villagers were risking their freedom to help sustain them a little longer.

At night, lying on the hard floorboards, watching the shadows on the ceiling dance to the tempo of the fireplace, they told each other stories until sleep enveloped them one at a time. On the night he died, Grigori, between agonising breaths, told them the story of his last encounter with his brother. The Democratic Army patrol unit he led on Mount Parnon, in south-eastern

Peloponnese, had come across a group of lost gendarmes. After a four-hour battle, the gendarmes, wounded and disheartened, surrendered. As his men were taking their weapons away, one of the wounded cried out: 'Brother, it's me.' Grigori did not even know his brother Vassili had enlisted. 'Whatever the outcome of this civil war,' Grigori concluded, 'our mother was bound to mourn a son – I am glad it will be me, not Vassili.'

Many nights later, as they were remembering Grigori, Yorgo spotted a large scorpion crawling upside down on the ceiling right above them. 'Don't move,' shouted one of the men who knew about scorpions. 'It is about to launch itself at us!' He then jumped up, pulled a chair, climbed on it and, with impressive dexterity, grabbed the scorpion by its tail and threw it into the fire. That's when Yorgo witnessed something that would stay with him: the scorpion, having landed amid red-hot logs, began frantically to sting its own head, as if striving to kill itself before the flames did. There was a desperate poignancy in the way the creature practised dignity in death. 'For a few minutes,' wrote Yorgo to Anna when he got a chance, 'we stared at the fireplace in silence, as if in a wake for a fallen comrade.'

A month later, in February 1947, upon arriving exhausted at the gendarmerie – as they did every morning, a little weaker than on the previous day – Yorgo was taken aside by a sergeant who handed him a written order to appear as soon as possible at their headquarters in Aghios Kyrikos, Ikaria's largest town. Without delay, he set off on an eight-hour hike across the beautiful mountainous landscape, past Steli and skirting the spectacular Rantis Forest. He arrived well after sunset. Having eaten nothing, he hardly had the strength to climb the steps of the police station.

'I have received orders from Athens to release you immediately and put you on a boat to Rhodes, and from there forthwith to Alexandria,' the chief of the gendarmerie told Yorgo. To add a little humour, he quipped: 'Unlike Icarus, who mythology says crashed and burnt around this island's waters, you are about to fly away safely. Sign those documents and you are off.' Yorgo did not need to look at them to know that chief among them was the same denunciation declaration. It was becoming tedious to summon the same answer: 'Sir, I could have signed this in the first place, as you know. I did not then and I shall not now.'

Fuming, the chief ordered that he be taken into an underground cell in which he was kept for months. He never saw his comrades at Lampsachades again. He was, however, now allowed to receive three academic books that Anna had sent him via Nina. During one of the regular cell inspections, a gendarme grabbed two of the books and held them up by the tips of his fingers with an expression of disgust, as if in fear of being contaminated. 'What language is this?' he asked angrily. 'German,' replied Yorgo: 'I am trying to improve my German by reading German-language books.' Impressed, the former Nazi collaborator cracked a broad smile: 'At last, you are coming to your senses.' Yorgo couldn't control his glee all night long. For while one of the books was a calculus primer, the other was *Das Kapital, Vol. 1*, with the first few pages mentioning the title and Marx's name excised – a gift from Anna that had somehow slipped past the security checks, probably because it was in Hitler's language.

20. The final plea

A gendarme Yorgo had never seen before burst into his cell with a strange order: he was expected at Aghios Kyrikos' only hotel within the hour. Oddly, he was told he could walk there on his own, unsupervised. That made him suspicious. Might the coppers be staging a phoney escape to justify gunning him down? The street was deserted, the afternoon summer heat keeping the locals indoors. For the first time in two years he was walking alone and unshackled in a town. With eyes burning in the bright sunlight, he struggled to get his feverish body to complete the short journey. At the two-storey hotel, an elderly receptionist who seemed to be expecting him smiled and pointed to the staircase. 'Room eleven,' he said. Yorgo climbed up to the first floor, his heart almost stampeding out of his chest. The door of room eleven was ajar. Through the opening, he saw her.

Elation can be as strong as a volcanic eruption or as mild as a budding flower. It can be pure, or it can be steeped in misgivings. But elation is never not a feeling that one can touch the stars. Seeing Anna brought happiness of an order beyond his soul's capacity. He felt self-conscious, worried that his sunken face and starved body would terrify her. However, her passionate embrace soon put paid to all that. Could she really be there? How had the army and the gendarmes allowed her to sail to an exile island? No mother of any other political prisoner had got that far.

Apparently, Anna had pulled out all the stops, and then some. She milked her connection to Nina and Costa for all it was worth.

She had also tried out Yango's business network, hoping for access to British or American government officials. But, in the end, it was the least likely path that led her safely to Ikaria: one of her union comrades knew a woman who waxed the legs of Egypt's Queen Farida. Queen Farida, in turn, was on excellent terms with Queen Frederica of Greece who, for some reason, agreed to give the order for Anna's passage to Ikaria.

The moment she held him Anna knew he was burning up. She commanded him to lie on the bed while she darted out to the town's pharmacy, where she bought aspirin and a homemade lotion of sorts. When she returned, she gave him the aspirin, forced a little bread into his mouth and began rubbing his scraggy chest and back with the lotion. Yorgo moaned with a mixture of pain – the result of a broken rib – pleasure and relief. 'Does it still hurt?' she asked eventually, but Yorgo had already sunk into a deep sleep.

When he woke up, it was past midnight. Time, Anna thought, for the talk they had to have. But, before that, there was one more thing. 'Do you know the date?' she enquired. Yorgo had no idea, having lost count in his underground cell. 'The twelfth of June has just dawned,' she continued. 'Happy birthday, my son!' Reaching into her bag, she took out a small red notebook adorned with a white bow. It contained poems that she had written after learning of his arrest. Yorgo began to open the notebook but Anna stopped him: 'Not now, there is no time.'

A week earlier, Costa had alerted Anna to Operation Purgatory. It was to commence on the morning of 12 June. All political prisoners would be transferred from Ikaria to the hell known as Makronisos – a barren, desolate, uninhabited island off the eastern coast of Attica known for its crippling northerly winds which make it impossible even for bushes to grow tall on its rocky surface. A navy landing craft commissioned for the purpose was already in the port. Waiting. 'Think of this', she told him as her eyes roved around the room, 'as our last-chance hotel.'

Anna talked more, mentally transporting him to Cairo. The war's end had sparked new movements that were bound to end the colonial regime. She told him of a new friend she had made, Doria Shafik, whose magazine *Daughter of the Nile* invigorated the cause by linking issues like childcare with the anticolonial struggle. She conveyed news of his best friend, who was now studying chemical engineering in Pittsburgh, and greetings from people he cherished, but also hilarious tales of woe involving their extended family who, when wanting to scare their children into submission, would say things like: Don't do such and such, unless you want to end up like Anna's Yorgo. Hearing this, Yorgo smiled a bitter smile and asked: 'Dad too?' It was Anna's cue to appeal to his concern for her isolation.

After Yorgo's arrest, predictably, Yango had adopted an 'I told you so' attitude to Anna. She spoke of her existential loneliness. Her comrades sympathised but, at a time of renewed hope and possibilities, the last thing they needed was a broken white woman unable to put the struggle above her mourning for a living son. Meanwhile, her social circle treated her like the womb that had spawned Satan. The longer Yorgo spent in prison the more Yango and their broader community treated Stavro as the good son and Anna as the wayward mother. Anna and Yorgo were talked about as people with a visible trail of wreckage behind them. 'Every tear that I shed for you', she intimated, 'is debited to the account they keep of my misplaced loyalty to the prodigal son. Every sigh I let out activates a fresh censure. Normally, I would blast them out of the water. But my gunpowder is soaked in the muddy tears over your withering.'

Yorgo saw where this was going when she, jokingly, opined that, contrary to myth, frogs *do* leap out of increasingly hot water, and stampeding cattle *do* come to a standstill at a cliff's edge. She was making a final plea for him to sign. To walk out of there alive. With her. She reminded him that he had not invented subversion. That she too was a dissenter, a nonconformist, as revolutionary as the next man. Yes, she was proud of his integrity, but heroism and virtue are not always synonymous. 'If you must, choose a heroic death, then damned be me and my sorrows,' she proclaimed. 'But, if you are to die fighting, at least die in the trenches – not on some godforsaken rock, hungry and alone, over a bloody signature.' Then, softening, she added: 'With fascism on the run, a new world is possible, my son. Don't stay here in the country where the last remaining Nazis are holding on. Come to Cairo. With me. This morning. And from there the world is your oyster.'

'Sweet Mama,' came his instinctive answer, 'you got me wrong.' Not blinking before his torturers might have been his initial motivation. But, of the French Revolution's triptych, he was now far more driven by liberty and equality's lesser sibling: fraternity. For two years, he had bled, starved and wept next to so many brothers and sisters who, too, had mothers and friends to rush back to – but who also refused to sign. He could not bear betraying them. Walking past them a freed man, as they were being shoved into the dark vessel headed for Makronisos, was beyond his calculus of right and wrong. It was simply undoable.

Having run out of words, Anna and Yorgo lay on the bed, staring at the mouldy ceiling in silence, holding hands. A couple of hours later the sun would rise. There was no point in prolonging the agony. As they embraced one last time, they caught a glimpse of themselves in the vertical mirror fixed to the back of the hotel room's door. For the first time Yorgo noticed how she had aged, her puffed-up eyes making her look at least two decades older than her forty-three years. Anna too recognised how her impassioned plea had burdened his haggard body. Without looking back, clutching her red notebook with the distinctive white bow, Yorgo left the room, descended the stairs and walked out into the street heading for his cell.

A few hours later, at the Aghios Kyrikos harbour waiting for the ferry to Piraeus, Anna saw him again. This time he was in cuffs and chained to another young man, part of a chain gang of two hundred prisoners at the quayside, waiting to board the roofless boat that would take them to Makronisos. 'Raise your soul, my boy,' she whispered. Yorgo winced, and quickly looked away, pretending not to have noticed her.

21. Double exile

It was many months before Anna received word from Makronisos. Her imagination yielded a reasonable approximation of the shocking reality: endless beatings by dehumanised military policemen, constant hunger, enforced thirst, weeks of sleeping out in the open on rocks lashed by angry waves and spiteful winds, and, perhaps worst of all, an occasional execution to enhance the petrifying effect of the frequent mock executions.

When the first army-issue envelope arrived in Cairo, it contained several heavily redacted letters that Yorgo had managed to write. Anna pored over the fragments with the zeal of an Egyptologist who had just discovered shards of clay adorned with hieroglyphs. She read between the lines that her little red notebook had been confiscated, as had everything else that was precious to him – his books in particular. The one fragment that touched her greatly was a passage reflecting the mood of the prisoners:

> Some remain as open and welcoming as a church at Easter; others as sealed up as U-boats. One will open his heart and let it all pour out; the other will swear at you if you so much as look at him, let alone ask him anything. One is more gregarious than the stars in the sky; another looks less sociable than a statue of Poseidon nursing a grudge against Athena.

In one letter, which a remorseful sentry had smuggled out uncensored, she was stunned to read that the commissioned officers and fascists running the prison camp hardly ever laid a hand on them. No, they kept their hands clean. Every single one of their torturers, Yorgo claimed, was a formerly left-wing partisan who had been broken under torture. 'That's how true brutality is reproduced,' he surmised. 'When I hear one of them call my name,' he lamented, 'I pray that he is not an until-recently-true believer in our cause. For he harbours the greatest rage and has the most to prove to his abusers.'

Even in decades to come, when he could talk freely, Yorgo avoided discussing what was done to him during his 'tenure', as he referred to his time on Makronisos. The occasional twitch under his right eye. The loss of feeling in his right leg. Evident revulsion at the sound of bouncing basketballs. The panic attack that, one evening, caused him to flee from a cinema at the sight of an elderly man sitting a couple of rows in front. The odd reference to the claustrophobia of sharing a sack with a cat or a snake as the sack sank in the sea – before being pulled out again. The frenzy of fear triggered by Johann Strauss' *Blue Danube*, despite having grown up waltzing to it with Anna. A single photo of him smiling among comrades taken by a smuggled-in camera. Those were the only clues of what he had endured. Rather than dwell on these, he focused, instead, on two silver linings: invaluable education and incomparable friendships.

Anna learned that, after the first weeks of sleeping rough, they had been given two-person army tents to be shared by groups of four prisoners, driving them ever closer together. By pure luck Yorgo was assigned to the same tent as Yannis Ritsos, one of Greece's greatest poets; Manos Katrakis, one of its greatest tragedians; and Spyros Lynardatos, a learned author and journalist. Three intellectual giants in one tiny tent who taught Yorgo many things: from dispelling the myth that intellectuals are physically timid (Katrakis, in particular, goaded his torturers as they were beating him, with cries of 'Is that all you have?') to lectures on literature, theatre, law, philosophy. In return Yorgo managed to excite their curiosity about chemistry, calculus and, of course, the political significance of Einstein's relativity theory. In a letter to Anna that she never received, he revealed cheerily that his comrades once threatened to catapult him into the stormy Aegean if he dared continue to spoil their sunset with explanations of how the colour red had a higher frequency which succeeded, through atmospheric refraction, to reach their eyes well after the sun had descended below the horizon.

In time, prisoners would form larger groups to discuss political economy late into the night – from memory, of course, since they were allowed no books. Their interest in economics was not surprising given, as Ritsos once put it, they were all there because of their 'slight, albeit rather costly, disagreement with capitalism'. Naturally, as most were members of the Communist Party, Marx's *Das Kapital* featured prominently in their discussions. Yorgo, who had read it recently in Ikaria, in the original German no less, happily recounted what he recalled of Marx's theory of surplus value, and the tendency of the profit rate to fall.

One thing puzzled him: those meetings also attracted folks with no education. Farmers from rural areas who couldn't even write or read Greek, let alone tackle these technical issues, stayed and listened intently into the wee hours. As tactfully as he could, he put it to them: Don't they get bored? Frustrated? No, came the answer. Of course, they had no clue what the learned ones were yapping on about. But they were gratified that they were sacrificing their lives to build a better world side by side with people who were on top of the theory of what that would take. Their trust moved Yorgo and made him take a decisive step – to approach the Communist Party's rep formally to request to join.

'Well, you have refused to denounce us at great cost – you might as well join us!' came the answer.

Meanwhile, within a year of her failed Ikaria mission, and with her mind full of the horrors she imagined were taking place in that distant purgatory, Anna's blood pressure ran amok. The first effective medicine for her heart condition would not arrive in Cairo for another eight years. By 1949, she could no longer leave the apartment. Imprisoned in a failing body, all she could do was scribble in her diary lines that might assuage the guilt filling Yorgo's soul, praying to see him one more time. It was not to be.

It was early 1949, the hideous civil war's final year. The partisans were facing ruin on the mountains of the Peloponnese, Epirus and Macedonia. The execution squads were working overtime. The camps were filling up. Their underground organisations in the cities were being dismantled, one by one. The cause was dying. 'We have a mission for you,' the party's two reps in his segment of the camp revealed to Yorgo one day. He was to leave Makronisos for Athens, lie low for a few weeks, return to university and, gradually, help rebuild the party's central Athens organisation. 'And how do you propose I get out of here?' Yorgo asked in disbelief. 'You will have to sign,' came the reply. Was this really happening, he wondered.

Had he signed at the Athens police station, where he was first rounded up years before, he would have departed as a gentleman. Had he listened to Anna in Ikaria, he would have walked away with her, hand in hand, as tourists whose holiday had come to an end. But now? Signing in Makronisos was no longer enough. To further break the spirit of those who signed, their sadistic keepers had devised a new ritual. New signees were now forced to walk between two rows of unbowed prisoners who would reliably call them traitors, spit on them, curse them, disgrace them.

For Yorgo, who had lost so much for a mere signature, who

had sacrificed everything to stand with his fellow prisoners, to sign and then to walk the gauntlet of humiliation meted out by comrades who had no clue he was acting under orders – no, that was a sacrifice too far. 'I won't do it,' he stated unwaveringly. To his dismay, they were unmoved. He was a card-carrying party member now. His inclinations were noted but played no role in the decision. He was ordered, a second time, to walk over to the control centre to announce his change of heart. Suddenly, he recognised an awful truth, as he told me decades later: had his side won the civil war, he would've probably ended up in the same prison camp, albeit with sentries parroting his own ideology. The realisation steeled his resolve to respond to the party's order with the most radical of words, which he had been telling his gaolers for years: 'No!'

As the rumour spread swiftly around the tents that he had been disloyal to the party, Yorgo was spoken to by almost no one. The other prisoners, ignorant of the details of his 'betrayal', refused to look him in the eye. Some spat on the ground as he passed by. The few who talked to him were disciplined, so Yorgo withdrew from them even more to spare them further punishment. The friendships that had sustained him all that time were gone. He was in a category of one, neither a signee nor a comrade. Two separate walls were closing in on him, one the crushing panoply of the fascist state, the other the frozen parapet that the Communist Party had erected around him.

All he could think of was that he had wronged Anna, that his rationale for not signing was flimsy, vacuous, bogus, his principles nothing more than an asset to be traded for some dubious organisational gain. Paradoxically, his determination not to sign grew even stronger.

22. And the ship sailed on

A year into his double exile, in May 1950, Yorgo received a letter with Yango's handwriting on the envelope. Anna, it turned out, was barely conscious. Several mild strokes had taken their toll. 'I thought you should know,' the brief, dry epistle concluded.

A couple of months earlier, against the backdrop of an international campaign exposing the Makronisos atrocities, with the civil war over and the left defeated, a new government decided to evacuate the island. Thousands of prisoners were to be released, with the exception of the Communist Party's upper echelons, who would be transported to Ai Stratis, an even more remote island exile. To be released, Yorgo would have to sign, but now, with the mass evacuation under way, there would be no humiliation to suffer. The die was cast. With a sunken heart but a clear conscience, he signed and, a week later, conditional on reporting weekly to his local police station, he was released to the wooden *kaiki* that transported him to Lavrio, a port on Athens' east approximately two and a half nautical miles from Makronisos.

From the open army truck that was struggling over potholed dirt roads to Athens, an unbearable fact began to sink in. Shops looked busy. People were going about their business. He spotted a group of youngsters in fancy dress frolicking in the streets. Music oozed out of tavernas. Laughter and, even worse, normalcy were in the air. People had carried on. An older fellow sitting next to him in the truck could see what was troubling him. 'Did you think people would stop living,' he asked rhetorically, 'just because we were put on ice? No, mate, the ship sailed on, as she always does. We fought for them but they wouldn't know it – and you shouldn't care that they don't care. Can you do that? If so, you will be alright. Otherwise, if you crave some medal, you will waste your life.'

Back in Athens, a shadow of the person he once was, he struggled to recover what he had lost. His bank account savings had been confiscated, but, astonishingly, his former landlady had kindly kept his belongings all those years and rented him his old room on credit. Hungry and tired, he visited the university to reactivate the enrolment cut short on the marble steps of the School of Chemistry almost five years earlier. But his main concern was that, with his Italian passport rescinded, his prison ID was the only identification he had. To reach Anna's bedside, he had to apply for Greek travel documents.

At the police station, his application was met with derision and threats of fresh detention. Out of options, he sought help from Costa. The timing was inauspicious. Army officers with a Venizelist background were keeping a low profile. While the new government had shifted closer to the centre, the military was purging anyone not demonstrably ultra-right. The last thing Costa needed was to be stigmatised by association. 'Don't contact me again, I shall contact you in the unlikely event I can help,' was the reply.

Cut off from Cairo, indeed the rest of the world, Yorgo's luck improved when he befriended a middle-class family with teenage sons struggling to pass their university entrance exams. They introduced him to another family with similar needs. Tutoring became a lifeline. He bought food, a few clothes, enough resources with which to return to the university. It was a difficult return. Gone was the unconscious swagger with which he had arrived in 1945. Instead of the cosmopolitan, confident youth, in the window of the main lecture theatre he glimpsed a ramshackle man with slumped shoulders and sadness carved on his face.

The building looked the same, the professors were the same, except a tad grumpier, but the students seemed different. His cohort had either graduated or disappeared and the new ones seemed better fed but less passionate. Unnervingly, no one recognised the student who was, in his first stint, the president of their union. The only people there who knew of him worked for the police and kept tabs on him. Keeping to himself felt like the best survival strategy. So, he sat alone on the far side of the amphitheatre, trying his best not to look like death warmed up.

This first lecture was on organic chemistry. As the professor lectured, two observations gave him some cheer. The first was that all the reading in Ikaria, and the thinking on Makronisos, must have paid off, judging by the ease with which he could follow the material. The second was a young, attractive woman – the first female student he had ever seen in there. That same afternoon, he bumped into her again in the inorganic chemistry laboratory. There, Yorgo realised that her shyness concealed a lion's heart.

Two students demanded from their lab instructor a re-evaluation of their previous week's grades, disputing that 'that woman' could have scored higher than them. Many in the group cheered. Just before Yorgo opened his mouth, the instructor spared him the risk: 'Eleni, would you be prepared to partake in a quiz?' 'Gladly,' she replied. Following a quick-fire round of technical questions, she emerged triumphant. Unable to repress a wide smile, Yorgo blushed when he noticed Eleni smiling back at him. Perhaps, he thought, it was a moment of recognition between two students suffocating, for different reasons, in a hostile environment.

Eleni felt it too. There was a kindness in his face that she had not seen in a man's before, and a quiet grace that made the X Group ruffians and their fear of him seem ridiculous. And when Yorgo blushed, his cheekbones jutting awkwardly from his undernourished face, her smile became a heartfelt signal meant only for him. The dialectic of recognition Yorgo had hoped for had come to pass.

A couple of weeks later, when the X Group organised a petition to expel Yorgo from the university, Eleni stood in the corridor, next to their stall, and delivered a judicious speech about the inappropriateness of students demanding the expulsion of peers who had never been convicted of anything, by any court, anywhere. Chastened, the X Group dropped their petition. When Yorgo later approached her, she gave his thanks short shrift. How could she explain that she had chosen to clash so publicly with the X Group to sever her links with them?

Before long, these brief exchanges had developed into a shy courtship in between their lab's benches. One morning, a dozen students were relaxing in that lab, waiting for an organic reaction to ferment. To pass the time, one of them suggested a game: 'If you had a magic wand that could conjure up one thing, anything, what would you have it create for you?' Answers ranged from a car to other magic wands capable of producing infinite goodies. When Yorgo's turn came, he answered: 'A passport.' Facing a wave of heckles demanding a more fun answer, he thought again and, influenced by the memory of that house in Lampsachades, replied: 'OK, I would ask for a fireplace, in front of which to sit during long winter nights with a good book and some music in the background.'

Later that day, as he was descending the marble steps leading to Solonos Street, his mind full of Anna, Eleni approached him from behind, undetected, to whisper into his ear: 'It will be *our* fireplace!' Before he could react, quick on her feet, she disappeared into a side street. His soul's aches melted away. The words of the poet Palamas that Manos Katrakis had taught him in their tiny tent came to him: 'Even within your fall, try to stay upright.'

23. We have much to do

Anna's illness underlined the segregation she had fought against all her life. After she descended into an intermittent coma, Yango insisted she be allowed to rest in their fourth-floor apartment where he, and the family, could afford her a dignified *telos*. Salma, her other union comrades and her Arab neighbours knew it would only cause surprise and consternation were they to attempt to visit her. Only Yorgo appreciated their central role in her life, and he wasn't there. So, they waited downstairs.

Yorgo wrote to Anna daily. Her joy at learning he was no longer alone burst out with every letter. Alas, it was not long before she stopped writing back. Time was running out. Pulling every string he knew of, calling in every favour, he managed, eventually, to secure a temporary travel document – not a passport – that allowed him a single visit to Egypt for no longer than a month. When, at last, on 12 June 1951, his birthday, he breathlessly made it to their fourth-floor Cairo apartment, a Greek doctor was with her, as were his father, brother and a niece. Her blood pressure through the roof, the doctor stuck a needle in her right arm to release some of that pressure. A thin geyser of blood hit the ceiling. Within hours, it was over.

Since he was a boy, Anna had made Yorgo promise that, when the time came, she would be buried in Cairo's *libres penseurs* ('free thinkers') cemetery. But Yorgo's pariah status rendered him powerless to sway the extended family – who wished he had stayed away altogether. Yango proved more amenable but had his own reason for resisting him, which Yorgo respected: as their stranglehold over Egyptian society weakened, the British authorities were agitated. Jittery that Thomas Cook in Egypt was run by the father of a certified communist, a nonconformist burial of his wife, in a cemetery for French-speaking atheists no less, could be the final straw.

The Greek Orthodox cemetery of St George's Church was an alternative that Anna might have approved – the next best thing to a non-sectarian, secular, multi-faith resting place. She had always marvelled at how Muslim pilgrims would visit Qiddīs Jurjī ('St George' in Arabic), camping respectfully on its grounds to pay their respects on special days to 'their' jurjī – often placing what little money they had in the collection box. On one occasion, to Anna's restrained aversion, a richer Muslim pilgrim slaughtered a bull outside the church to thank St George for healing his daughter. Of all the theist cemeteries, this one was most in tune with her commitment to pluralism and to Egypt's true owners.

On the day, it all looked like a typical Greek-Egyptian funeral. A few dozen relatives and friends had gathered in the church waiting for Anna's coffin, a freshly dug grave in view just outside. Back at the apartment, the immediate family and a few helpers carried the coffin downstairs and onto a six-horse carriage. The first sign that something was afoot was the silence. The street was deserted. Every shop shuttered. On a working day? In the midst of central Cairo? As the carriage started on its way, with Yango, Yorgo and Stavro walking slowly behind, it began. Groups of women, most veilless and dressed in white, appeared from the side streets to join the procession behind the three men. They kept coming along the route. Within minutes, they numbered hundreds, then thousands.

Yango worried aloud about what the people waiting at St George's would think. 'People are going to believe what they need to believe,' Yorgo whispered back. Exalted, in proud disbelief, he looked back repeatedly at the white torrent of strangers that had come to celebrate Anna. It was the most fitting of funerals, after all. A year later, the same people were part of the masses that joined the revolution which brought down the government, expelled their Quisling King Farouk, got rid of Egypt's colonial masters, introduced land reforms and restored their country's independence. The army officer Gamal Abdel Nasser fronted the revolution that Anna's feminist comrades had worked so tirelessly to foment.

Yango and most of the Greek community experienced Nasser's revolution as a calamity. Within a decade, the vast majority had emigrated, most to Greece, many to Australia, some to parts of Africa still under British control. To this day, the community and their descendants believe that Nasser, and the revolution that Anna had backed, expelled them from Egypt. Yorgo begged to differ. Nasser's government was all about liberating Egyptians from the British that had laid siege to their country since 1879. Yes, Nasser's revolution, like almost every revolution, ended up eating its children and spawning new malignancies. But, at the very least, Egyptians were now responsible for their own affairs.

When Nasser nationalised the Suez Canal, Britain, France and Israel invaded Egypt, paving the ground for the British Empire's final humiliation. Following that invasion, British and French companies, along with their functionaries, were expelled from Egypt. As the Greeks had tied their fates to British and French neocolonial rule, they could not engineer a new modus vivendi for themselves within the emergent post-colonial Egypt. In a letter to Eleni written the day after Anna's funeral, Yorgo had anticipated this: 'Judging by Dad's awkwardness in front of the crowd who joined us to honour Anna, I doubt that he and his mates will be able to coexist with emancipated Egyptians no longer willing to tolerate our lot's entitled arrogance.'

Even if his travel document had not compelled him to return to Greece, Yorgo would have been eager to leave. His family and entire community had failed Anna. Bereaved and traumatised, he had no stomach for further confrontations with any of them. As for Anna's Egyptian comrades, they did not need him. If the spirit they displayed during her funeral was anything to go by, they had it all in hand. His Cairo, the city that would forever dominate his heart and mind, had died with Anna. It was time to go.

Back at the apartment, having packed his small suitcase, he spent what time remained going over Anna's poems, essays and diaries. In their midst, he found a note addressed to him. It read: 'I tried to stop you from going to an Eleni bent on destroying you. Now, my hopes rest with *your* Eleni.' What did she mean, he wondered.

When he returned to Athens, Eleni deciphered Anna's cryptic message. In ancient times, Makronisos was called Eleni. Upon hearing this, Yorgo fell to pieces. Eleni put an arm around him and said: 'Come, come, life is ahead of us. Raise your soul now. We have much to do.'

PART THREE

Trisevgeni

24. Run with it

Trisevgeni had never initiated a telephone call until that day. The Siemens phone her son Panayis had proudly installed was still too alien a presence in her living room. At most, she would reluctantly take the handset whenever it was handed to her by one of her children, and only after they announced who was on the other end. But on that December day in 1954, she did not hesitate to call Yorgo's work and ask to speak to him urgently. Why would Eleni's mother be calling him, Yorgo wondered. 'Come home, my boy,' he heard her sad, tender voice tell him. 'You are getting married this afternoon.'

Konstantinos, Trisevgeni's husband, had been suffering from a weak heart since the Axis Occupation. That morning, the visiting doctor had given him days, not weeks. Had he died before Eleni and Yorgo wed, Eleni would be expected to wait a year before marrying, draped in black. Ever since Yorgo's final return from Cairo, Trisevgeni had welcomed him into her family. Unwilling to delay his formal induction by a whole year, she organised Eleni's wedding on the very day she was losing the light of her life.

Before they walked from their home at 102 Naiadon Street to Panayitsa, Paleo Phaliro's main church, the wedding party gathered around Konstantinos' bed. Panayis and Yorgo stood behind Trisevgeni and Eleni, looking at one another in silent vigil. Grief-stricken, Eleni clutched her father's hand. Meanwhile, next door, Eleni's sisters, Marika and Georgia, fussed over what the bride and groom would wear. Miraculously, as they were about to depart, leaving behind a second cousin to stay by his side, Konstantinos came out of his haze. With a faint but telling gesture he gave his blessing for his daughter's imminent marriage. Without it, Eleni would not have found the strength to leave him.

At the church, Trisevgeni instructed the priest to deliver the ceremony's briefest version. The wedding was short and melancholy, but warmth broke through when Eleni repeated, in place of vows, a reminder of her promise to Yorgo that they would soon build a fireplace together. And as rice was being tossed at the newlyweds – a time-honoured Greek Orthodox tradition – Konstantinos' heart stopped.

By the time the wedding party had returned to Naiadon Street, a swarm of neighbours, led by their diligent cousin, had already washed and dressed the body, laying it on a floral bed in the living room for the obligatory all-night wake. Eager to join them, Eleni lost no time getting out of the off-white dress her sisters had procured for a wedding of which not a single photograph was taken. When she appeared in the living room in the black attire she would wear for months, the room already stood still. Trisevgeni summoned her and Yorgo to where she was sitting, next to Konstantinos' ashen face. As the couple knelt on the floor next to her, she took their heads in each hand and said:

> Civil war brought you together. Your wedding merged with a funeral. It is a sign. A good sign. The universe is determined that you shall be happy come what may. Take this sign to your hearts. And run with it.

25. What if the bastard exists?

Trisevgeni could hardly have had a background more different from Anna's. A frail and pudgy woman, looking older than her age courtesy of a malnourished childhood and a life steeped in interminable manual labour, it was easy to miss her inner strength. I shan't forget how, to protect five-year-old me from an approaching viper, she sprang out of her chair, grabbed it by the tail and, with the speed of an action hero, smashed its head on the stone wall of the country cottage we were renting that summer.

When Kostis Palamas, Yorgo's favourite poet since his Makronisos days, put together the words 'thrice' and *eugenia* ('gentleness'), to compose the name *Trisevgeni* as the title of his sole play, he could not have known how well it reflected the character of the woman who would take Yorgo in. With Anna gone, Yorgo chose to be a lifelong refugee in Athens, with Trisevgeni's home his refuge.

Unable to read or write until she was in her sixties, innocent of the Enlightenment's principles or Marie Curie's achievements, without a word of French, English or Italian, never having travelled south of her northern Peloponnesian village, or north of Athens, Trisevgeni was the epitome of the propertyless girl who had moved straight from an arid farm into the inner city. Lacking formal education, she had to discover wisdom from first principles.

One Sunday, I noticed she had spruced herself up, put on her Sunday best, with the obligatory hat complete with Parisian-style black veil, and was heading for the door. 'Where to, Grandma?' I asked. 'Off to church,' she replied. Her churchgoing being noticeably sparse, I asked: 'Do you believe in God's existence, Grandma?' She gave me a playful look impossible to construe as an affirmative answer. 'So, why waste your Sunday morning?' I insisted. 'What if the bastard exists?' she whispered cheekily. Trisevgeni had worked out Pascal's wager without knowing a thing about probability theory.

A hard life can harden people or, as in Trisevgeni's case, instil a soft touch. Trisevgeni's touch was the softest, her diplomatic skills a rare virtue that she struggled to pass on to Eleni, and then to me – sadly, with little success in both cases. Who else could have secured the family peace after taking into her home a stigmatised, unemployed communist to live out of wedlock with her daughter, the sister of Panayis – a rightist, multinational company director who considered himself the family's paterfamilias?

Having learned the art of bringing warring sides together, Trisevgeni's home remained an oasis in the midst of war. Extending it to their Naiadon Street abode in the much calmer 1950s was a piece of cake – often literally as her baking placated family and neighbours.

The 1950s are, to this day, remembered as Greece's 'stony years'. For the first time in half a century the country was not at war, but the price of peace was unremitting repression. Scores of Yorgo's comrades higher up in the party hierarchy were executed by firing squad. Police informants spread terror in working-class neighbourhoods, in factories, in schools and in universities. Being seen to read even centrist newspapers, the Greek equivalent of the *Washington Post* or the *Guardian*, often meant losing a job, a trading licence or a passport.

The elected bourgeois ministers, especially the prime minister, were in government but never in power. Paramilitaries and the palace were running the state. To get anything from a passport to a licence to sell watermelons required a clean bill of 'ideological health' from the former Nazi collaborators that dominated your local police station. Even then, you had to sign the declaration denouncing communism and its fellow travellers, the very same that had indelibly marked Yorgo's life but brought him into Eleni's path. Politics, in short, intruded in every nook and cranny of every family. Trisevgeni's family was not an exception, but she was rather exceptional.

General elections, which in Greece traditionally take place on Sundays, always threatened her family's equilibrium. Panayis would come to Naiadon Street to drive his mother to the polling station, a state school opposite Panayitsa, the church where Yorgo and Eleni had wed. On the way he would mansplain the country's political situation in no more than thirty seconds and then proceed to put in her purse a completed ballot paper picking the libertarian rightist party of his choice.

During their drive, Trisevgeni unfailingly reassured him that his pick would be her command, that he knew best, that of course his party choice was her party choice. Little did he know that, before leaving the house, she had approached Yorgo conspiratorially, whispering in his ear: 'Don't forget to slip into my bag the ballot paper,' meaning that of the United Greek Left which contested the elections on behalf of the banned Communist Party.

In similar fashion she would collect ballot papers from her other children, but also from neighbours and even friends, making each feel they directed her vote. Then, at the polling station, behind the ubiquitous blue curtain, she would do as she pleased – votes that she never revealed to me, despite eventually confiding how she played us all off against each other.

26. To keep you in lipstick

The Naiadon Street two-bedroom house was bursting at the seams well before the bittersweet wedding-funeral. Besides Trisevgeni and her ailing husband, it housed four unwaged youngsters: Eleni, her younger sister Georgia, Yorgo and his brother Stavro, who had arrived from Cairo to enrol at the Polytechneio and whom Trisevgeni, as was her wont, insisted on taking in.

Without a single salary coming in, and with only a small monthly stipend from Panayis, putting food on the table was a Herculean task which she somehow accomplished daily. However, Trisevgeni's harder tasks were keeping at bay the shame Yorgo and Eleni felt from failing repeatedly to land a job and persuading young Georgia to attend university.

The mid-1950s was a boom time for science and engineering graduates. Funded by Marshall Aid monies, factories were springing up in new industrial zones hungry for skilled workers. Towns like Elefsis, the holiest place in ancient Greece, or Lavrio, the site of the ancient silver mines which enriched classical Athens, morphed from archaeological delights to loci of Burkean mills and cement factories belching black smoke. They needed chemists, engineers and foremen to keep them going, but Yorgo was a marked man and Eleni was, well, a woman.

Yorgo was hired twice or sometimes thrice weekly, and fired with the same frequency. Waking up at five every morning, he would catch two or three buses to some factory. There, he sought an audience with the head of personnel, occasionally managing to see the top man. The story was the same everywhere he went: the hiring manager, or the boss himself, impressed by Yorgo's degree, his languages, his cosmopolitanism, would invariably snap him up. But, upon returning the next day to take up the position, Yorgo would be shown the door. For in the meantime, compelled to contact the local police station, the company had been instructed to lay off the treacherous commie. The stigma was so powerful that, despite Eleni's prodding, even Panayis refused to give Yorgo a reference, let alone consider him for one of the many positions his office was looking to fill in companies doing brisk business with Siemens.

Eleni's rejections were as monotonous, only they manifested differently. Minutes into an interview, threatened by the chemistry degree under her belt, the manager's eyebrows would be raised at the idea that she was daring to seek a graduate's position, rather than a secretary's spot or a blue-collar post. The final straw, which led her out the door, was that she was married. Women were tolerated in the labour force only while in search of a husband. Aping her first professor at the School of Chemistry, every manager she came across found her interest in a decent position an affront, an audacity tantamount to trying to steal the bread from a family's breadwinner. 'Have you no shame?' one of them asked as he was slamming the door behind her.

Eleni's luck changed in early 1954. A fertiliser company in Piraeus was desperate for a chemist to oversee production on the factory floor among unskilled workers handling dangerous chemicals. But the conditions were so atrocious that none of Eleni's male graduate cohort would risk life or limb for a salary they could secure in safer workplaces. Eleni took the job, spending years on a hellish shopfloor, often knee-deep in water replete with poisonous chemicals, feeling her lungs burn during the day and coughing herself to sleep at night – and all for a wage set by law at exactly half of what a similarly qualified male would be earning.

One day, after having prevented serious damage to the factory by detecting early the rapid accumulation of methane in one of the boilers, Eleni coyly suggested to her boss that, perhaps, a pay rise was in order. He smiled, reached for his wallet and gave her a smudged banknote, adding: 'That should keep you in lipstick for at least a fortnight.' She did not take it. She did not quit either. She just made a mental note never to forget it.

Seven months later, Yorgo had his improbable breakthrough. On 20 September 1954, he went through his usual ritual once again. This time he had secured an interview with a certain Mr Angelopoulos, the boss of Chalyvourgiki, Greece's first (and, at the time, only) steel plant – a buccaneering businessman whose entrepreneurship, ruthlessness and sheer tenacity made up for his almost complete lack of education or finesse. Like so many before him, he hired Yorgo on the spot, making him manager of the plant's fledgling quality control department. But, unlike his ilk, out of stubbornness and an inflated ego, he did not fire Yorgo the next day.

The police were, naturally, peeved. The police's chief commissioner drove all the way to Chalyvourgiki's factory in Elefsis to meet Angelopoulos and convince him to get rid of the subversive miasma. But Angelopoulos would not buckle. Despite his ultra-rightist politics, Angelopoulos grabbed the opportunity to score a small victory in the pissing game between himself, a self-made former shitkicker, and the very authorities that used to look down on him as a teenager. With his internationally expanding business and high-level ministerial connections granting him immunity, he could afford to play the liberal card: 'Who are they to tell us what to do?' he told a jubilant Yorgo afterwards, patting him reassuringly on the back. Nonetheless, Angelopoulos cut his salary by half, to the level of an unskilled shop-floor worker. In his mind, it was a mutually advantageous move: Yorgo got the job and he bagged a quality control director at a proletarian's salary!

Thus, Eleni and Yorgo ended up supplying their labour to Greece's post-war industrial miracle for the going salary of one person. Yorgo tried to laugh it off with a romantic spin: 'We were always meant to be one person.' Trisevgeni was not amused. She did not mind that her kids' salaries had been cut in half. By the standards of her household's past financial inflows, they were bringing home unprecedented sums. What she did mind was the clipping of their wings at the moment they should be soaring.

Of the two humiliations, it was Eleni's that she found harder to take. Yorgo, she used to say, could take solace from his standing among both enemies and comrades as a political animal paying his dues for resisting despotism. Eleni, on the other hand, was paying the price for the crime of being a woman, treated like a whore kept in lipstick.

On the night Yorgo kept his job at Chalyvourgiki, Trisevgeni told the couple: 'Now, get Eleni out of that toxic factory – that's my prayer and my curse.' They promised to engineer a career change. To make it so, Eleni enrolled for a postgraduate night course in biochemistry. It proved a sound investment. In the summer of 1960, just before they discovered she was pregnant, with me, she was offered a biochemist's position at a posh military hospital in the city centre, which treated higher-ranking army officers.

27. You might as well summon *Sputnik* back from space!

Motherhood meant different things to Eleni than it had meant to Trisevgeni. For the older Peloponnesian woman, giving birth was the beginning of a new serfdom within the walls of isolated domesticity. For Eleni, motherhood remained compatible with romance. Trisevgeni felt no jealousy, only surprise that it was possible for a woman to escape the drudgery without losing the husband. Mindful of this, even as her body grew heavy, Eleni took pleasure in the whirr of the hospital centrifuges, in the precision of her work. And when back at home, with Yorgo by her side, she carried domesticity lightly, like a happy burden.

With the newlyweds in respectable jobs and expecting their first child, her son flying high, her youngest daughter Georgia about to graduate as a dentist and Stavro, Yorgo's brother, in his last year at the Polytechneio, Trisevgeni's turn had come. 'My work with you lot is done,' she told them sternly during a Sunday lunch in December 1960. 'You are all educated citizens making your way usefully in a world moving too fast for me to fathom. It's payback time. I want you to teach me how to read and write.'

And so they did, taking turns to help her master textbooks meant for young children. Two years later, at the ripe age of sixty-four, she passed the primary school examinations. Liberated from 'un-alphabetism', her term for her illiteracy, she soon ploughed through novels she had heard people rave about. A skilful tale-spinner herself, she became obsessed with what she called her 'hitherto inaccessible windows to other souls and minds' – her prized books. One day, I was calling her to come and play with me, to no avail. Eleni stepped in instead, saying: 'Your grandma is immersed in Nikos Kazantzakis' *Christ Recrucified*. It would be easier to summon *Sputnik* back from space. Let her be.'

Sputnik had left its mark on Naiadon Street, on Trisevgeni in particular. The first artificial satellite in Earth's orbit, its successful launch caused waves of panic across Washington. It also marked a long paradox whose beginnings she first noticed on the day when her husband passed and her daughter was wed: while her life was slowing down, the world was changing at an alarming rate.

In 1954, as Nasser was reclaiming power from the British, and the Vietnamese were routing the French colonialists, Trisevgeni sensed the excitement in the streets of Cairo and Hanoi. In 1955, she was impressed that Germany and Italy, two countries whose soldiers she had seen occupy her country, joined France to found what we now know as the European Union. Change was afoot. In 1956, Trisevgeni's household echoed with ruminations on a tale of two cities surprisingly close to their hearts: Tehran and Budapest. As Soviet tanks crushed demonstrators in Hungary's ornamental capital, Panayis lost no time in exacting his rhetorical revenge on Yorgo and Eleni. They had been on his case for three years, ever since the CIA and MI6 had overthrown the democratically elected government of Mohammad Mosaddeq – the first act in a never-ending catastrophe that engulfed Iranian society.

Trisevgeni watched and listened carefully. As the Soviet *Sputniks* and the American *Explorers* crisscrossed the skies in a game for cosmic dominance, in Naiadon Street her children were holding Iron Curtain debates under the cloud of the Cold War, which in Greece, a country positioned right on the seam, was inordinately thick. Everyone wondered which side of the fence, if any, Trisevgeni would fall. Her son's? Her son-in-law's? Or that of her daughter, Eleni, who campaigned for people and countries to remain non-aligned, though never neutral?

Trisevgeni focused instead on the chasm between her two boys' psychological make-ups. Panayis dismissed his side's coup in Tehran as a necessary evil. His confidence never wavered, steeled by professional success and a fat bank account, until, of course, it dissolved into apoplexy in the early hours of 21 April 1967. Trisevgeni was glad that her son had risen above the need, angst and doubt that had preoccupied her ancestors. Secretly, however, she sympathised with Yorgo's position: believing in socialism, while fearing that its implementation may violate his humanist ideology.

Yorgo was haunted by the images of the Red Army tanks taking out his freethinking comrades in the streets of Budapest. The former peasant girl detected this. 'There's a lonesomeness at Yorgo's core', she once said, 'that invokes an overwhelming urge in me to want to throw a protective shield around him. I just can't help myself!'

In 1956, in the fog of the Suez war, Trisevgeni recognised in Yorgo a sadness: on the one hand, he celebrated that Egyptians were rising up, but on the other, he mourned the demise of the expatriate community which nurtured, then spurned, Anna and him. To boot, he foresaw a difficult scene: Yango appearing on their doorstep on Naiadon Street.

Five decades later, when I authored *The Global Minotaur*, a book about how the post-war world begat the financial crash of 2008, I took it for granted – like most economists of my generation – that the 1950s and early 1960s were capitalism's golden era, a rare period of stability, relative prosperity and falling inequality. From a macroeconomic perspective, I was not wrong.

But now that I am revisiting those years through Trisevgeni's eyes, I feel embarrassed.

The world was moving almost as fast as *Sputnik* circumnavigated Earth, except on a far less predictable trajectory. For Trisevgeni, the end of the 1950s must have seemed like watching a newsreel on fast-forward: Fidel Castro expelling the Mafia from Havana; US marines entering Lebanon; Éamon de Valera's rising to the Irish presidency; the assassination of Ceylon's first president; Cyprus gaining independence; Patrice Lumumba liberating Belgian Congo, where European colonial evil had reached its apex.

Closer to home, a domestic edition of the same newsreel projected the meteoric rise of the United Democratic Left party (EDA) in the general election of 1958. Trisevgeni knew that the left's comeback, this time through the ballot box, would unleash an almighty backlash from a regime known for its brutality. The signs were everywhere. Panayis was becoming more irritable in Yorgo's presence and especially rude to Eleni. Since the 1958 election, Trisevgeni also noticed Grigoris, our neighbour across Naiadon Street, whom I envied for his old black BMW motorcycle, intensifying his surveillance of her family – reporting our movements to the local police station had become something of a part-time job for him ever since Yorgo moved in.

A day after the Soviets' *Lunik 2* became the first human-made object to land on the moon's surface, Yorgo arrived in Naiadon Street with *Sputnikaki* – as Trisevgeni would christen the sandyellow Renault 4CV. Like the phone in her living room, the new car parked at night in her front garden pushed her into a state of ambivalence. She only began to make sense of it by studying the front cover, and then the inside, of a magazine Eleni had brought home.

The cover was Paul Klee's painting *Angelus Novus*. Along with

Walter Benjamin's interpretation of the sheep-like angel contemplating the repulsive past while being forcefully dragged forwards into a future, Trisevgeni recognised in that painting her own mixed feelings towards progress – a path that is neither linear nor reliably a good thing.

28. Sacred snakes

At the beginning, there was Chaos. Existence began with Gaia, Mother Earth. Then came Uranus, the limitless dark blue sky up there above the clouds. Those two begat the tall Mountains and the Pontus, the endless sea. Don't be fooled by their beauty, my son, for they never fully defeated non-existence. Chaos still lives inside of us, jostling for position in our soul, threatening to gain the upper hand during our darkest moments. And when your life's thread runs out, you, like me, like everyone, will be returned to Chaos. The question is: What will you accomplish before then despite the void within? So, let me tell you the story of . . .

This is how Trisevgeni would begin every one of the bedtime stories in the Naiadon Street bedroom I shared with her. Lyrical, often gory, they were my introduction to the lure of existentialism, the violence of politics, of geology even. The Earth, epitomised by Mount Helmos in whose shadow Rododafni, her village, nestled, was important to my grandmother, not least as a metaphor for the women in her life that history forgot in a community culled by malaria, her father and two siblings included. Gaia had protected her from despair. Trisevgeni was determined to extend her protective shield over me.

Inspired by the sight of hundreds of snakes jolting out of their hiding places minutes before her village was hit by a powerful earthquake in April 1928, Trisevgeni made up a suitable Hesiodic tale to help me overcome my snake phobia.

> Once upon a time Gaia fell ill, her whole body shaking violently. Chaos was making a comeback. In her belly! What had happened was that Uranus and their son Cronus had been at loggerheads, engaged in a violent political powerplay over control of the Cosmos. It turned so nasty that Cronus castrated Uranus and, as if that were not enough, Gaia was impregnated by the spilled blood. Thus an abomination of a child was born. Enceladus.
>
> Every time Enceladus came near her, Gaia would shake violently, the houses of us humans would tumble and fall, crushing our young; our blood turning into bile that poisoned our bodies. But wise old Gaia thought of a remedy. She consulted Athena, the goddess of wisdom, who suggested they enlist her sacred snakes. It was agreed.
>
> Whenever Enceladus – now fully entrenched on Mount Olympus as the god of earthquakes – approached Gaia, she would summon Athena's snakes. They would lose no time before jolting out of their holes to warn us humans, giving us a scare that never failed also to restore our blood's purity.

Snakes never terrified me the same way again. Trisevgeni's fables transported me in a television-free country, a country where even black and white TV arrived as late as 1969. Miraculously, their magic remained intact upon contact with the images that Yorgo would bring back from his travels: silent but beautifully coloured Super 8 flicks.

During my first six years, Yorgo was away for much of the time. Angelopoulos, his boss, was adamant that Chalyvourgiki should grow into a modern steelworks. With no English or engineering background, he needed Yorgo to accompany him, again and again, to Duisburg, Rotterdam, Pittsburgh, Seoul and Yokohama, where they bought machinery; and to Australia or Indonesia, where they secured adequate supplies of iron ore and coking coal. Yorgo would film everything he could – and then screen it in our living room upon his return.

In my child's mind, those silent masterpieces from the four corners of the planet merged flawlessly with Trisevgeni's stories. Her ecumenical myths of Hephaestus' exploits were at one with Bessemer furnaces; the great ships launched in Yokohama were tributes to Poseidon.

To prevent Angelopoulos from fully hijacking his spirit, Yorgo decided to embark on a second life. In Makronisos, his survival strategy included doing higher mathematics or chemistry on the dirt, using a stick. Later, he was moved to tears when he read Primo Levi's account of how he too had survived the concentration camp by doing chemistry in his mind – an escape into a world of unalloyed truths. So, during his lunch break he would leave Chalyvourgiki and head for the nearby Elefsis Archaeological Museum, where he luxuriated in the discovery of ancient steles full of clues that antiquity's technologists were more advanced than previously thought.

Trisevgeni was mesmerised by the discoveries Yorgo would come home with. She lapped up his findings from experiments and chemical analyses of ancient artefacts (javelin tips, swords, instruments, jewellery) that he carried out after hours in his lab. In time, these led to a doctorate in archaeometry and several significant discoveries of how the ancients created their material world, such as the metal rods that held the Parthenon's columns together.

With Trisevgeni always there, I hardly noticed my parents' absences: the picture shows, stories and magnificent toys, especially from Hamleys in London, that Yorgo brought back proved ample compensation. Eleni's long hours at the military hospital were also compensated by my boyish delight whenever an army jeep whisked her away to deal with some urgent issue. Those were exciting times.

Later, I realised that they were also interesting times in the sense of the Chinese curse. While I was still in Eleni's belly, the CIA murdered Patrice Lumumba, and John Fitzgerald Kennedy entered the White House before reluctantly embarking on the folly of the Vietnam War. Closer to home, doctor and long-jump champion Grigoris Lambrakis was elected to parliament, on the EDA ticket, where he initiated the Greek peace movement, paying for it with his life at the hands of state-sponsored thugs two years later in the streets of Thessaloniki – soon after the Cuban Missile Crisis nearly wiped us all out. Unbeknownst to the boy under Trisevgeni's tutelage, the world was brewing heavy weather.

29. TWA Flight 800

For Trisevgeni, nothing could be further from her truth than Scottish philosopher David Hume's allegation that it is 'not contrary to reason to prefer the destruction of the whole world to the scratching of my finger'. Ever since she learned to read newspapers, she would be moved to tears by reports of the suffering of faraway peoples, whether victims of China's famine after the disastrous Great Leap Forward or hapless Vietnamese whose limbs were blown off by American bombs. If she could have saved them by chopping off her right hand, let alone a lone finger, she would have. In contrast, when minor disputes in Naiadon Street blew out of proportion, she would first get bored, then annoyed.

One such quarrel began when Panayis and Eleni, in a rare show of unity, went ballistic over the news that Georgia, their younger sister, and Stavro, Yorgo's brother, were an item. Trisevgeni was shocked by her children's social conservatism, their readiness to espouse the Greek Orthodox tradition that considered Stavro and Georgia siblings, their marriage only sin-free if it had coincided with Yorgo and Eleni's wedding. 'I am the ancient one who should be outraged,' she protested. 'Why are my secular children getting so hot under the collar?' Indeed, their reaction was so unpleasant that Stavro and Georgia chose to elope to Switzerland where they lived and, in fact, prospered for more than a decade.

There was, however, one development that threw Trisevgeni off balance. Yango's arrival. She feared that Yango would look down on her as uncouth. In Trisevgeni's eyes, his impeccable manners confirmed the disdain he must have felt that destiny had condemned him to end his life in her world. During the seven years I observed my two grandparents waltz carefully around one another, I never saw Trisevgeni relax properly around him.

For several years before his arrival in Athens, Yango had been struggling in Cairo. Following Britain's 1956 invasion of Egypt, Thomas Cook ceased to provide him with the income or authority to which he had been accustomed. The ruling class he had belonged to no longer ruled. Every week, some friend or relative would up stumps and leave for Europe, Lebanon, Israel, South Africa, Rhodesia or the Americas. By his own account, Yango decided to move to Athens when he heard of the birth of his first grandchild – me.

Humour, Yango's weapon of choice, crashed into the shoals of Trisevgeni's cheek. When she wanted to push back, she would insinuate that, unlike her late husband, who had grown up in Crete and was a bona fide Venizelist liberal from cradle to grave, Yango's Cretan roots were too obscure, a Venizelism which arrived in Cairo distorted. 'Enriched, you mean?' a smiling Yango would retort through his pince-nez glasses.

Their passive-aggressive altercations dissolved when, one evening, Yorgo announced that Eleni had been diagnosed with an aggressive thyroid cancer – possibly due to the toxic fumes she had inhaled during her fertiliser factory years. Naiadon Street went into overdrive with Trisevgeni at the helm. Panayis, who was living in Thessaloniki at the time, managing Siemens' hydroelectric projects in northern Greece, returned to hover, offering moral support as best he could. Yorgo and Eleni soon made tracks for Switzerland where a Lausanne-based specialist, whom their long-departed siblings had pinned down, would treat Eleni. For a couple of months, it was all systems go.

Eleni hardly had a chance to take in what was happening in

her body. Adrenaline drove every move and masked all emotion. It was not until they had laid her on the stretcher outside the operating theatre, where the cold, antiseptic air pressed against her skin, that the machinery of thought re-engaged. And then, strangely, it was not fear of the knife, nor even the looming spectre of mortality, that seized her. Prompted by the itchy hospital gown, her mind travelled to the dreary dresses Trisevgeni had sewn for her in childhood. How they had chafed, not just against her skin, but against her deeper, unnameable longing to escape a world that, through the coarseness of that fabric, and its dull hues, cautioned her against aiming for a place above her station. 'As if wings were not meant for the likes of me,' she told a bewildered Yorgo when she came round later, unaware of the small fact that, in the meantime, she had had a tumour removed.

The operation was a success, even if the prognosis gave Eleni a decade to live. To celebrate, Yorgo decided to fulfil Eleni's wish to visit Firenze, travelling south from Switzerland in a hired car towards Rome where there they would, eventually, board a plane to Athens. On the twenty-third day of that mild November, Trisevgeni, Panayis and Yango were preparing to take me to Athens' old seaside airport to welcome them back, collectively to turn that bleak page.

Minutes before getting into Panayis' car, the wireless, which Trisevgeni kept on at all hours, spewed news that sucked the air out of our living room. Athens-bound TWA Flight 800 from Rome had crashed on take-off on the tarmac of Leonardo da Vinci Fiumicino Airport. Most passengers, the radio announcer said, were incinerated in the burning fuselage.

Within minutes, Panayis announced that he, and his wife Sophia, would immediately draw up the adoption paperwork. 'I shall need you to move to Thessaloniki to help us with the boy's transition,' he told Trisevgeni. 'Not on your nelly,' came her answer. 'The boy stays with me, here, in his home. If you want to adopt him, you need to move back to Athens.' Yango looked on, quietly, but not without admiration. Realising how premature this disagreement was, Panayis instead focused on extracting information from the authorities.

Eleni's and Yorgo's names were on the passenger list but, for twenty-four hours, the authorities would not release the names of the confirmed fifty dead or the twenty-three badly injured passengers. Then an oversized grey taxi, straight out of some 1950s Hollywood flick, pulled up on Naiadon Street. From it the smiling couple emerged, along with their considerable luggage.

It turns out that, on the spur of the moment, Eleni had suggested that they stay an extra day in Rome to visit the Sistine Chapel. So, after arranging to fly back the following day on an Alitalia flight, without bothering to cancel their TWA booking, they spent a carefree day in Rome without, of course, listening to or reading the news. Only as they were boarding their Alitalia flight did they hear of the previous day's TWA disaster. By then, the best way to contact us was to convey the good news in person. 'I never thought I would be in the debt of the Vatican,' murmured Trisevgeni that evening.

30. Anna's wake

Yango's Thomas Cook pension, when it eventually began to flow, was modest but sufficient for a small, stand-alone, rented house in Glyfada – a picturesque seaside suburb not too far from Paleo Phaliro. As for the lump sum that came with his pension, in an attempt to reconnect with his childhood on Leros, Yango invested it in *Anna* – a wooden boat he commissioned featuring a small cabin and a noisy diesel inboard engine.

The half hour it took to drive from Naiadon Street to Yango's Glyfada abode, which he shared with several formerly stray cats, was a journey to a world of mystique and freedom. Yorgo and Eleni would take me there often and let me spend days, sometimes a week, with the 'old man and his sea', as Trisevgeni put it.

The act of taking *Anna* out of Glyfada's small fishing port as the sun rose behind us over Mount Hymettus, heading east towards the Poseidon Temple on Cape Sounion, was a mental canvas on which to concoct my own fables. Mostly in silence, we would spend the whole day at sea, me swimming and he fishing, until the sun disappeared into the water – our cue to head back. Then Yango would fry the fish he had caught before ceremoniously feeding them to his cats, while I ploughed into his vegetarian Cretan pasta. Occasionally, when the sea got angry, the anxiety and effort to return safely to port gave me a taste of danger that Trisevgeni had made it her late life's work that I never experience.

One late summer evening, a storm hit us with ferocious

winds. *Anna*'s little engine could hardly counter their power, its bow plunging into terrifying waves, the low cloud reducing visibility, making it hard for Yango to see where he was heading. Time passed quickly and, as the winds grew stronger and the waves taller, the pitch-black night engulfed us. 'Go to the front, hold on tightly and try to make out twin red lights,' he instructed me. Petrified, I did.

For what seemed like an aeon, I squinted to see through the darkness. Nothing. But then, I spotted them. 'There,' I shouted, pointing in their direction. To this day, every time I pass by Glyfada's Konstantinos and Eleni church, perched just behind the coastal road connecting Glyfada to Athens, my eyes squint until I spot those same twin red lights that still stand next to the cross atop its dome.

Greek family law ran on the reprehensible dowry custom, like many other Western countries. Societies that treated women as property until very recently had difficulty recognising women's property rights. As Eleni told me: 'Your grandmother has worked harder than all of us put together, but she has no income. She doesn't even own her home.' The law stipulated that the Naiadon Street home passed from Trisevgeni's husband to their firstborn son, Panayis. Panayis did not want the house for himself but not for a moment did he consider passing the deeds to his mother. Instead, weighed down by a patriarchal sense of responsibility to his sisters, he handed the house over to Eleni and Georgia. Thus, Trisevgeni was left with no income and no assets, relying on the kindness of her children. It was the joy that Eleni saw in my eyes, every time I returned from Glyfada, and Trisevgeni's incapacity to compete with Yango in this regard, which alerted my mother to the injustice unfolding in her own home.

Influenced by Virginia Woolf's *A Room of One's Own*, which she had read in the mid-1970s, Eleni lamented how Trisevgeni's lack of a small pension, even a room in her own house that she could call hers, had turned a proud, wise woman into a vassal of children and men. Around that time, Eleni quit her hospital job and threw her lot into the second feminist wave which, by 1983, after years of campaigning, forced radical changes to family law, expunged dowry from the statutes, and granted peasant women a small, but liberating, pension.

31. Fireplace marvels, interrupted

When parts of our roof caved in in 1965, a civil engineer declared our Naiadon Street home structurally unstable. Within hours we were evacuated to a tiny, rented apartment nearby. Lacking access to the banking system, or any savings to speak of, Yorgo and Eleni had to approach everyone they knew to seek microloans, mostly in the form of hoarded gold sovereign pounds. Even though they gathered less than a quarter of the estimated rebuilding cost, they proceeded anyway. Within a week, I remember cheering on a bulldozer while, next to me, a glum Trisevgeni was crossing herself.

By chance, our old house's demolition coincided with the demolition of our stunted democracy. Unhappy with the election of a centrist government in 1963, plans were afoot at the CIA, the State Department and the Pentagon to contain it. Their first symbolic step was to encourage their local proxy, the king, to demand that one of his courtiers become the new defence minister. When the elected prime minister rejected this royal show of no confidence, suggesting instead that he himself take on the sensitive defence ministry, the king sacked him – ending any pretence that we lived under a constitutional monarchy. It was July 1965. Massive demonstrations erupted that summer. For almost three years, the cities, towns, highways and byways up and down the country became stages for marches, processions and vigils. My first memory of a political rally revolves around the sound of our Sputnikaki's horn getting hoarser and hoarser from overuse as Eleni drove us to one of these protests, a small part of a convoy of thousands of cars whose horns created a gloriously unruly cacophony.

While democracy faltered, our home had better luck. With help from Trisevgeni's favourite niece, who had just qualified as an architect, and various builders and plumbers willing to work for nominal sums, the house on Naiadon Street was rebuilt – complete with red-brick fireplace. Eleni had fulfilled the promise she had made to Yorgo more than a decade earlier. Besides its sentimental value, it proved mightily useful when, in late 1966, two months after I started primary school, we moved into the not-quite-complete house in the middle of winter. The new fireplace had more of an educational impact on me than my poor schoolteacher, besieged as he was in a class by fifty unruly boys caged in a dilapidated state primary school.

Huddled in front of the fireplace every night, listening to Anna's favourite Verdi, Beethoven, Bizet or Mozart tunes on a new Philips stereo, Trisevgeni and Yorgo took turns to entertain me – since Eleni either was lost in some book or had already made her excuses. While embroidering yet another mantelpiece cover or some fancy tablecloth, Trisevgeni would tell us one of her stories before passing the baton to Yorgo and his friends – as he called the lumps of ore or the metal rods that he brought back from the steel plant in a grey sack. Trisevgeni, who insisted that Yorgo's friends be laid down reverentially on one of her embroidered creations, watched attentively as he introduced me to the magic of melted metals and, in particular, the mysterious properties of iron.

As I have recounted in my last book, it was my most peculiar introduction to historical materialism: the way technological advances, from metallurgy to electromagnetism to artificial intelligence, clash with society's outdated social arrangements to generate historical change. Trisevgeni was spellbound. Though she had witnessed ironsmiths at work in her village, she had not realised how truly miraculous it was that, by simply 'baptising' red-hot, soft iron in a pot of cold water, we transformed it into cold, hard steel.

Of course, the wonders of chemistry would not have fascinated her so much had they not been accompanied by Yorgo's evocative tales of Hesiod, the original compiler of ancient Greek mythology who feared and loathed the coming of the Iron Age more than today's technophobes fear and loathe AI. Or Homer, who likened the sound emitted by the burning wooden stake which Odysseus plunged into Polyphemus' only eye to the baptism of hot iron. Trisevgeni was so taken with this, that for years to come, she would recite the relevant line from the *Odyssey*: 'And as when a smith dips a great axe in cold water amid loud hissing to temper it—for therefrom comes the strength of iron—even so did his eye hiss round the stake of olive-wood.'

It was a winter so marvellous that some vengeful deity must have been irked, making it its business to lash out. The year was 1967. On that April's twenty-first day, shortly after four in the morning, thugs broke down our new front door to hunt down and abduct Yorgo.

32. Get out of my home, mongrels!

While the rest of us froze, watching the military police dash through the house, cuff Yorgo, throw a hood over his head, and drag him to a waiting jeep, only Trisevgeni resisted them. She grabbed her favourite broom, chased them down the corridor and, almost comically, hit them about their heads, shouting, 'Get out of my home, mongrels!' Out on Naiadon Street, she took aim at their speeding jeep, catapulting her broom in its direction. Then, leaving the broom in the street, perhaps as a symbol of her defiance for the neighbours to see, she walked gracefully back into the house to make camomile tea.

Strangely, Yorgo's violent abduction from her home destabilised Trisevgeni less than the litany of small cruelties which unfolded *after* that fateful morning in April 1967. The ban on Darwinism, Einstein's relativity theory, quantum mechanics, modern mathematics, the philosophy of Epicurus and some of the most poignant ancient Athenian plays puzzled her. She could make sense of the ban on listening to the BBC or Deutsche Welle radio broadcasts as the instinctual decree of insecure thugs. But the prohibition of some of the novels she had grown to cherish, including *Christ Recrucified* – *that* she took personally. Fortunately, she found light relief in the surreal criminalisation of whistling tunes by popular musician Mikis Theodorakis and, to top it all, the banning of the letter Z – for daring to allude to the Greek word *zei* ('he lives') which youths spray-painted on walls in memory of the slain Grigoris Lambrakis.

A few days after the coup, and his abduction, Yorgo turned up at our (still busted) front door. He explained that the military police had dragged him to a football stadium where they had rounded up several thousand potential subversives – a practice pioneered by Latin American dictators with a proven fondness for blending football and brutality. Eleni was incensed that, while her mind was racing to barren islands, rural prisons or underground rendition sites, he was sitting, jaded and forlorn, a stone's throw from Naiadon Street.

Minutes later, it was Trisevgeni's turn to lose her nerve when an army jeep screeched to a halt outside the house and two uniformed men walked energetically towards her. 'Don't worry, Mum,' Eleni reassured her, 'they're here for me.' It was a time of delicious absurdities: one parent abducted by the same military that sent a jeep to take the other parent to work.

With Yorgo still in one piece, Trisevgeni extolled Eleni to do something to protect me from being picked on at school as the son of a subversive. Eleni complied, acting on rumours that the owner of a la-di-da private school in Athens' northern suburbs was secretly taking in the children of dissidents. A few weeks later, I was yanked out of my local school and off I went, enduring more than an hour's bus ride each way, to a school packed with posh establishment kids. 'Why would the owner of such a school do that?' a suspicious Trisevgeni asked.

As he explained to me many years later, Antonis Moraitis, the school's owner, had been badly shaken by the April 1967 coup. Unlike Panayis, Moraitis, a young philologist and classicist afficionado, had been a member of EPON, the leftist student resistance group to which Yorgo had drifted soon after arriving from Cairo. Marriage into an industrial dynasty put clear water between him and the civil war's losing side, allowing him also to buy a prominent private school, which he named after himself and turned into his oyster. Although he had long since left behind the radical politics of his youth, when the tanks rolled in on 21 April 1967, he, like Panayis, was disgusted. His resistance took the form of turning an already established high-society school, to which even ministers of the fascist regime sent their children, into a secret refuge for around fifty children of dissidents, purged university professors and enlightened high school teachers.

Meanwhile, Yorgo was conflicted. Trisevgeni sensed his unease. His son was safe, he was back at work. But so many others were running for their lives or languishing behind bars. Despite my tactless joy at growing up in interesting times, I was always aware of his sadness. Like scenes from an Ingmar Bergman movie that the mind cannot shed, they endure in me. One such cinematic sequence harks back to a winter's night in 1968, when a stranger appeared on our doorstep: his tattered raincoat dripping on the floor; a battered leather briefcase in his left hand; his eyes dull with exhaustion; the long, silent embrace with Yorgo; the whispers; Trisevgeni serving camomile with honey; pamphlets and a book taken from the briefcase; the swiftness with which the stranger rose to his feet to leave; not looking back as he walked out into the unrelenting rain. And Yorgo, standing at the front door long after his visitor had disappeared, drenched, staring aimlessly into the cold night.

Later I learned that he was Kostas Kouloufakos – the EPON man who had drafted Yorgo into that ill-fated student union leadership position, and who had ended up in Makronisos with him. One of the few who never signed, never settled down, never found comfort in a post-civil war Greece pretending to be a normal country. A constant fugitive, seldom sleeping in the same bed twice and always at the top of the list of people the military longed to get their hands on. It was only a decade later, when his friend found recognition as one of Greece's notable poets, that Yorgo could smile again at the mention of Kouloufakos' name.

Eleni was less sympathetic to Yorgo's guilt. 'The struggle', she would say, 'needs living hearths, not just broken hearts.' Saving Yorgo from a life in damp cells and on friends' couches was what she could do to change the world. Her guiltless pursuit of as much normality as she could create was, she believed, entirely consistent with empathy for the fugitives and the imprisoned – even before Panayis joined their ranks. A bizarre consequence of this empathy was our Red Blanket Days, as Trisevgeni called my parents' strange ritual every night just before nine.

Hungry for news that might shed light on whether the regime was loosening or tightening its grip, with all of what that meant for detainees and renegades, Yorgo moved a bulky state-of-the-art short-wave wireless that he had bought in Tokyo into our living room. Placed opposite the fireplace, the device's receiver proved capable of overcoming the regime's jamming waves. As if by magic, the BBC World Service and Deutsche Welle broadcasts filled the living room.

Mindful of Grigoris, the snitch across the street, whom Trisevgeni had once caught with his ear pressed against a window on the eastern side of our house, Yorgo and Eleni decided on a low-tech but, to me, electrifying means of dampening the crackling sounds of the wireless: they covered the device with a thick woolly red blanket and huddled under it, ears straining.

Diving under the red blanket to join them, the muffled jingle followed by a German announcer's voice or the chimes of Big Ben propelled my six-year-old self to a mythical place called Europe. A place I had yet to visit, apart from the tantalising glimpses offered by an illustrated Brothers Grimm book I had in my bedroom and,

Anna, 1923

Yango, at his Thomas Cook office, 1923

Yorgo and Anna on Poros, 1932

Anna and Yango, Alexandria, 1927

Greek expatriate society on a riverboat cruise on the Nile

Yorgo, Makronisos, 1947

Marble steps on Solonos Street leading to the old School of Chemistry building

Anna's diaries and her small red notebook

Eleni and Panayis, Syntagma Square, Athens, 1945

Panayis awaiting his bride, with Eleni (far right) and Trisevgeni (left), 1956

Running with Eleni

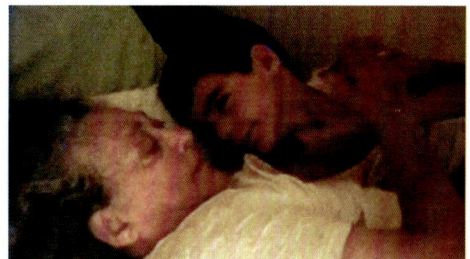

Trisevgeni's stories at bedtime

Trisevgeni the younger with Eleni

Panayis with his fellow defendants at their court martial in 1970 were front page news

Yango sailing on *Anna*

With Yorgo, Olympia, 1976

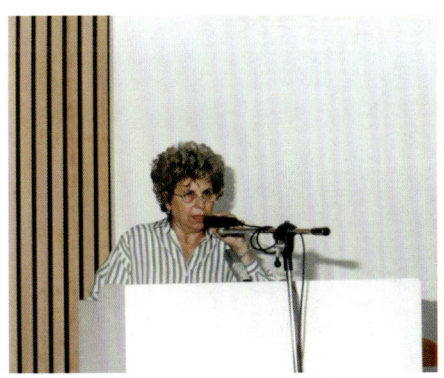

Eleni at a hustings, 1984

Georgia with my daughter, Xenia, 2005

Danaë working at her studio

Kashmir, 2006

of course, my copy of *Robinson Crusoe* that Yango had insisted I read. In time, I learned to appreciate that to discover what was happening to our people, in our backyard, I had to travel to foreign lands – that the only way truly to know your country is to see it through a foreigner's, especially a refugee's, eyes.

33. Murder in Los Angeles, slow train to Munich

A little over a year after the coup, Trisevgeni decided to do something novel. Parisian youths had just lit the fuse of an uprising that spread across Europe like a Mediterranean bushfire, when she staged her own rebellion. On a cloudy May morning she caught the number 32 bus from Naiadon Street to the centre of Athens. For no reason. Just to experience that strange thing the young called leisure. Her first taste of freedom from domestic labour gave her a thrill. To share the buzz, she began to take me along. For a few weeks, before my planned midsummer disappearance with Yango on *Anna*, Trisevgeni and I would spend the mornings wandering the ancient ruins around the Acropolis or the Agora, occasionally catching a matinee.

During one of those sojourns, on a hot afternoon in early June 1968, Eleni joined us for a stroll outside the revamped ancient stadium where the first modern Olympic Games were held in 1896. A newsboy suddenly broke the calm announcing, at the top of his voice, that some American was dead. Eleni's eyes filled up with tears. 'He was our last chance,' she said.

Eleni's grief was genuine. Bobby Kennedy would have made a difference, she believed. He had openly castigated the CIA for organising our colonels' coup. That, along with his support for the civil rights movement in the American deep south, gave her hope that, were he to enter the White House the following January, he would issue the appropriate order to underlings who were keeping our patch of southern Europe in chains. The news that he had been gunned down in cold blood hit her like a wrecking ball. 'If they can take out another Kennedy, weeks after Martin Luther King, imagine what they will do to us,' she muttered as she removed her sunglasses to wipe her eyes.

Trisevgeni was circumspect. She knew nothing of the second slain Kennedy. But she didn't think she needed to look to a foreign politician for hope. Indeed, she thought little of her daughter's fascination with father figures from abroad who would magically deliver us from tyranny. Every time Eleni and Yorgo waxed lyrical about Willy Brandt, the then West German foreign minister who later became chancellor, or Bruno Kreisky, the Austrian Socialist Party leader who decriminalised abortion, or Olof Palme, the Swedish prime minister, Trisevgeni rolled her eyes. She did not so much question their good intentions, acknowledging how they had embraced many of our political refugees, as she focused on a darker side of our predicament.

Even before the Occupation, she had learned to focus on the brutality of our own people, especially towards women – in the homes, in the villages, in the cities. During the Occupation, she was struck by the zeal of the collaborators, men even more vicious than the German Nazis. She wasn't convinced that a telephone call from Washington or a fiery speech in Bonn, Vienna or Stockholm would wrest power from the tyrants who were turning the screw on us.

A couple of months later, in August, after I had had my fix of the Saronic Sea with Yango, Yorgo and Eleni announced that they were desperate for a breath of 'democratic' air. Having secured passports for all of us, with Panayis' help, they had a plan: we would spend their annual holiday in Vienna and Munich, in the beating heart of European social democracy. It was a ritual that we would repeat, with slight variations, every summer until the junta's collapse in 1974.

The Acropolis Express, travelling majestically at a snail's pace, took us through northern Greece into Yugoslavia and then across the border into what the adults called Europe. Perched on my top bunk bed, I spent day and night transfixed by scenes that can only be relived today by watching Emir Kusturica's *Time of the Gypsies*. It is so hard to imagine now, and yet communist Yugoslavia was freer and more prosperous than Greece.

Trisevgeni, who accompanied us on that first trip on the sleeper train, grew obstinate as we crossed into Austria. Her mind understood the changed political circumstances, but her spirit refused to see Austrians and Germans as our reliable defenders against fascism. During the three weeks we spent in Germanic lands, she never missed an opportunity to moan about something or other. On the way back, in a rented car that took us through northern Italy to Brindisi, where a ferry to Patras was waiting, it was only when the landscape became less green, the first olive trees appeared and the voices of the people grew louder that she relented.

For years I dismissed Trisevgeni's attitude as that of a woman born in the dying years of the nineteenth century, unable to join in my parents' celebration of Europe's post-war democratic makeover. Yet, as I now know, Greece was not the only country where a latent totalitarian instinct proved hard fully to eradicate.

34. Like vermin in a zoo

On our return to Greece, Eleni sprang her canon on me. A list of good books that I had to read in quick succession, by authors from Fyodor Dostoyevsky and Penelope Delta to Mark Twain and Menelaos Loudemis. German-language lessons were thrown in too, echoing Eleni's own immersion in Goethe. Aghast that my last summer days would be spent on dry land, Trisevgeni was my last resort. She rose to the task valiantly.

'You are not doing this *for* the boy,' she lambasted Eleni, 'but just to show off our boy to the new fancy school.' Sparks flew before a peace treaty emerged, granting me one precious full day with Yango in Glyfada. That evening, after the blazing sun had traded places with the brightest night sky, Yango took me to an open-air cinema to watch Sergio Leone's *The Good, the Bad and the Ugly*. Our leisurely walk back to his sedate house and unruly cats is my last memory of him.

That autumn landed early and hard, doing a good impersonation of winter. One particularly cold evening, *Anna*'s anchor got stuck on the rocky seabed of a nearby island and Yango dove in to retrieve it. On the way back, dripping wet against a frosty headwind, he caught pneumonia, which swiftly colluded with his lifelong asthma to procure a massive heart attack. Eleni and Yorgo kept it from me. To Trisevgeni's horror, they did not tell me until after the funeral.

While clearing out Yango's cupboards, Eleni discovered a secret cache of robes and artefacts that proved Yango had been high up in Cairo's Masonic fraternity. Yorgo was embarrassed but unsurprised, meekly remarking that Masonic shenanigans were commonplace among the minions of the British Empire. Thinking back, I can't remember a single moment when he and Yango chatted as father and son. Rather, they avoided each other, speaking through others. Consequently, the task of including Yango in our family had fallen on Eleni. It was, therefore, surprising that it was she who reacted to the discovery of his Masonic paraphernalia no less furiously than if she had caught him in full Ku Klux Klan Grand Wizard regalia. I was just angry at my grandfather's posthumous demonisation.

So I staged a pathetic little mutiny. Instead of *Crime and Punishment*, which was at the top of Eleni's canon, I plunged into *Robinson Crusoe*. But Eleni's wrath crashed on the sandbanks of Trisevgeni's defences. Like a new Antigone, she rose up to guarantee Yango a sacred passage to the other side – and my right to read Defoe's Protestant 'boy's own manual', as Eleni referred to *Crusoe*, on condition that I would then move on briskly to the dark Russian masterpiece.

That winter felt milder than the autumn. The seeds of Panayis' *peripeteia* were taking root. Trisevgeni, who knew nothing of her son's hidden conversion from scion of the establishment to urban guerrilla, was investing much of her attention in my new school. She made it her business to know that the long bus journey to the school felt like a wormhole ride sucking me into an alternative universe. She listened as I merrily recounted the clandestine recognition game that we, the kids of dissidents, played. Sworn by our parents never to reveal ourselves, we had to devise a protocol of mutual acknowledgment. It was a good game that made me special friends, such as Erifyli – the daughter of an imprisoned philology professor – with whom I later explored a whole world of film, music and edgy culture.

Antonis Moraitis was so enamoured of his school that he ran Berkshire, his successful nylon and stocking factory, from the school office staffed by two secretaries: the gentle soul who dealt with teachers and pupils, and a sterner one who dealt with nylon clients and managers. I remember waxing lyrical to Trisevgeni that, in a country where the parliament was mothballed and unsolicited speech could land you in gaol, Moraitis insisted that pupils elect our class representatives, organise debates and read banned books. She appreciated all this, but her cynicism lingered.

She wasn't wrong. In an oral history published in the late 1990s, a woman who had worked in Moraitis' Berkshire factory described the conditions she and her fellow proletarian women worked under, as I was cocooned in a liberal bubble a few miles away: 'We laboured at breakneck speed, for a pittance, terrified of the forewoman who behaved like a Nazi sentry and whom I had to beg every afternoon for a bottle of milk to take home to my daughter.'

Even nice liberal men cannot avoid reproducing nasty violations of liberty when exercising power. In retrospect, my freedom was not much different from that of vermin in a zoo: free to roam around while the larger animals, the adults around me, were caged, exploited, driven into the ground – a forlorn metaphor that Yango, who always felt a little like that too, might have appreciated.

35. My own special Miss Havisham

One evening, as Beethoven's *Moonlight Sonata* was playing on our stereo, I expressed an idle interest in the piano. Trisevgeni took note. Without telling anyone, she did her research. A neighbour told her that a Mrs Jenny, a former concert pianist, offered lessons at her home four blocks away at the corner of Halcyon and Ivy Streets. Before I knew it, I was crossing Mrs Jenny's threshold.

The stand-alone two-storey house, in the neoclassical Athenian architectural style of the 1920s, exuded old money that had dried up long ago. The heavy front door opened to a long corridor, high ceilings, a wide staircase the likes of which I had only seen in American movies, and strains of several pianos coming at once from different wings of the house. Feeling like a trespasser, I waited outside the living room. While finishing up her previous lesson with a young woman, whose mesmerising playing I had been listening to in the corridor behind the living room's shut double doors, she summoned me to enter.

Even though the sun was beating down on Paleo Phaliro that afternoon, the large room was dim, courtesy of wooden shutters ably assisted by heavy velvet curtains that had seen better days. An ornamental Louis XV-style couch resting against the long wall opposite the large French windows was the only furniture of note besides two enormous Steinway grand pianos. Nestled in each other's curved cases, the two grands were positioned so that the two players faced one another, able to stare into each other's eyes but not see each other's hands.

Sitting behind the grand whose tail faced the living room's entrance, with her back to the deep bay window, Mrs Jenny did not look up as I entered. With a theatrical wave of her left hand, while her right continued to play, she directed me to the couch where I waited while she instructed the young woman how to practise the Béla Bartók piece. As my eyes grew accustomed to the low light, and my nostrils registered the rising damp, I caught my first glimpse of the striking woman in her late fifties. Pale beyond words, impeccably attired, the whiff of thick French perfume hanging over her, Mrs Jenny was forbidding and otherworldly.

Once we were alone, again without looking at me, she gestured that I approach her. Reluctantly, I circled the two grand pianos and stood awkwardly above her, not realising I was meant to kiss her hand. With a stern nod, she made me understand. For a good twelve years, every Tuesday and Thursday at exactly six in the evening, before taking my seat in front of the second Steinway, I would kiss her hand in the way she demanded that day. And then do so again on my way out. Two things won me over immediately, making this a gesture of heartfelt respect.

The first was Mrs Jenny's unmistakable delight in music, which she insisted should be our common end-in-itself, the only driving force in the room. Unlike conventional teachers who follow a preordained canon, she would play one piece after the other until one spoke to me. Then, I would raise my hand and say 'this one please', at which point she would smile and proceed to help me learn it.

The second idiosyncrasy was her teaching method. During that first lesson, once I was sat on my piano stool opposite her, seeing that I was trying in vain to see her hands move on her Steinway, she smiled and commanded me to stop. At first it seemed unreasonable. Like every beginner, I needed her to place my fingers on the right keys, to let me watch her hands while trying to imitate them. Yet in all the years she taught me, not once did I see her hands play or feel them manipulate mine! 'Your ears, my dear boy, your ears,' she would say melodically. 'Train your ears and then your fingers will find their way to the right keys.' Gradually, as I heard her play, my fingers learned their way around the keyboard as if an invisible hand beyond my control were guiding them.

For several years, our conversations were limited. Yet nothing rewarded me more than the odd smile with which Mrs Jenny's face revealed a degree of satisfaction with what I had played. The only aspect of our arrangement I disliked was her insistence that, on Wednesdays, in between our Tuesday and Thursday *séances*, as she called our lessons, I should practise scales with her husband, a man twenty years her junior who, even in my child's eyes, seemed out of place. Nevertheless, solely to satisfy her, on most Wednesdays I grudgingly rode my bicycle to their fading mansion, walked up the stairs to a dingy room, and played one scale after the other on a less than well-tuned upright, supervised by the talentless husband. To mitigate the boredom, I trained my ears to ignore my piano's sounds and focus instead on whatever music was floating up from the living room downstairs.

In time, once she decided I was worthy, Mrs Jenny told me about her musical studies in Paris, her first recitals. And when she found out that, as fate would have it, her beloved brother shared a prison cell with Panayis, and later sat in the same dock during their court martial, our bond grew stronger. So much so that she talked to me about her desperate decision to return to Greece when her mother fell ill and her father committed suicide after the family business went bust.

As she opened up, I was shocked to discover she had not left that house for years. Her pianos being the only world she cared for, she saw no need ever to step outside. 'This house is my mausoleum,' she once said melodramatically. 'But, surely, you must want to hear soloists, orchestras, choirs perform?' I dared interject. 'No, the jealousy would be too great to bear,' she confessed. 'Even if one of your students is performing?' I continued. 'Especially then,' she confirmed.

Trisevgeni was mightily pleased with my growing obsession. Once a cheap, Soviet-made lacquered black upright piano found its spot opposite our red-brick fireplace, she made a point of sitting in her armchair for as long as I practised, her hands busily embroidering, her ears tuning into every false note, every harmony, every hesitant arpeggio. When I complained that Mrs Jenny banned me from playing volleyball, insisting that I study towards becoming a professional pianist, Trisevgeni beamed with pride and made a point of telling Yorgo and Eleni to drop any ideas they might have that I would be a scientist. They reassured her I was, for better or for worse, free to choose, free to lose, free to do as I pleased.

Flattered by Mrs Jenny's approval, even her directive to give up my beloved volleyball, which, I confess, I never heeded, I warmed to the idea of making the black and white keys my universe. And as the joy from playing burgeoned, the word 'pianist' rolled off my tongue when grown-ups asked the insufferable question: 'What do you want to become when you grow up?' Until one Thursday afternoon, I discovered the truth.

Towards that lesson's conclusion, I was feeling pleased, having performed a difficult Chopin piece to Mrs Jenny's satisfaction – judging by her suggestion that it was time for me to graduate to Rachmaninoff's preludes. As always, she began playing one piece after the other until I raised my hand, choosing the one I wanted to start learning the following week. 'Ah, a splendid choice,' she remarked. 'Number 32 appassionato, a very difficult piece that will challenge you, my dear boy, in the most delightful of ways.'

Pleased with myself, I began walking towards her to kiss her hand when, suddenly, I heard him play.

An eight-year-old boy, who had been sitting on the couch waiting for his first ever lesson with Mrs Jenny, had walked up to my Steinway, sat down and, by golly, started playing Rachmaninoff's Allegro appassionato – without ever having listened to it before, let alone practised it, going on nothing but Mrs Jenny's rendition. At that point I knew: no amount of love or dedication could make up for such a chasm in natural ability.

That same evening, I confided in Trisevgeni that I had come face to face with my pianistic nemesis and that theoretical physics would have to be my new love. Not one to be strategically passive-aggressive, her disappointment was sincere. But it only lasted until the next morning when she cheerfully turned the page to whatever new chapters awaited.

Today, five decades later, every time I sit in front of the piano, I am transported back to the enchanted living room of my own special Miss Havisham. Overflowing with gratitude to Trisevgeni for opening those double doors for me, my nostrils fill up with the whiff of mildew from the velvet curtains. Suddenly, every sea of troubles is calmed under the spell of Mrs Jenny's sweet voice which still rings in my ears, telling me to block out the world, to relax my shoulders, to ignore my fingers, to concentrate on the melody, not the notes.

36. Riveting darkness, nauseating light

The year 1969 arrived with the news that I was to have a sibling and, more worryingly, that I would have to swap German for English lessons to cope with my school's Anglo-Saxon orientation. The only constants were the piano lessons with Mrs Jenny, running amok after school around Paleo Phaliro with a pack of local boys and a few girls, and Trisevgeni's phlegmatic comments aimed at Eleni and Yorgo's hands-off parenting. But the highlight of 1969 came on 20 July when Panayis invited us to his house to see the Siemens television set he had just installed for Neil Armstrong's much-anticipated 'giant leap for mankind'.

Television had just arrived in Greece over a decade after it had become commonplace elsewhere. For Trisevgeni, it was a double whammy: a man walking on the moon, whom she could watch in a magical box in her son's living room, caused her to cross herself more vigorously than ever before. Only Eleni noticed Panayis' standoffishness, which she explained away as the product of some work-related anxiety. Which, of course, it wasn't.

A few days earlier, Sakis Karagiorgas, a renowned sociology professor and founding member of Democratic Defence, the underground organisation Panayis had secretly joined, had been badly injured in his basement as he was putting the final touches to a homemade bomb – one of several explosive devices they planted around Athens. With his right hand blown off and an eye missing, he was rushed to hospital where a police informer alerted the cops. Panayis knew that his own arrest, along with that of his other comrades, was a matter of time. Having us at his home, immersed in the excitement of the first moon landing, was his way of saying goodbye, silently.

Later that summer, soon after our obligatory stay in Vienna, and a week of decompressing on Rhodes, Yorgo was the first to receive the shocking news of Panayis' arrest. Fearful of Eleni's reaction, seven months into her pregnancy, he suggested a romantic drive. Pretending to be lost, he drove to the vicinity of the maternity ward where I was born, parked close by, and broke the news to her – in close proximity to the obstetrician whom he had also alerted, just in case. Eleni was furious with him, probably because it was easier to take it out on Yorgo than to fathom the thought of Panayis under torture. 'Trisevgeni can't know this,' was the first thing she said after she had calmed down, adding: 'she won't survive it.' And so began the saga of lying to Trisevgeni, with myself as a willing co-conspirator.

For two years, Eleni, Yorgo and I, along with the whole extended family, connived to tell Trisevgeni that her only son was 'away on business', that Siemens had moved him to Hamburg where he had been handed responsibility for the company's Latin America operations. Before a newspaper or magazine was allowed into our home, Eleni made sure that any articles mentioning Panayis' trial, especially any photographs of him, were excised and that visitors were read the riot act lest they mention his actual whereabouts.

A few days after we visited Panayis at Hotel Pefkakia, Eleni went into labour. It was a girl – a little sister whom everyone fussed over. When the time came to name the newborn, Eleni suggested Anna but Yorgo insisted on Trisevgeni. As the baby grew into a toddler, and then attended kindergarten, fearful that her hard-to-pronounce name might embarrass the child, Eleni began calling her Evi. Today, I seem to be the only one who continues to call her Trisevgeni – and I think she likes it.

With Panayis rotting in prison and his court martial a sword of Damocles over Eleni and Yorgo, Trisevgeni kept herself busy with my sister while trying, and usually failing, to keep an eye on me. Feeling guilty that Eleni was working long hours at the hospital, and that he too was either at the steel plant or immersed in some research paper, Yorgo decided it was time to buy us a television. Soon, my grandmother and I were hooked on two programs: *Star Trek*, Hollywood's timeless celebration of a future liberal communism, and the regular propaganda broadcast by the regime's chief anti-communist theoretician, George Georgalas.

One afternoon, Yorgo caught us watching Georgalas attentively. An embarrassed Trisevgeni tried to downplay it, lying that we were only waiting for the next program to come on. Yorgo was neither fooled nor vexed. Instead, he sat down with us to watch the riveting albeit nauseating tirade. When Georgalas finished, Yorgo said: 'He was always a fine orator,' before proceeding to startle us with a story.

Georgalas was Cairo born and bred, he told us, three years Yorgo's junior at the Ampeteios high school. 'Did you know him?' asked Trisevgeni. 'Not only did I know him,' replied a red-faced Yorgo, 'but, in fact, it was I who recruited him to the Antifascist Vanguard', the banned underground movement set up by Greek, Arab and Jewish youths. And that was not all. Just after Yorgo moved to Athens, so did Georgalas – to enrol at Athens University Law School.

Yorgo's arrest, among others, was Georgalas' cue to flee to Cairo and from there, in 1948, to Paris. Sentenced in absentia to a long sentence by a martial court, the Greek Communist Party ordered him to move first to Prague and then to Hungary. There, he taught Greek and lived among the leftist political refugees while attending the ruling Hungarian Communist Party's School for Political Cadres. Upon graduating, he went on to serve as an announcer for Budapest's main radio station and, in 1951, was seconded to the Propaganda Department. During the Suez crisis, on the strength of his Arabic, he was dispatched to Cairo as a correspondent for the official Hungarian State News Agency.

In October 1956, the Soviet invasion of Hungary, unleashed by Moscow to crush the reformist locals, found Georgalas in Budapest. There, he sided with the pro-Soviet hardliners and soon won a spot in the Soviet leader's entourage, eventually accompanying Khrushchev to Egypt. Once back in his hometown, he sought political asylum at the US Embassy. Before one could say 'defection', he reappeared in Greece, his sentence rescinded. After proving himself valuable to the ultra-rightists around, he rose to the rank of our fascist rulers' chief propagandist, Minister for Propaganda, and became a regular TV regime evangelist. For the rest of his life, he remained a staunch apologist for those tyrants – even when it was not fashionable. 'Hardliners can change their spots but they will always remain hardliners,' was Yorgo's last word on the matter.

A year later, as Trisevgeni the Younger was approaching her first birthday, dark news reached us from Genova. On 19 September 1970, Kostas Georgakis, a twenty-two-year-old student, walked up to the entrance of the courthouse on Mattcotti Square, emptied a can of petrol over his own head and lit a match, after shouting: 'Viva democracy! Let every Italian cry out *Free Greece!*' His agonising death was celebrated by democrats and mocked by Papadopoulos, our crazed dictator-in-chief, as the act of a lunatic. Trisevgeni was incensed both with the regime's callousness and by the reality that had pushed a young man to do such a thing. It was only when she read the poem Nikiforos Vrettakos dedicated to Georgakis that she made peace with what he had done:

> You dressed like a bridegroom
> You lit yourself up like a celebrating nation
> You became a soul's show
> Stretched out like a horizon
> You transformed into the bright summary of our drama.

37. You two, pack a bag and run

The winds of change began to pick up in early 1973. Discontent boiled over that February when law students occupied their school in direct defiance of the police. It then spread to the military, prompting the crew of a destroyer to hijack the battleship and sail to Italy where they sought political asylum. To shore up his regime, our supreme tyrant Papadopoulos turned to the oldest trick in every dictator's playbook: he staged a rigged referendum.

As long as we consented to him writing a new constitution that endowed himself with all the powers he craved, he promised us . . . free and fair elections. All we had to do was to vote 'yes' in a late-July referendum, which he 'won' handsomely – prompting Trisevgeni to dub him Europe's greenie because, as she put it, only if the trees had voted for him could he have secured the official 78.4 per cent.

To sweeten the poison, our new 'president' released most of the political prisoners. A few days later, as Panayis' car pulled up at Naiadon Street, Trisevgeni gave us a lethal look, screaming: 'How dare you think I didn't know?' During the years of Panayis' incarceration, Trisevgeni had been playing along, humouring the lot of us as we lied through our teeth. Somehow, she knew everything and only pretended to be fooled to lessen Eleni's heartache. Even when her son appeared on our doorstep, Trisevgeni stuck to Eleni's script, playfully asking Panayis about his exploits in South America. However, beneath her wry humour, she was hurt.

'Has your mother forgotten', she asked me when we were alone again, 'of the night of the twenty-first of April 1967, when those mongrels burst into our home to grab your dad? Did I turn into a blob of jelly then? Why did my daughter think I was less able to withstand the terrible news about my son?' Attempting to defend Eleni, I mused: 'Well, Grandma, maybe because Panayis is . . . your son.' With daunting disdain in her eyes, she thundered: 'And you think my heart would prove weaker over one of my boys' suffering just because he had come out of my womb? Is that what you lot think of me?'

To change the subject, I asked her how she managed to stay so composed and play along with a subterfuge that she, clearly, considered insulting. She explained that, in addition to finding no tangible purpose in having it out with Eleni, she had noticed that when people thought she was in the dark, their demeanour around her unwittingly revealed more information than straight talk ever could.

Trisevgeni's strategic aptitude was my introduction to the unbearable wastefulness of patriarchy. Here was a woman whose diplomatic skills and principled rejection of DNA-based favouritism would have made her indispensable to any municipality, national government or, even, international organisation. Like Anna, she had been held back less by a benign husband than by a system working overtime to limit her ability to contain pain and spread justice.

Trisevgeni's mind then turned to the future. What would it take to prevent her boy being snatched from her again? Eleni was quick to reply that the price our mad dictator demanded was our consent to his revamped tyranny. 'Will we pay it?' Trisevgeni asked. The answer came from the street: we would not! Soon after our dictator installed a straw man as his 'prime minister', hours before the Yom Kippur War broke out, students began protesting. Trisevgeni was torn. She wanted them to go all out. But she couldn't bear the thought of Panayis on another long business trip.

On 14 November 1973, hundreds of students barricaded themselves in at Panayis' alma mater, the Polytechneio, and immediately began broadcasting from the basement on a makeshift radio station which Yorgo's sophisticated wireless could pick up. Life at 102 Naiadon Street paused. All we could do was listen. The announcers read poetry, issued economic analyses, incited citizens from all walks of life to join them. And as the regime's violent response kicked into gear, the little radio station began to report on the multiplying incidents of police and paramilitary brutality around the Polytechneio – but also how the police were swamped by the tens of thousands who rushed to supply the students with food, medicines and invaluable solidarity.

Seeing that only the army could defeat the crowds, our rulers rolled out their tanks. At three in the afternoon on Saturday 17 November, three tanks appeared, one behind the other, right in front of the Polytechneio's iron gate on which students were clinging like grapes waiting for the harvest. Back in Naiadon Street, clinging to the wireless just as tenaciously, we listened to the announcers' heart-wrenching pleas:

> Our brothers in arms, our message goes out to you. To the driver of the tank. To the soldiers manning it. Those of you uniformed children of this land hiding behind its armour. We are your brothers and sisters. You cannot fire upon us. We are driven by the same duty.

And when the first tank rolled forward, at exactly the moment it crushed the gate along with the students on it, we heard the radio announcer recite Dionysus Solomos' 'Ode to Liberty' – Greece's national anthem which Rudyard Kipling translated thus in 1918:

> We knew thee of old,
> O, divinely restored,
> By the lights of thine eyes,
> And the light of thy Sword.
>
> From the graves of our slain,
> Shall thy valour prevail,
> As we greet thee again,
> Hail, Liberty! Hail!

And then, silence. Not a dry eye in our house or countless others. Even my four-year-old sister knew it was a time for reflection. Panayis looked at Yorgo, who was staring at Eleni, whose eyes reflected an abyss. Trisevgeni shattered the silence with a resolute order to the men: 'You two, pack a bag and run.' They understood. The regime was mortally wounded. Like a ferocious beast, it was bound to lash out as it struggled to survive. Political prisoners would be reinterned. The secret police could be knocking down our door any day now.

Two duffel bags were stuffed with a few clothes, some tinned food, whatever cash there was in the house. The idea was for Panayis and Yorgo to reach Rododafni, Trisevgeni's village in northern Peloponnese, where a distant cousin awaited to hide them. 'I will drive you to the intercity bus station,' said Eleni. When they got there through unlit backstreets, no buses were running as the army had blocked the main roads. Among the stricken crowd, they bumped into a friend of a friend who offered to take them via a tortuous road. It took two days and nights, but they got there.

On Sunday night, forty-eight hours after the tank had entered the Polytechneio, Eleni had to work the night shift at the military hospital where officers with loose tongues let it slip that the morgues were filling up, the torture chambers were jam-packed and a new coup was in the offing. On Monday morning, at the crack of dawn, Dimitris Ioannidis, a shadowy brigadier-general who had personally tortured Yorgo on Makronisos and had known links with the CIA, overthrew Papadopoulos along with the other colonels and, in a textbook counter-coup, took over power.

On hearing the news, Trisevgeni decided we should stick to business-as-usual. With Eleni still at the hospital, she made sure that at half past six, as on every other morning, I was spick and span and awaiting the school bus on the corner of Naiadon and Parthenon streets. As the bus meandered its way across Athens, glued to the window, I got to see what a city under occupation looks like. I counted every one of the armoured personnel carriers, the military trucks, the tanks. There were hardly any civilian vehicles. I wondered what I was doing going to school when my father and uncle were on the run.

Like every other school day, we walked to the back of the main school building where we assembled every morning for the obligatory prayer and headteacher's pep talk. On that morning, however, there were fewer of us, no attempt at prayer, no headteacher – just Antonis Moraitis looking sombre. As silences come, it was the eeriest. Even the birds in the pines opposite had hushed up, waiting.

With his hands joined behind his back, his eyes fixed on the ground, he walked heavily up the five steps leading to the podium. Then, he looked at us – a few hundred youngsters stemming mostly from a ruling class that was, directly or indirectly, complicit in the regime's six-and-a-half-year reign. After another long pause he spoke:

Last week, a few miles from here, young people stood up so that you can be free – so that we can be free. Had they prevailed, light would have pierced the darkness and we might have moved forward into the broad vistas where lies wither and liberty gets a chance. Alas, two nights ago, the darkness prevailed again. All that we strive to teach in this school is now imperilled. All that matters melts into ether. Go home. Reflect. And come back tomorrow with a plan to avert our New Dark Age from becoming your permanent prison.

Moraitis knew that many of my fellow pupils would report him to their parents. Sure, he was a well-connected man, a captain of industry, but, with a monster like Ioannidis in power, there were no guarantees that Moraitis would not also disappear into some hole in the ground. That he spoke out anyway was perhaps the most valuable lesson any teacher has taught me.

38. Off to Blighty

In July 1974, the dictatorship that had been our bitter backdrop for seven long years collapsed as suddenly as it had commenced, spurring the long-awaited restoration of Greek parliamentary democracy. Just over a year later, I was walking down Solonos Street with Manolis, a school friend. Little did I know that in the same spot where Yorgo was first arrested and, years later, Eleni took him under her wing, a chance event would seal my passage to England.

Manolis and I were on a mission to distribute leaflets we had printed ourselves in support of that week's general strike, which had been called in protest against the new government's decision to pardon the fascist regime's 'ministers' and functionaries, and almost all of its torturers. When two policemen appeared at the corner of Solonos and Themistocles Streets, Manolis urged me to run. Ignoring Trisevgeni's warnings that regimes may change but the police stay the same, I decided to stand my ground. Half an hour later, at around eight in the evening, I was in a windowless police cell. Alone. Sweating it out.

My watch had been confiscated, so I lost count of the hours. Suddenly, the solid iron door opened and a pudgy gendarme took me to the sergeant's office, where a tall, balding man smelling of garlic and burnt caramel received me with a self-satisfied smile – his eyes fixed on a bulky folder sitting on his desk. 'Quite a family history is weighing you down, young man,' he said. The clock above his head showed just after four in the morning. Trisevgeni would be driven around the bend, I thought to myself, worrying more about her than about my parents.

A surreal conversation ensued. 'Who penned the text on these leaflets?' the sergeant asked. I confessed it was me. 'They are well written,' he said, almost approvingly. After toying with me for a while longer, he came round to the gist: he would release me if I were to promise that I would never publish anything ever again. 'Nothing? Not even a gardening manual?' I asked impertinently. 'Not even that,' he replied before adding: 'You commies have this remarkable talent. Even when you begin to write about courgettes, you just can't help yourselves. Before long, your convoluted argument turns to Marx and calls for revolution – so, no, not even a gardening manual.' 'OK, I promise not to publish any gardening manuals,' I pledged.

It was already six in the morning when I arrived at Naiadon Street on foot to find Trisevgeni wearing away the pavement as she paced up and down. That evening the three of them, Eleni, Yorgo and Trisevgeni, sat me down after dinner to give me the news. 'Right,' Yorgo opened the proceedings, 'you are to study in England. I don't care what. Read anything, from Anthropology to Zoology. The one thing that is non-negotiable is the country. We can't allow you to stay in Greece given today's irrefutable evidence that you are on a path deadly similar to mine.'

It made sense. Greece's return to democracy was terribly recent and awfully fragile. The fascists were still in control of the police, the army, most of the state. Grigoris still threw menacing glances from across the road. The tanks itched to roll back onto our streets. The universities could become battlegrounds again, the Polytechneio's corridors filled with fallen students. Besides, there was something utterly compelling about the prospect of living solo in the land of the Rolling Stones, Pink Floyd, Genesis,

Jethro Tull, Brian Eno, Liverpool Football Club, not to mention the place to which Marx escaped to pen *Das Kapital*.

When the Ioannidis regime collapsed in July 1974, two parties on the left rose up to dominate my world. The Communist Party, legalised for the first time since 1946, and PASOK, a brand-new radical socialist party founded by Andreas Papandreou – a charismatic, US-educated academic who had once chaired the University of California, Berkeley's Department of Economics before returning to Greece to enter politics, easily becoming the conspiring putschists' top target at the time of their 1967 coup. Papandreou's appeal, in my impressionable eyes, was enhanced when I discovered that legendary American economist John Kenneth Galbraith had personally asked President Lyndon B. Johnson to tell our tyrants to release Papandreou from prison and let him leave Greece – a request to which Johnson responded with a hilarious message to Galbraith's secretary: 'Tell Ken I have asked my people to tell those sons of bitches in Athens to let go of his son of a bitch of a colleague, whatever his name might be.'

During the 1950s and early 1960s, before our dictators banned all political parties in 1967, Eleni and Yorgo both supported the same party – EDA, the Unified Greek Left. However, after 1974, they diverged. Yorgo stuck with the recently legalised Communist Party, mostly for sentimental reasons, while Eleni enthusiastically joined Papandreou's new socialist outfit. A bemused Trisevgeni kept her distance from both, while simultaneously resisting Panayis' efforts to enlist her to the more centrist party he favoured. For my part, I sided with Eleni. Before long, I joined the fledgling socialist party's high school students' wing, whose weekly newspaper I helped edit.

When I began the process of applying to English universities for a place to read theoretical physics, my history teacher at Moraitis' school, who was close to Andreas Papandreou and high up in the socialist party, offered to arrange for the great man to give me an academic reference letter. Asked to pick it up from the party's office at Parliament House, I entered our tortured democracy's temple and took a seat in Andreas' waiting room. While the secretary looked for the letter, Andreas walked in, stopped momentarily in front of me and, to my astonishment, invited me to join him in his office.

Taking his time to light up his signature pipe, he eventually looked up to confess he had no memory of having written a letter on my behalf or who I was and, with the gentlest of manners bade me to tell him what subject I was proposing to study. 'Theoretical physics, hopefully at Imperial College,' I replied in a trembling voice. 'No, you will study mathematical economics at the University of Essex,' he stated emphatically.

I was incensed. What audacity, I thought. Who did he think he was telling me what I should and what I shouldn't study, and where – when, by his own admission, he knew precisely nothing about me? But then, as he began to explain, my fury evaporated fast. 'I assume that, to be here, you are a political animal,' he began before pointing out that theoretical physics and mathematical economics employ identical maths. Same methods, same geometry, same underlying logic – the only difference being that instead of plotting acceleration versus mass and energy, as the physicist does, the mathematical economist plots things like inflation versus unemployment and investment.

But if they are so similar, why economics? Because, he continued, in the heat of a political debate, people exercised by economic crises – personal or societal – would take me seriously only if the word economics featured in my degree's title, especially if it was a type of economics expressing what everyone really knows in equations few can understand. As for why no-frills Essex, his answer was equally compelling: a couple of outstanding mathematical economists of his acquaintance had moved there, plus an excellent game theorist.

Later that day, I redrafted my application. Trisevgeni was not pleased, convinced that if physics was my thing, I should pursue its mysteries. Moreover, she stubbornly refused to accept that 'studying Nature' was equivalent to 'studying money', as she put it. Of course, her deeper objection stemmed from not trusting any politician with my future, or the nation's for that matter. But, as was her wont, once she had aired them she let her objections scatter in the breeze. Ten months later, in the autumn of 1978, I arrived in Colchester to read mathematical economics at Red Essex – the derogatory nickname given to Essex University in the circles of the prime minister-in-waiting, Margaret Thatcher.

39. The blacks of Europe

Weeks after moving to Essex, an industrial strike broke out at Ford's main factory in Dagenham, an industrial town sandwiched between north-east London and south Essex. Today, it is remembered as the trigger of Britain's 'Winter of Discontent' – four months of industrial strife which, in the following April, brought down a brittle Labour government and begat Thatcher's landslide election victory, fought and won under the fiendishly smart slogan 'Labour Isn't Working'.

Eager to join the picket line, I headed for Dagenham in a hired Ford van with a dozen scruffy students. That evening, soggy and miserable after a day's picketing in the rain, I found myself at the pub sat next to a long-standing trade unionist. I struggled to decipher his thick Scottish accent, and it was not until the following day that a friend informed me I had been chatting with a legend – Mick McGahey, the heart and soul of the National Union of Mineworkers, who had led the successful miners' strike of 1974 that toppled the government of Ted Heath.

Hearing me express relief to be in a country where I could picket without the fear that the secret police would be breaking down my front door in the wee hours of the morning, Mick scolded me: I had not grasped the real difference between Greece and Britain. Britain's ruling class, he opined, had honed a skill that Greece's rulers hadn't: getting poverty voluntarily, and consistently, to deploy its political freedom to keep wealth in power.

His words reminded me of something Trisevgeni had said

after the tanks had crushed the gate of the Polytechneio – which I took the liberty of sharing with Mick. Amused by the ease with which the regime snuffed out its own pathetic process of democratisation the moment a group of students challenged its power, Trisevgeni surmised that the powerful revere democracy as long as the *demos* are kept out of it. 'Your grandma's a smart woman,' Mick said. Then, after a swig of his pint, he added: 'Make no mistake, my lad. If democracy ever threatens their power through the ballot box, our rulers' secret police will break down not just our front doors but our very spirit too.' Later, I learned that Mick had been under constant MI5 surveillance for years.

Back at the campus, the spectre of the looming Tory government was radicalising students. As Thatcher touted her project to turn Britain into a 'shareowners' democracy', they saw through her sugar-coated words her ironclad intent to dismantle all public institutions, including our maligned university. The ensuing student union general meetings were heated and, to me, a joyous baptism of fire in the English language.

One day, my friend Winston approached me at the Union Bar, accompanied by two other British-born Jamaicans I used to hang out with, some Irish mates and Mike, a tall London-born Cypriot whose obsession with reggae convinced him he was Afro-Caribbean. 'We've got a proposition for you,' he said. Their outrageous proposition was that I become the spokesperson for the local branch of the Black Students Alliance – a black consciousness movement affiliated politically to ComSoc, the university's communist society which dominated our student union.

'Are you serious? Have you ever even looked at me with sufficient quantities of blood in your alcohol?' I asked facetiously. They were dead serious. That my skin was pale, at least during the long British winter, was the very point, they said. 'The BSA's *raison d'être*', Winston continued, 'is that black has nothing to do with colour and everything to do with colonial conventions of discrimination functional to the smooth operation of exploitative societies.' I saw his point – a point which, of course, only a black person had the right to make. After a couple of briefings, I was ready for my first gig: an extraordinary general meeting of the Essex Student Union convened to discuss sharp rent hikes.

When my turn came to take the floor, I was trembling. But as I rose to my feet to speak, the enterprise steadied my nerves – as did the knowledge that it would take only four words to accomplish the intended effect. 'We black students demand . . .' was all I had to say for the house to come down with laughter, derision, boos and hisses. It was the perfect, fully intended, opener. All I had to do then was smile, pause and, once the ruckus had subsided a little, add:

> Come, come comrades. Black is a state of mind, remember? We Greeks are, after all, the blacks of Europe – something the skinheads and the British National Party thugs remind us of every Saturday night as they chase us with ill intent down Colchester's High Street.

Right on cue came David, a Belfast lad who sprang up to my defence: 'And so are we Paddies and Mickies! We are the blacks of Britain, aren't we?' 'Yes we are!' screamed a choir of David's Irish mates waiting in the wings. That was it. Point made.

When I gleefully recounted that scene back on Naiadon Street during the Christmas holidays, my audience was split down the middle. Eleni was unimpressed. Though she lacked today's critical terminology of 'cultural appropriation', she opposed my 'stunt' on the grounds that blacks and Greeks must fight their own battles, not each other's. Before I could defend myself, Trisevgeni took her to task: 'Are you saying that a man cannot defend women?'

she asked rhetorically. While Eleni pondered her rejoinder, Trisevgeni continued.

Trisevgeni arrived in Athens in 1924 to wed Konstantinos as part of an arranged marriage package deal. Athens, she explained, was more alien to her in 1924 than London could ever be to me in 1978. Arriving alone not just as a woman but as a peasant bride earmarked for domestic labour, her passage to the big city was tortuous. On the bus that took her from Athens' railway station to Konstantinos' home in Gouva, she made the mistake of sitting near the front. A few stops later, a middle-class couple boarded the bus, looked at her disdainfully, and ordered her to move to the back of the mostly empty bus.

'So, when I read about that black woman who stood her ground on another bus somewhere in Alabama,' she said sternly, 'I knew that I had been one of the blacks of Athens – so, yes, I can see why Irish, Egyptian, Greek lasses and lads *are* the blacks of Europe.'

Decades later, after reading Susan Scafidi's *Who Owns Culture?*, Eleni asked me if I would do it again – appear as a spokesperson for black people. 'Today I wouldn't be asked, Mum,' I replied instinctively. As she digested my answer, I caught myself thinking: are we white enough now, we Greeks? Or has the struggle against prejudice lost the unity of purpose it once had?

40. Fiona

Unlike Anna, a clandestine member of the Egyptian Feminist Union since the 1920s, Eleni did not, at first, warm to the word 'feminist'. Her proto-feminism was visceral, a survival instinct, a reaction to a brutal civil war which snuffed out every advantage that women had won during the Occupation through their active participation in the Resistance. Like most Greek women of the second feminist wave, it was only after the dictatorship's collapse in 1974, and her induction into the Union of Greek Women, that she embraced the word.

Eleni's newfound feminism took a most practical form. Leaving grand theoretical debates to others, she focused her energy on organising around two specific issues: setting up shelters for abused women and their children, often in abandoned orphanages; and getting herself elected Secretary of the old League of Women University Graduates, to turn it from a bourgeois women's club into a radical campaigning vehicle.

With explicit engagement in feminist politics came the need to navigate political minefields that Eleni's background and disposition had ill prepared her for. For instance, when a group of young lesbian feminists stormed into her office, it was the first time Eleni had met a woman who openly identified as a lesbian. 'Imagine my shock when five of them confronted me to demand a clear position from the union on lesbian rights. My knees buckled,' she confessed, with a voice ringing with shame. 'My mouth dried up, my head told me I had to come up with the goods, but my heart had sunk.'

Eleni's feminism was a constant struggle against her innate social conservatism. But it was the first time I had heard this inner conflict so vividly conveyed in the tremolo of her voice. 'When you are back in Athens for the summer, we need to talk,' she stated before hanging up. She sought my advice because she knew that England had exposed me to the right people – Fiona for example.

Fiona was a contrarian's contrarian. A lesbian who occasionally had sex with men out of 'a penchant for solidarity with the defective sex and a predilection for pissing off lesbians'. She was a Marxist who despised most Marxists for using Marx's emancipatory narrative to abuse other comrades, build their own power base, gain positions of influence, bed impressionable students, eventually take control of the Politburo and throw anyone who questioned them into the gulag. Above all, Fiona was a thinking radical's thinking radical. Energetic and brilliant one moment, vexatious and maddening the next.

Back on Naiadon Street for the summer, sitting in our living room with Eleni and Trisevgeni, I told them how I first met Fiona. It was at a general meeting of the students' union, when I stood up to speak on a resolution against the apartheid South African regime. 'Oh dear, another male socialist explaining oppression? How original!' I heard a pulsing voice taunt me from somewhere in the large crowd. I tried to ignore it and spoke of the heroic resistance of the women of Soweto when their men were snatched by the police. 'By golly, you almost mentioned women unprompted! Progress!' the same voice shouted. It was only then that I saw her, her bright red hair, her scornful smile making me both laugh and feel tiny on that stage.

Realising her heckling had worked, she went in for the kill: 'Is this the part where you say, "Not now, sister – the real enemy is imperialism, the true class struggle!"?' she asked before eviscerating men who, like me, have no qualms about speaking authoritatively on subjects they know nothing about. Struggling, I resumed my rehearsed speech. 'You cite Gramsci on hegemony but still interrupt women? Curious!' she threw back at me. Not knowing whether to feel wronged or deservedly put in my place, I tried to reclaim the high ground with a few sentences about how we were allies, about the pointlessness of infighting. 'Oh, we are allies, are we?' she snapped back. 'Then prove it by shutting up and passing the mic.' Which I did, without another word spoken. It would be the beginning of our friendship.

A graduate anthropology student, Fiona was appalled and galvanised by the realisation that we were all in on it: not just the City, Whitehall, the boardrooms of the monolithic corporations, or the arts councils and think tanks, where the more sophisticated forms of greed are cultivated, but the student unions, the BSA, the Communist Party, even feminist organisations. Her intense disapproval of me was systemic, not personal. This is why we became close.

Trisevgeni, evidently amused, was knitting with ears pricked up. Eleni winced. Fiona sounded intriguing but also a challenge to her petit bourgeois concern for the company her son kept. However, I ploughed on.

A year after Fiona had heckled me, we met again at one of the countless meetings called by left-wing activists at the London School of Economics to counter the onslaught of Thatcherism. Fiona was billed to address the meeting. After two hours of tiresome speakers denouncing Thatcher's social and industrial vandalism, she rose to speak. Essentially she told the assembled radicals that they could not hold a candle to Thatcher. Her opening line said it all: 'While listening to the previous speakers, I was thinking to myself: "Give me Maggie Thatcher any time!"'

Eleni, for whom Thatcher was a menace to the women's cause, was ever more agitated. But she let me explain why I was the only one in the audience who applauded Fiona: because she was juxtaposing Thatcher, who had a forward-looking plan, with her comrades, who were backward-looking, defensive, boringly attached to dead-end politics. 'Unlike you, Maggie gets it,' Fiona told her audience.

> We live in a revolutionary moment. The post-war class-war armistice is over. If we want to defend the weak, we can't be defensive. We need to advocate as she does: out with the old system, in with a brand-new one. Not Maggie's dystopic system, but a brand-new one nevertheless. You lot are bandaging corpses while she is digging graves. If I had to choose between you and her, I would choose her every time. Monstrous as she is, Thatcher can at least be subverted. You wouldn't recognise subversion if it came at you with a barge pole.

Intrigued, and beginning to see why I chose to bring up Fiona and her exploits, Eleni asked me how I could handle my new friend's scathing attitude towards her comrades, towards me.

In lieu of an answer, I related something Fiona had told me during one of her mellower moments. When she saw me down at the Union Bar, or in the union meetings, interacting with mates like Winston, Mike, even Bianca, a brilliant Chilean refugee from Pinochet's henchmen, Fiona saw decent people in the process of unwittingly turning into brutes. Our organisations, she believed, earnestly professed feminism, anti-racism, socialism, veganism, pacificism, you name it. But, at a deeper level, Fiona saw them function as the organised left's finishing schools, country clubs, Rotary Clubs – their purpose being to offer people like me the illusion of social significance and revolutionary virtue while preparing us for subjugation to someone else's authority. The only way she could remain sane, untouched by arrogance, was as a lone woman blighter.

Eleni was reticent. She appreciated Fiona's pathos, her free-spiritedness. But she could not but reject Fiona's denunciation of the organs of collective action. For Eleni, a woman who had faced down organised misogyny alone for so long, organisations like her union were a sanctuary. Sure, she could see how any institution was subject to personal agendas and overinflated egos. But without an organisation in which to crowdsource ideas, life was dreary and unbearably long.

When I told Fiona of Eleni's reaction to my interpretation of her musings, she made a telling remark: 'Your mum', she said, 'is lucky not to be afflicted with my condition: by *not* being a subject of the bloody queen, a citizen of the imperialist European North, she has a freedom I can never have. Tell her I envy her.' In retrospect, I think that Anna might have appreciated her remark even more.

A few months down the track, on a miserable December night in 1982, Fiona rang to say she was helping plan a mass women's rally outside an RAF base against the deployment of American cruise missiles aimed at eastern Europe. Could I turn up to support them? I arrived at Greenham Common late the next day. In the pouring rain, thirty thousand women were trying to join hands around the base in the face of police violence. Just when I thought it would be impossible to locate Fiona in the chaos, I spotted her on the stone-cold, muddy ground, two women kneeling beside her, holding a handkerchief to a bleeding gash on her forehead. 'A gift from an overzealous defender of the realm,' she told me, grinning proudly.

A couple of weeks later, in January 1983, Eleni summoned me to Athens. Trisevgeni was in hospital, the prognosis grim.

41. To Serbice!

The drab hospital waiting room reeked of mould and chlorine. The day broke slowly as Trisevgeni struggled through the night to emerge from a stroke-induced daze. Sat there, opposite Eleni, Yorgo and Panayis, I peered into each of their eyes.

Just over a year earlier, in October 1981, Eleni's socialists had won a landslide election victory. Andreas Papandreou was now prime minister. His ministers rode to work on mopeds, and some even kept portraits of former enemies of the state in their offices. The minister of police, whose first decree was to abolish the hated paramilitary gendarmerie, was, like Yorgo, a former EPON member who had spent three and a half years in internal exile during the colonels' dictatorship. Whatever else one might have thought of the new government, it was the nearest to regime change that elections can deliver.

Of the three, Eleni was the most pleased. The Union of Greek Women, of which she was a spirited member, led by the prime minister's formidable socialist-feminist Illinois-born wife, was essentially dictating government policy on women's issues. One of the new government's first moves was to bring in a small, but unconditional, monthly pension for peasant women over fifty, which could not be collected by a man and could only be delivered by the postman into the woman's hands, in cash. When Trisevgeni received hers, it rocked her assumption that nothing good can come from politics. However, for Eleni, what mattered more was their grassroots activism.

Modelled on the freedom rides of the 1960s civil rights movement in America's deep south, Eleni and her union comrades rode buses into rural spots were women did not dare imagine, let alone assert, their newfound rights. There, they held clinics to persuade peasant women that, no, their husbands had no divine right to rape, beat or bully them. Domestic violence shelters were set up, packing a century of feminism into a few months. On the day a sweeping new family law banned dowry, granted women equal rights in property law, introduced no-fault divorce and even decreed that married women keep their surnames, Eleni brought a copy to Naiadon Street as a present for Trisevgeni: 'We did it, Mum, we did it!'

Yorgo was more ambivalent. He was grateful that, for the first time, he could breathe easily, free of fear of the secret police, our neighbours and the constant urge to self-censor. The state had awarded him, along with thousands of others, a medal 'for conspicuous service to national liberation and democracy', Papandreou's shrewd tactic for honouring the defeated leftists without ever mentioning the civil war. His election to the post of honorary associate professor in the School of Chemistry, for his research into ancient technology, made him swell like an excited peacock.

Nonetheless, Yorgo continued to support the communists because of a strong suspicion that, once the excitement had died out, the steady encroachments of the economic ogres that capitalism always breeds – inflation, unemployment, sickening inequality – would eventually lead to the restoration of the *ancien régime*. Already, he could see how the steel industry was being buffeted by the waves of the global crisis gathering pace ever since, on 15 August 1971, President Richard Nixon had blown up the global post-war economic system known as Bretton Woods.

Panayis was the least enthusiastic of the three. Unlike leftists, who had to wait until 1981 for a modicum of empowerment,

Panayis' power had been fully restored in the summer of 1974, when the army reluctantly returned to their barracks. Alas, prison had changed him. But Greece had changed too.

As we sat in the waiting room, Panayis revealed why it was impossible for him to enjoy democracy's return to its birthplace. Feeling the pinch of the 1970s global manufacturing crisis, Siemens was eagerly eyeing the lucrative digitalisation of Greece's arthritic telephone system. So the company set up a vast slush fund and instructed Panayis to use it, at his discretion, to line the pockets of every politician or bureaucrat central to the task at hand. Panayis reacted pugnaciously, not only tending his resignation but also doing something perhaps even more drastic than when he opted for armed struggle in 1968.

In 1977, the day after he left Siemens, he went into business with another German-trained engineer. Their idea was to secure large cost savings for the Greek state by approaching Siemens' East German competitors, whose technology was much cheaper and, by Greek standards, advanced enough. But Panayis soon sensed that his new business partner was open to shady deals, not to mention a certain whiff of association with the notorious Stasi. A year later he ditched his dodgy partner, who soon went on to great heights of wealth and influence, to concentrate on less high-profile business ventures. For Panayis, this was a disappointment too far.

Following the socialist party's 1981 electoral triumph, Panayis watched as his former prison mates, one by one, almost to a man, traded their past heroics for a parliamentary seat, a ministry, a lucrative government post. Today, hardly anyone remembers Panayis, the result of his deliberate choice not to lever up his resistance record. The Greek Siemens franchise had been his identity. The business world he had traversed with relish during the authoritarian pre-dictatorship era had given way to a cesspool of spivs.

Every breath that Trisevgeni struggled to take in intensive care, Panayis felt as his own last gasp. His mother had always been his grounding rod. The last thirty years of his high life, spent mostly away from her, now felt like a boozy party that had lasted too long. Judging by how Eleni held his hand rather than her dying mother's, I could tell she too had noticed his cry for redemption. What she could not have known was that a vile motor neurone disease was already eating him up. Very slowly. From the inside.

Standing alone further back in the intensive care unit, Yorgo looked lost. As he confessed later, he was mentally in Cairo. For my part, untouched by past loss, I was determined to make the most of my granny's last drop of consciousness. I was lucky. Before she passed, she came round one last time when I was alone in the room. 'Tell me, *Yaya*,' I said: 'where would you like me to take you when we get out of here?' 'Home, my boy,' she replied, valiantly playing along. 'Take me to my village, to Serbice!' 'But', I protested, 'your village is Rododafni, have you forgotten?'

Giving me her trademark conspiratorial look a final time, she clarified: 'Rododafni? That's a bullshit name. When I was a lass it was Serbice. Then the wise men came from Patras and threatened us that we were not to call it that again. That, from then on, it was Rododafni.' I understood. 'I shall take you to Serbice,' I promised. Only much later did I realise what Serbice meant: *the Serbs*, in Serbian.

'You do that,' she concurred and closed her eyes.

42. To Australia

Back in England, the future was taking shape one defeat at a time. Thatcher was on a relentless mission to make it impossible to imagine anyone doing anything unless there was something in it for them – a price tag. The last remaining obstacles in her path were two trades unions: the miners, who, under Mick, had already defeated the previous Tory government, and the printers, who could still stop the newspaper presses dead.

The miners were defeated in 1984, in scenes resembling a nationwide civil war. As for the printers, Thatcher's alliance with Rupert Murdoch bulldozed them out of existence in the 1986 Wapping dispute. Democracy's fragility, which had made Trisevgeni doubt there was ever any room for the *demos* in our democracies, was now plain to see in the country that had revived it after the Middle Ages.

My English eighties were a reality check on the unbridled optimism Eleni had instilled in me in a Greece where, however terrible things might have been, progress seemed inevitable, liberation a matter of time. Thatcher's project made me appreciate Trisevgeni's playful cynicism about the concept of progress. My decade in Thatcher's England was indelibly marked by the 105 weeks, between 1984 and 1986, when along with Fiona, we picketed, fundraised and floundered non-stop on history's losing side. Those bitter days were my crash course in the left's permanent defeat – a process that Papandreou's 1981 landslide election victory delayed in Greece by two decades.

Around the time I managed to wrap up my doctorate on mathematical economic models, which Fiona dismissed as 'fine exercises in logical-positivist masturbation', I remember visiting her in hospital after mounted police had trampled her outside Murdoch's Wapping site. Perched at her bedside, I asked her if the fear of physical harm had ever brought her close to giving up. She replied that when you join in a good struggle, you learn to live life in near proximity to giving up without ever actually giving up. No, her only regret was that we were putting up a splendid fight in defence of communities that deserved defending, but in pursuit of causes that screamed 'anachronism'. 'Why can't we bring the country to its knees to demand clean energy and a free press, instead of defending filthy coal-fired power stations and the male trades union bosses of right-wing newspapers?'

I realised I did not need grand victories to fuel the good life. Little victories did nicely. Defeat was OK. Especially when I had Eleni screaming softly in my mind's ear that 'no good cause is ever lost'. And yet Thatcher's Britain was proving a hard place to exist in – especially after I transitioned from graduate student to lecturer in a university system so stricken with budget cuts that panicking older colleagues, whom I revered, saw only one thing in me: a younger, cheaper lecturer who would make it easier for cost-cutting managers to make them redundant. And that's how the die was cast. When a job offer came from the University of Sydney, I took it.

Soon after I emigrated to Australia, all hell broke loose in Yugoslavia. The newspapers were replete with stories of massacres, mayhem and ethnic cleansing. Greece was portrayed as the tip of the Balkan Peninsula, seemingly innocent of these inhumanities – an image I too would have bought had it not been for Trisevgeni's dying words, which, in the face of the Yugoslav tragedy, piqued my curiosity. So I started asking questions.

Eleni knew nothing about Serbice, the Serbian word for 'the Serbs'. Older relatives didn't want to talk about it, or didn't know the dark truth. Eventually, with the help of British historical archives, I got to the bottom of it. Trisevgeni's village, it turned out, was not an outlier. Many villages in the Peloponnese had been renamed at the end of a Hellenisation campaign in the early 1900s – a polite term for ethnic cleansing. From the eighth century onwards, at the height of the Eastern Roman Empire (which a British academic later christened the Byzantine Empire), Slavic peoples, mainly ethnic Serbs, moved to the Peloponnese. It was only when the fledgling Greek state began to expand northwards during the Balkan Wars in 1912–13 that the Hellenisation drive sought to erase this history, replacing Slavic names with invented Greek ones, such as Rododafni, Terpsithea etc.

It is a contested history that none of us learned at school. A history I cannot raise, to this day, without being labelled a self-hating Greek. A history that says so much about our present moment in which ethnic cleansing is the order of the day, not just in the Balkans but in Ukraine, Georgia, Armenia, Syria and, of course, Palestine. A history that Trisevgeni's final words brought close to home, alerting me to the importance of questioning my tribe's official version of everything.

PART FOUR

Georgia

43. To the serpent's lair

Georgia was dreading our first meeting. But I was dreading it more. The drive from Athens over winding mountain roads traversing the Peloponnese was arduous but beautiful. Margarita, Georgia's maternal granddaughter, was anxiously silent throughout the journey. Just married, the visit was meant to be our pilgrimage to her Greek roots. It ended up being much more than that.

Georgia's farm was nestled between a heavenly sprawling mountain range and the fabled Ionian Sea. Heading south from Kyparissia, we turned left off the coastal road and up the unsealed drive leading to the farmhouse. With the sun setting behind us, we reached her gate under an enormous eucalyptus tree that stood there as if to highlight the Australian connection. Georgia came out to greet us with a broad smile and extended arms. For a fleeting moment, her outline illuminated by the crimson twilight, I thought I saw Trisevgeni – or, rather, what Trisevgeni might have been like had she not left Serbice for Athens.

After she hugged her granddaughter passionately, Georgia embraced me warmly, which thawed her trepidation, and mine. That's when I caught a glimpse of him lurking in the shadows. Kapnias, Georgia's second husband, stood some twenty yards away, surrounded by his goats, his eyes fixed on me. A hawk hovered motionless over the farmhouse.

A dishevelled yet not undistinguished figure adorned in the work clothes poor Mediterranean farmers think of as their uniform, Kapnias' weather-beaten face, covered in white stubble, smiled at me. Sensing his presence, Georgia tried to usher us into the house, away from him. But Kapnias, ignoring the two women, stepped up to me, stretched out his arms, and at the top of his voice shouted theatrically: 'Welcome to my poor abode. We meet at last!' I have seldom felt so vulnerable.

That an unnerving story hovered around the picturesque farmhouse, I knew. Maria – Georgia's daughter and Margarita's mother – had told me the story of Kapnias a year earlier, shortly after I first met her at her home in Sydney. Instead of the typical coy niceties, Maria threw me in at the deep end.

My reputation having preceded me, Maria was dying to let the Greek leftie dating her daughter have it as soon as I stepped inside their home in suburban Earlwood: 'So that you know,' she told me, 'when I was only two, and my baby brother had just been born, the communists abducted my father from my mother's arms and had him killed. Then, they killed my mother's father.'

Maria's salvo was only the beginning of my introduction to Georgia's story. Stunned by what I had already heard, I urged her to tell me more. Maria obliged. In April 1948, she continued, at the height of the civil war, a company of communist partisans arrived at their house in Alvena, a mountain village north of Kyparissia, where Georgia and Xenos, her beloved husband, were nursing their newborn son and raising two-year-old Maria. The intruders demanded that Xenos join them, leaving his family behind. He refused, protesting that his wife would not cope in her state without him. 'The cause is above family,' they barked back and led him out of the house and into the night. A few days later, he was found dead in the woods – the rumour being that he had been shot and left to bleed to death. As if that were not enough, Maria concluded, a week or so later the same band of guerrillas returned to the village to execute Georgia's father.

All I could do upon hearing Maria's grisly account, was to hang my head in shame. Yorgo and Eleni's own account of the late 1940s oozed with the cruelty that a civil war wreaks on both sides. Painful as it was, I urged her to continue.

Widowed and orphaned, in the midst of war and famine, Georgia's survival, along with that of her two children, was touch and go. It was a time when a single mother needed a male protector to survive, especially in those harsh mountain communities. With her husband and father in early graves, Kapnias made himself available, offering to help raise her orphans if she agreed to marry him. Having worked for Georgia's father as a farmhand before the war, he had coveted the village belle for years. Now a fully fledged member of the national gendarmerie, sporting a uniform and in receipt of that rarest of monthly gifts – a state salary – Kapnias was something of a solution.

Not long after they wed, Kapnias showed his spots. Abusive to Georgia's children, then to her, he felt no compunction to veil his inner brute. Then, within months, he was fired from the gendarmes for 'excessive violence' while interrogating communist captives – a real feat in the paramilitary context. The dismissal, not to mention the loss of income, led to drunken frenzies that left Georgia spending months indoors, lest a neighbour notice her bruises. Instead of divorce, a legal impossibility at the time, she gave him Dimitri, a son. But any hope that a boy he could call his own would pacify Kapnias dissolved when, in a show of atrocious non-discrimination, he abused all three children equally.

Maria, Georgia's eldest, was the first to escape Kapnias' cruelty. Without consulting Georgia, she sought refuge with Georgia's sister who lived with her teacher husband in Sparta. From there she reached Athens where, taking advantage of Australia's open call for migrant workers, she emigrated to Sydney in the early 1960s.

Maria's younger brother, George, had resigned himself to tolerate Kapnias' violence, internalising the notion that a stepson had no right to expect anything better. However, something in him snapped one day during the olive harvest, when Kapnias took his rage out on his own flesh and blood, Dimitri. Though only fourteen, George stood up to Kapnias to protect his half-brother. Kapnias punched him but, failing to capture him, he ran back to the house to fetch his shotgun. 'Run my boy, run as far away as you can,' screamed Georgia. He ran. Never to return. At Georgia's prompting, a neighbour helped the teenager make his way to Macedonia, where, miraculously, he fended for himself, found work, enrolled at night school, eventually married and had his own family.

With all that swirling in my head, I had not known what to expect upon arriving at Georgia and Kapnias' farm. The one thing I had not expected was the power of a frail old man to project fear onto those around him using nothing more than a broad, welcoming smile. What an innocent outsider might have mistaken for a quiet weekend in the countryside felt like entering a serpent's lair with an overwhelming urge to extract its captive, Georgia, before making a getaway. If only it were that simple!

44. The white angel

After settling into the bedroom that Georgia had lovingly prepared, we made our excuses, pretending to be meeting friends for late-night drinks in Kyparissia. In reality, we were escaping Kapnias' suffocating presence hoping that, by the time we returned, he would be fast asleep. When we returned to the farmhouse, well after midnight, I was relieved to hear his distant snoring accompanied by a chorus of overexcited cats meowing. Exhausted, I too was ready for a good night's rest in the lap of the Peloponnesian countryside. Then I saw them: two books resting on my pillow.

The first one I picked up was entitled *Memoirs of a Prime Minister*, in Greek, and authored by the man Brigadier Ioannidis had anointed 'prime minister' two days after the tanks crashed their way into the Polytechneio. It was laughable, both the book title and the gesture. The second book, however, extinguished whatever smirk was on my face. It was a small leather-bound volume, in German, in an advanced state of disrepair. Incredulous even after I had read the title, *Mein Kampf*, I opened it. An original German edition, published in 1934, it was obviously intended to shock the visiting leftie. Kapnias had outdone himself, I thought, marking his territory with a rare form of excrement.

Next morning, hoping that he would have headed out to tend to his animals, I delayed getting out of bed. When all sounded quiet, I tiptoed downstairs. As I entered the small kitchen, I saw him, sitting on a wooden chair, with a triumphant smile. Had I really imagined he would miss the joy of gauging my reaction to his late-night offerings? And so we started talking over coffee. 'I was an untouchable,' he began proudly, before adding with menace: 'until a man of genius touched me.'

The reference to his untouchability was an allusion to the time, in the late 1930s and 1940s, when he used to work for Dimitroulas, Georgia's father – the village nobleman. Kapnias despised him. 'I didn't exist for him,' he said 'I was invisible to him, unworthy even of chastisement.' Similarly with his daughter, 'the Alvena Princess' as he mockingly called Georgia: 'She worked so damned hard to not see me either.' As the Nazi occupation entered its third winter, Kapnias' hatred boiled over.

In late 1942, in preparation for a possible Allied invasion of Greece, the British government decided to forge a military alliance with Greece's left-wing partisans, who were already conducting sabotage operations on the nearby Wehrmacht and the Italian battalions. British officers parachuted into Greece to seal the alliance, organise weapon drops and coordinate operations. One of them, Sergeant O'Donnell, an Irish Catholic engineer with a mission to build secret airstrips in the Peloponnesian mountains, was hosted by Dimitroulas. Seeing O'Donnell enter the farmhouse in full British military garb, sometimes accompanied by bearded communist partisans, Kapnias knew that something was afoot. Something big that he was unceremoniously excluded from. Soon he discovered the 'Made in England' military-grade radio transmitter operating from the main house's basement, proof that Dimitroulas had been a British intelligence asset for some time.

'Would you have liked to be part of all that?' I asked. 'For sure!' he concurred. 'But they wouldn't touch me. These up-themselves aristocrats look at people like me and all they see are insects. What they don't understand, what you commies don't grasp,' he continued, as he looked into my eyes with the air of someone convinced he knew me inside out, 'is that we, the insects, always survive long enough to savour our sweet revenge.' To speed up the conversation, I interrupted to ask: 'So, who was the genius that gave you a chance? Who "touched" you?' A little disappointed that I wanted to cut to the chase, Kapnias switched gears.

'Their arrogance, their outrageous self-importance, their hubris led myriads to their death.' On 17 October 1943, communist partisans ambushed and captured eighty-one soldiers, mostly Austrian, of the Wehrmacht's 117th Jaeger Division near Kalavryta. A few of the captives fell in the ensuing battle but most were killed later as three thousand German army reinforcements began encircling the partisans. Once the German rapid response battalion entered Kalavryta, the newly appointed operations commander, one Major Ebersberger, gave the order to implement 'atonement measures': they rounded up all males aged twelve and over and marched them out of Kalavryta just beyond the town cemetery where concealed machine-gun posts had been set up. When flares rose into the sky, released by Ebersberger from a balcony in Kalavryta's *Kommandatura*, the industrial killing began. Four hundred and sixty-three boys and men died on the spot. In all, including in surrounding villages, more than fourteen hundred were executed, while thousands of houses were torched – including the magnificent Aghia Lavra Monastery, where the spark of the Greek Revolution of 1821 had, according to legend, been ignited.

'This is what real men do!' Kapnias proclaimed elatedly. To my horror, I realised his real men were the Nazi executioners. 'Real men eliminate those who wrong them, and thus survive. Those who die declare, through their death, their unfitness to live.' It made perfect sense. Kapnias was not just wasting my time with war stories. No, he was proudly narrating how he had turned into a Nazi, not only in deed but also in spirit. How his marginalisation in Alvena had opened him up to the distorted logic of the superhuman race whose time had come. How the murder of hundreds of men and boys was a glorious reflection of the 'will to power', the moral equivalent of his own personal legacy – his serial abuse of Georgia and her children. Ultimately, he wanted me to know that the 'white angels' sporting slick SS uniforms were his saviours from a life in the shadows.

'The Germans were above God,' he informed me, his face lit up like a Christmas tree. 'Unlike the Italians or our own mob, they did not hesitate to use *any* means to get the job done. Without wincing! With no fear! No passion! No love! No hatred! You had to see them with your own eyes. They were magnificent.'

'You still have not told me who the genius that "touched" you was,' I egged him on. 'His name was Hans – but you are not to speak the name of my white angel – you are unworthy of the honour,' he snarled back. 'Do you know why they call me Kapnias? Because I was always bitter, always at war with a world that denied me – everything,' he said, answering his own question.*

After the Kalavryta massacre, by his own account, the twenty-three-year-old Kapnias left Alvena behind to join the notorious Security Battalions, or *Tagmata Asfalias* – a Greek collaborationist force the Nazis had put together to help them contain the partisans. There, he was handpicked by Hans, a Gestapo liaison, who offered him a chance that Kapnias grabbed with both hands: to follow him to Crete where he would be trained in the dark arts of interrogation and countersubversion. It was in Crete that Hans, who also acted as his instructor, gave him the leather-bound copy

---

* Kapnias, his nickname, was a play on *kapnos*, the Greek word for tobacco – a substance famous for its bitterness. His real name was Yorgo, like my father – indeed like Georgia's first husband too, who went by Xenos, his surname (which, in Greek, means 'foreigner').

of *Mein Kampf*, like preachers who hand out copies of the Bible to illiterate natives before moving on to proselytise others.

That Kapnias could not read a word of German was irrelevant. That little book was like a free pass into a European Brotherhood of Evil. The type of evil that, when absorbed by armies and bureaucracies, not only elicits a hideous outpouring of violence, but gives cowardly men a priceless sense of belonging, of having arrived at last.

Years later, when reading articles in *The New York Times*, the *Washington Post*, the *Guardian* and *Le Monde* that tried to make sense of how fascism made its comeback in the West after our generation's 1929 – the financial crash of 2008 – I thought of Kapnias and his monologue in Georgia's small kitchen over a tiny cup of Greek coffee.

It was all there. From how Donald Trump could so effortlessly weaponise so many naked lies to inspire hatred in so many dispirited people, to how Viktor Orbán, Marine Le Pen and the rest of the Xenophobic International could stir up mass animosity against refugees, migrants, 'others'.

45. A red flag is raised, another lowered

Having said his piece, Kapnias disappeared with his goats, allowing me to get to know Georgia better. Her good cheer and resilience were disconcerting, especially when I asked how she could live with such a man.

For decades, Georgia told me, she pretended to turn a blind eye to Kapnias' violence. Keeping her head down, she worked singlehandedly to create everything they now had: the house, the farm, two lovely olive groves, a small vineyard, the animals. He, on the other hand, with his drunkenness, brawling and womanising, ended up owning absolutely everything. Could she exercise her new legal rights? With a withering look Georgia reminded me that only the bourgeois think that a change in the law changes the balance of power.

Not only could Georgia not afford a lawyer but, even if money were no issue, the local court would chew her up and spit her out, while the local community rallied around him – such were the prevalent patriarchal norms, as well as the terror Kapnias instilled in their hearts and minds. Leaving him would mean becoming a refugee and, at best, a dead weight on one of her long-suffering children who had escaped him. She would rather die.

When I pushed a little, she snapped at me: 'If you want to blame anyone, blame the communists who took my Xenos away, shoving me into Kapnias' trap.' She then added: 'But, I must admit, I do owe the left a debt of gratitude' – referring to her monthly pension for peasant women over fifty.

Back in Athens, in the few weeks left before I was due to fly back to Australia, I spoke to Nikos Petralias – a German-trained economics professor at the University of Athens who hailed from that part of the Peloponnese. It was he who raised the red flag on Georgia's story. Over drinks at Au Revoir, Athens' oldest bar, I recounted her story as best I could. Did it seem plausible, I asked. 'It's suss,' was his instant response. By the time of Xenos' alleged abduction in April 1948, he explained, it would have been suicidal for the partisans forcibly to recruit unwilling fighters.

The tide had turned against the partisans when the United States took over the prosecution of the Greek Civil War from the exhausted, and bankrupt, British. It was the first manifestation of the Truman Doctrine – the new policy announced in March 1947 by President Harry Truman that broke with America's isolationism. Truman's first step in projecting US power globally, which three years later begat the NATO alliance and set the scene for America's involvement in the Korean War, was to declare that the United States would not allow communists to prevail in the Greek Civil War.

Soon, the partisans found themselves bombarded relentlessly by the US Air Force during the day while, on the ground, day and night, the Greek nationalist army, armed to the teeth with sophisticated American weaponry carried on the backs of countless improbably large mules the Americans had shipped over from Italy, swept the forests, the ravines, every nook and cranny of the Peloponnese. The partisans had to move fast, silently, in small loyal bands. An unwilling partisan could have easily run away, thus condemning the whole platoon.

'I just can't believe they took an unwilling man from his wife's arms, not at that phase of the civil war,' Petralias surmised. After taking down the details on the back of his cigarette pack, he promised to get back to me if anything interesting turned up. With that task in hand, I focused on catching up with Yorgo and Eleni during the Christmas break before my scheduled return to Sydney.

Pinching myself that I was back on Naiadon Street, as if Australia had never happened, I feasted on the fierce, fleeting joy of being among them again. On New Year's Eve, as we chatted over dinner in front of the red-brick fireplace, we heard on the old wireless that, in the dying moments of 1991, the red flag had been lowered above the Kremlin. For good. With the triumphant news bulletins playing in the background, featuring a parade of celebrities cheering on the new era of freedom, I asked Eleni and Yorgo what freedom meant to them, on a personal level. Eleni replied first. To her, freedom was the ability to choose your partners and your projects. Yorgo was looking on approvingly when the phone rang. It was Georgia with wishes for the New Year.

Behind her festive chatter, I detected a longing. Our recent visit, I imagined, had rekindled a hankering for contact with people from the outside world. To give her something to gloat about, I mentioned the collapse of communism. Ignoring me outright, she asked to speak to Eleni – whom she had never met or spoken to before.

Eleni listened to Georgia in an awkward silence. Minutes passed without a noticeable change in her expression. Then a tear rolled down her cheek, her left hand moving swiftly to wipe it dry. Eventually she spoke into the handset: 'Everything I do I do for women like my mother, like yourself – but, Georgia, it is all to no avail if *you* opt to live in fear.' Eleni was right. But Georgia was not wrong either. The free, especially the bourgeois, cannot begin to fathom how terrifying liberation can seem to solitary women in the clutches of male violence.

Georgia's call changed the mood. Yorgo and I reflected on how the wave of optimism released by the Greek socialists' triumph in 1981 had fizzled out by 1989. Sensing that Yorgo was enjoying an 'I told you so' moment, Eleni stepped in. 'No good cause is ever lost, remember?' she thundered. 'But if the victims remain wedded to their victimhood, there is only so much progressive politics can achieve.' She had a point, of course. But was it ever right to blame the victim? That conversation did not go well.

Eleni had little time for my suggestion that we needed to be careful before burdening the silenced with the personal responsibility of regaining their voice, of utilising the new progressive laws as efficiently as veteran lawyers, of turning to the movement for help with the sure-footedness of seasoned activists. I could see her point that liberty cannot be spoon-fed to the unfree. That they must grab it with both hands once it is close enough. I too might have felt as she did, had I not shared a roof with Kapnias. But that experience changed me. It had given me a whiff of how easy it is to underestimate evil's gravitational pull. No, Georgia's was not a classic case of Stockholm Syndrome. It ran deeper, and was far uglier.

46. Red widow

A year later, the phone rang at my Sydney home. It was Petralias. 'I have news,' he announced. 'Are you sitting down?' I said I was. Xenos was not abducted. He was a volunteer. And more. A member of the Communist Party since his late teens, he had fought against the Nazis during the Occupation as an EPON foot soldier – the same youth organisation Yorgo later joined. After the war, he re-enlisted in the Democratic Army as soon as the civil war began, almost to the day Yorgo was transferred to Makronisos. By the time of his death, in April 1948, Xenos had risen to the rank of second lieutenant. There was a small plaque in his memory somewhere near the ravine where he died. And an official medal, like the one Yorgo was awarded, still awaiting collection.

Once the startling discovery was verified, one question loomed large: what on earth was Georgia on about? At first I wondered, perhaps Xenos had kept her in the dark to protect her. It only took a split second to dismiss the possibility. In tiny Alvena everyone knew what anyone was up to. Xenos could not have concealed that he was a Resistance fighter from the woman he courted during the Occupation. How could he have when Georgia's home was the meeting place of British officers and local Resistance fighters like himself? And there was no way she did not know during the civil war, which spanned three long years, including their marriage and the birth of their two children. What about his alleged abduction? It would be absurd to think

Xenos staged it for Georgia's benefit – and that she fell for it. No, there was no doubt. Georgia knew!

Piecing together the truth felt like I was watching a Ken Loach film where, just as you think the protagonist has hit rock bottom, a plot twist entangles her in webs of tragedy thicker than your soul can bear.

During the civil war, the widows and orphans of fallen partisans were referred to as *miasmata*, an old Greek word intended to signify something defiled, disgusting. For women like Georgia and her children, once Xenos was dead and the partisans in retreat, the southern Peloponnese resembled an endless valley of rape, beatings, starvation and death. With the countryside teeming with former Nazi collaborators who ran the gendarmerie and manned the paramilitary death squads, there was nowhere to run. So when I worked out that Georgia knew, another question hit me. Did Kapnias know too? Did he know he was marrying a red widow?

The only explanation of why Kapnias married Georgia, I thought, was that her *miasma* status meant he could dominate the Alvena Princess – the perfect revenge for the shunned boy whom Georgia's father wouldn't give the time of day. But, then again, to gain this power, Kapnias would have to engineer a big lie.

Rudimentary research confirmed that the gendarmerie would never have granted one of their men a licence to marry a red widow. Kapnias' buddies would regard Georgia's young children as the seeds of Satan, and would intern them, with Georgia, in some prison camp. Kapnias must have lied to his superiors, presenting Georgia as the victim of the reds, rather than the widow of one of them. Although I had no evidence as to who had invented the story that Xenos had been kidnapped by the communists, it was a lie that served Kapnias' designs.

It explained why Kapnias imagined he could get away with brutality uncommon even in those brutal times – and why Georgia stayed with him, decade after decade. She feared exposing her kids to the truth about their father. But more disturbing was the possibility that she felt indebted to Kapnias. For if Kapnias had lied to his superiors on her behalf, I could see how Georgia could have fallen into the trap of feeling a perverted sense of gratitude. The worst slavery is one where the slave feels she owes the master a debt. Kapnias' hold over Georgia suddenly made more sense. As did his rage, and his cruel confidence that Georgia would take it.

I wanted to cross-check the details before confronting Georgia. Elena, a niece of Xenos that Margarita and I managed to locate, confirmed Petralias' findings, but also mentioned a memoir authored by a Captain Belas, the nom de guerre of one of the very few partisans in the Peloponnesian Division of the Democratic Army who had survived the civil war. I remember taking down the book's title over the phone: *The Dead Division*.*
Anxiously, I called my favourite Athenian bookstore. Did they have a copy? It was out of print, but they could locate one. A few weeks later, I was holding its two thick volumes in my hands. When I started reading, I grew frustrated: how could I not have known about this masterpiece?

The Dead Division had been authored in 1986. Like Trisevgeni, Captain Belas learned to read and write as an adult, And yet his book comes ever so close – at least in my estimation – to being Greece's answer to Tolstoy's *War and Peace*. Penned breathlessly, it grabs you by the throat and drags you kicking and screaming into a cinematic cornucopia of comedy, drama, resistance,

---

* *The Dead Division: The 3rd Division of the Fallen of the Democratic Army of the Peloponnese*, Volumes 1 & 2 (Η Νεκρή Μεραρχία: Η ΙΙΙ Μεραρχία των νεκρών του Δημοκρατικού Στρατού Πελοποννήσου, Τόμοι Α' & Β'), Athens: Alfeios.

betrayal, stupidity, brilliance, cruelty, kindness. As I read Belas' memoir, immersed in his epic tale, I almost forgot about Georgia and Xenos. Then, on page 620 of the first volume, Belas slapped me back to my original quest.

47. One of seven

Belas was recounting his platoon's involvement in the raid of Kalavryta in April 1948 – the same town where the Nazis had exterminated more than a thousand people five years earlier. Belas' raid had three aims: to demonstrate that the Democratic Army's Peloponnese Division remained capable of taking a major town; to assuage the partisans' outrage that, four years after liberation from the Nazis, their collaborators in one of occupied Europe's worst civilian massacres remained in control of Kalavryta, only this time wearing fresh Greek gendarme uniforms provided by the US army; and, of course, to restock their pitiful supplies of ammunition, food and medicine.

The raid was a success. The partisans took Kalavryta in the dead of night with minimal resistance from the much larger force defending it – most of whom were captured as they slept in their bunks. But a tactical blunder during their withdrawal, which Belas blamed on their commander, whom he described as a paper-pushing party commissar with little military experience, allowed the gendarmes to strike back as the partisans were retreating. Many partisans were injured, some seriously. Slowed by their captives, but more so by their wounded, they missed their chance swiftly to transport their precious cargo to their strongholds in the surrounding mountains.

So they released their prisoners and headed for a ravine, where they buried and carefully camouflaged their ammunition. There they regrouped to decide how to evacuate their wounded, before returning later to retrieve their prized ammunition. Belas, blind in one eye from an explosion and with a bullet lodged in his left leg, was given the task of leading a group of twenty injured partisans to safety. With the assistance of the unit's doctor and two able-bodied men, he struggled to keep the company on the move, especially the seven of them who were hurt badly.

Setting aside, for a few paragraphs, the facts of their struggle, Belas' prose takes a deep breath and then pauses to bring to life Asimakis from Arcadia, focusing on his jokes rather than the gushing machine-gun wound in his lower abdomen, and Andreas from Megalopolis, who recited Palamas' poems to take his mind off his shattered knees, and 'Xenos, from Alvena, a father of two young children, his left leg smashed to bits'. Xenos' name leapt off the page shattering my reading pleasure and burdening me with new duties. So I read on, no longer a mere reader of some fascinating story but a pained seeker of something far more intimate.

Belas could not continue with the seriously wounded in tow. His new plan was now to hide the seven in a natural crypt, a small cave, on the north ridge, hidden from below by the cliff face, escape to the ridge opposite, and then return for them once the army had moved on. The walking wounded slowly climbed up Mount Helmos, home of the sacred snakes in Trisevgeni's fairy tales.

The tall Christmas trees were covered with thick spring snow, as was the ground below. Seeing the enemy approaching from afar, they cut branches to hide under, lying on their backs and struggling to remain motionless for hours on end. If by sunset the enemy had not discovered the seven, they would make a dash for the top of the mountain as the last light faded, to reach the villages on the other side that were still under the partisans' control. And then, in the middle of the night, they would send a fresher, better-equipped team to retrieve the wounded from their crypt.

It was not to be. Around midday, Belas spotted two army companies enter the ravine. At six in the evening the gendarmes and the army were under the cliff just below the crypt where the seven lay. That's where they stopped. Their dogs must have picked up the scent. Before long, two soldiers started climbing towards the cliff. To delay them, Belas ordered four men to move their two machine guns to positions from which they could strike the crypt's entrance eight hundred metres away. As the bullets flew, the soldiers scattered in panic, almost falling into the ravine. The army returned fire at random, using parabolic mortars from deep inside the ravine. Then their machine guns went into overdrive. They weren't even close. Soon it was dark and all went quiet, the army lighting fires and erecting plush tents. A new plan had to be concocted.

Ten partisans and the doctor descended into the ravine and then climbed up to the crypt. They helped the seven out. The doctor changed their dressings. They gave them food and water before hiding them in another place covered by thick foliage. They stayed with them until two in the morning, then they joined Belas and the rest on the mountain opposite. The sun rose. At eight the army came out and began searching again in earnest.

At around ten they found them. From where he was perched, Belas saw the seven being dragged out of their hiding place and laid on the ground. For a couple of hours, nothing. Soldiers came and went, their officers barking mindless orders. Then they loaded them on mules and slowly led them back to where they had come from in convoy. But, before long, they stopped again at a spot just out of sight. Half an hour later Belas heard machine-gun fire. It was over.

Subsequently, Belas and the partisans met up with the army's muleteers, local people who told them what had happened. At first, the seven were not mistreated. But as the army were transporting them back to base, they came across a US army brigadier and his entourage. He ordered them to be taken off the mules. He demanded they tell where the weapons were hidden. All seven told him to get lost. He ordered that they be tortured. Sure enough, the gendarmes were all too happy to kick them, aiming their boots on their wounds. The seven swore at them. To buy time for his comrades, Asimakis asked to be held up, explaining that standing was the only dignified way to tell the American brigadier what he needed to know. As soon as he was upright, he spat in the brigadier's face. That's when they shot them.

Belas concludes this part of his memoir, and with it the first of his two volumes, thus:

> They were seven. I remember only three of them. Xenos from Alvena. Asimakis from Arcadia. Andreas from Megalopolis.
>
> The day before, we had confronted them in battle and we defeated them. Today we confronted them as humans, and we humiliated them.

This is how Georgia had become a red widow. What remained uncertain was how she lost her father too – the well-heeled Alvena chief who could have provided sanctuary for her, her two-year-old Maria and her newborn son George.

48. Double jeopardy

Against all odds, two of Xenos' surviving comrades turned up in 1995. One was Patra, a sweet one-legged grandmother who in a previous life was a seasoned partisan with years of battlefield experience. Thousands of women had fought tirelessly for the Democratic Army, inciting fear among the nationalists for whom the very sight of gun-toting women was ungodly and unnatural. The other was Takis, who had been in prison for two decades, and whose only way to regain a modicum of autonomy in a hostile post-civil war society was to build a thriving aluminium business from scratch. Between them, they filled in the gaps – Patra providing the broad strokes, Takis painting in the grim details.

After the battle of Kalavryta, and the execution of the seven, the partisans regrouped in one of their strongholds. Takis, who was at the meeting, remembered the consensus: the enemy must have got wind of their raid. Someone had betrayed them. But who? Simeon, a commander from Messinia, pointed an accusatory finger at Dimitroulas, Georgia's father. He admitted he had no proof but offered a plausible rationale.

Dimitroulas maintained close relations with partisans since the days of the Occupation, when his home was a Resistance hub, where a motley crew of communists, centrists, British officers and anti-Nazi fighters passed through, for shelter or for information. Simeon's point was that many of those fighters who, four years later, continued the fight as soldiers of the Democratic

Army, erroneously assumed that Dimitroulas was still a friend, his home still a sanctuary. Was it not possible that as partisans began to gather from all over the Peloponnese in preparation for the April 1948 Kalavryta raid, one or more of them met up with Dimitroulas and, still considering him one of them, disclosed critical information on the raid? Were they sure that every partisan, even those who had come from Sparta or Corinth, knew that Georgia's father had always been an asset of the British intelligence service and, subsequently, had turned against the partisans in 1944, siding with the gendarmes and the national army?

The commanders, while sceptical, decided that Simeon's theory constituted reasonable grounds for bringing Dimitroulas in for questioning. Takis and another partisan were dispatched to Alvena to bring Dimitroulas to their headquarters. Dimitroulas was despondent. He and Takis had known each other for years. 'How dare you come to my house to whisk me away?' he protested. When Takis assured him that he was not taking him to some kangaroo court, Dimitroulas relented, and they set off on the long trail back to the partisan stronghold.

Once in front of the partisan commanders, Dimitroulas remonstrated that they were mad to suspect him. Yes, politically he was now on the other side. Yes, he wanted them to surrender. But, no, he would not rat on them when he knew that the life of his son-in-law, Xenos, was at stake. And not just Xenos. Several of the partisans were the sons and daughters of cherished friends. He disagreed with their actions and their politics but would never, ever jeopardise their lives. He disliked the collaborators who swarmed the streets of Kalavryta pretending to be patriots, and he did not want the death of former comrades on his conscience. In any case, he concluded, he had no prior knowledge of the plans to raid Kalavryta.

The commanders, even Simeon, agreed they had nothing

solid on Dimitroulas. After breaking bread with him, and talking politics like old friends, Takis was given the order to escort Dimitroulas back to Alvena, and to make sure he got home safely to his wife, to his two sons, and to Georgia.

Takis and Dimitroulas had to take a meandering mountain trail for two nights, spending the intervening day hidden in the woods from the nationalist army crawling the lowlands and hiding from US Air Force reconnaissance planes. After a hard night's trek, just before sunrise, they set up a rudimentary campsite to rest. Munching on bread and goat's cheese, the two men reminisced. Nostalgia was in the air. Both missed the days before the *dichonia* – the post-liberation discord between former comrades-in-arms. The Cold War had similarly erased the warm embrace between American and Soviet soldiers when they met at the River Elbe on 25 April 1945, just before the fall of Berlin. Lubricated by a little raki that a villager had provided to keep them warm at night, the two men lamented that their civil war was far worse than the Cold War because, as Dimitroulas put it, 'here the division runs through families like a butcher's knife through a goat's spleen'.

They gossiped shamelessly and toasted the fallen, one by one with a sip of raki, lest oblivion swallow them up. As their defences weakened, Takis took the risk of broaching a sensitive subject. Referring to Xenos, known to his closest friends as Tzortzi, Takis said:

> Now that we are putting all our cards on the table, I need you to know that I know. No point in keeping it from me. Tzortzi put you in a tight spot – that's obvious. I can never condone what you did but I understand it. Dionysi told me everything. But worry not. It will stay between us. We have enough on our plates after so much death and misery.

Dimitroulas changed colour. In the spring sun, Takis noticed that the blood had drained from his cheeks, his upper lip was trembling and his eyes were watering. In a broken voice, Dimitroulas asked: 'You know? Dionysi told you? What on earth was he thinking?' Takis immediately realised they had been talking at cross purposes. Dimitroulas had just confessed to something hideous.

Takis' reference was to a rumour related to him by a man named Dionysi who worked for Dimitroulas. The rumour was that Dimitroulas had tried to persuade Xenos to desert from the partisans. Moreover, he had offered to transfer to Xenos full ownership of the estate, on condition that Xenos stowed away his rifle and his communism. Evidently, Dimitroulas thought that Takis was talking about something else. Reacting calmly to his friend's shocked reaction, Takis went along with him, hoping to get to the bottom of whatever Dimitroulas thought they were talking about. As Dimitroulas spoke, the truth soon surfaced.

On the night of the raid on Kalavryta, a seasoned partisan named Tzortzi (no relation to Xenos), whose unit had come from the faraway Mount Taygetus to join in, was injured in the chest. Having lost track of his unit, bleeding and disoriented, he wandered in the vicinity of Alvena looking for help. When he saw Dimitroulas' house, he recognised it as the safe house where he had taken shelter once during the Occupation. In his state, he had to take the risk of assuming that it was still safe.

As he entered the orchard behind the house, Dimitroulas' son Dionysi (not the foreman with the same first name) saw him and panicked. The sight of Tzortzi's bloodied torso didn't help, but that wasn't what frightened him – he was a young man who knew about serious injury, having lost his right arm before the war after falling off a horse. What if Tzortzi had been spotted by the ex-Nazis who now manned the Alvena gendarmerie, scoundrels who never fully trusted the Dimitroulas family? Goodness knows what they might do if they thought Dimitroulas' family were harbouring a wanted and wounded *miasma*.

Thinking on his feet, Dionysi urged Tzortzi to stay put, rushed to the stables to fetch a mule and some supplies, and then carried the wounded partisan to a hiding place in the woods. Then, he went back to the house and told his father what he had done. Dimitroulas commended his son but began to worry that the gendarmes would discover Tzortzi, who, under torture, might give them up. Without exchanging a word between them, Dimitroulas and Dionysi armed themselves with a knife and an axe and headed for the woods. Half an hour later, they were burying Tzortzi's corpse.

With every word of his confession to Takis, a burden was lifted from his soul. Takis did not need to say a word. Dimitroulas knew he would not be going home after all. No partisan turns a blind eye to the murder of a wounded comrade, not even by a panicked friend. Once it was dark again, Takis marched Dimitroulas back from whence they had come, to the partisan headquarters.

The two walked in grim silence, Dimitroulas ahead, Takis behind him, his rifle at the ready. Dimitroulas did not plead, did not protest, did not make a run for it. Only when the partisan firing squad was formed at dawn, following a rudimentary trial, did Dimitroulas look in Takis' direction and nod. Thus Georgia lost her father too.

49. Demonic women

The romantic in me expected Georgia to be relieved that Margarita and I knew. To be keen to share her side of the story with those she could trust after five decades of hiding her red widow status in the open prison erected by Kapnias. I was dead wrong. She denied everything.

Patra hardly knew her, Georgia claimed, and she hadn't met Xenos. Takis was an impressionable man who invented heroic tales in search of self-importance. Belas' book was pure fiction. Even the state medal did not sway her. 'You have been taken in,' she insisted. 'My sweet Xenos was taken by the communists who left him for dead in the woods after he was shot.'

Despite her denials Georgia looked and sounded cheerier. Whereas during our previous visits she would baulk at suggestions of coming along to a restaurant or on an excursion, she was now keen to partake. Kapnias noticed this too. Whether Georgia had told him that we knew I am not sure. What I am sure of is that Kapnias, the cunning weasel that he was, had worked it out for himself. To milk this common knowledge, for sport if for no other reason, he indulged in mind games, such as when he referred to Dionysi as the 'one-armed prince that the Erinyes', the ancient Furies, 'were bound to devour'. Or when he mocked the holier-than-thou pretensions of Dimitroulas.

Meanwhile, the civil war erupted again. In suburban Sydney. Forty-six years after its conclusion on Mount Vitsi, in Macedonia. It happened when we relayed the truth to Maria – Margarita's mother and Georgia's daughter. Faced with the overwhelming evidence, Maria's model of the cosmos shattered like a sheet of glass falling from a great height. Her life and identity had been built on the assumption that her passage to Australia was the last link in a chain of events triggered when heinous communists murdered her father. Discovering that her father was one of them, and a victim of the side Maria considered to be her own, was hard to swallow. What made it even harder was her own husband's history.

Two decades older than Maria, Nikos was drafted into the nationalist army days into the civil war, just shy of his twentieth birthday. With no connections in the state or the military, he was thrown straight onto the front line. At every major battle he was assigned reconnaissance duties – a polite term for being treated like human fodder – with explicit orders to draw the partisans' fire that would expose their position before the artillery took over. During the three years of war, his fellow conscripts dropped like flies around him, often over him. On one occasion he was pinned down in a foxhole for forty-eight hours by enemy fire, with the severed head of a friend in his lap. Only by a sequence of miracles did Nikos survive the civil war.

As soon as he was decommissioned in 1950, physically and mentally scarred, Nikos jumped on the first ship to Australia. Like my father, who never ceased talking about Egypt but also never returned there after Anna's funeral, Nikos talked about Greece incessantly but could never find the courage to return. Life had been kind to him in Sydney, where he built a decent life, married Maria and had three children. But he never really shook off the textbook symptoms of shellshock. Even to his family, he appeared closed, remote, happier to sit alone at the bottom of the garden and watch them from afar.

As long as Maria thought her father was killed by the partisans, she and Nikos had shared an identity. A bond that tied their fates inextricably together. It didn't matter that their neighbours in Earlwood neither knew nor cared for what had happened in their distant, beautiful, ravaged homeland fifty years earlier. But it mattered to Maria and Nikos. It was important to them that they were on the same side, the *right* side, of a vicious civil war that defined them, that was responsible for their being on the other side of the world together.

After reading Belas' memoir, Maria turned to other sources. The more she read, the angrier she became at Nikos, threatening their Antipodean equilibrium. Sure, she knew he was also a powerless victim. But he had been there, at the front. And now he was here, in her house. Whom else could she question? Whom else would she confront? One moment she was picking his brain, the next she was accusing him. One day, hearing Nikos' account of one of the campaigns in the Peloponnese, Maria worked out that there was a high probability that her husband and her father were, at some point, shooting at each other.

Margarita was writing her doctorate on the Greek women who had raised arms. She had scoured the archives for testimonies. One afternoon, unexpectedly, she got an avalanche of oral history from a source she had never thought to tap: her dad. It happened when Nikos heard, for the first time, of his daughter's dissertation. 'They were the hardest to kill,' was his odd compliment about the female partisans he had encountered on the battlefield. Against the grain of his usual reticence, he volunteered a lengthy recollection.

It was early 1949, towards the civil war's conclusion, when the remaining partisans had been cornered on mounts Grammos and Vitsi. By that stage, the nationalist army had overwhelming advantages in terms of artillery, air support, supplies and men, compared to the last few thousand decimated, emaciated and undersupplied partisans. The end was well and truly nigh. Except that the partisans would not give up, explained Nikos. One day, as usual, his unit was on reconnaissance duties when they stepped into an ambush. Two machine guns from two different directions and a handful of snipers pinned them down. The accuracy of the shooters was unsurpassed. Every time they tried to move more than an inch, they were hit within an inch.

As they lay helplessly waiting for reinforcements, they noticed something strange. The enemy fighters seemed to have long, flowing hair. Could they be women? When they realised that they were indeed women, the soldiers became even more anxious, for they had heard stories of women partisans who fought much better and harder than men. Many hours passed before help arrived.

When help did arrive, in great numbers and with plenty of mortars, guns and air cover, the women partisans quickly withdrew into a nearby gorge, hoping to make their escape on the other side. However, they had not counted on a second army regiment arriving from the other side of the gorge. The women were now surrounded. With a glimmer of shame in his eyes, Nikos recounted how the army and air force bombarded the gorge where the women partisans had taken cover for hours on end: 'We couldn't see the sky, such was the dust and the smoke from the bombs, the shells and the mortars. No living thing could have survived the pounding.'

A reconnaissance aeroplane flew over without being shot at, a sign that the enemy had indeed been eliminated. At least three dozen bodies were spotted strewn across the gorge's bottom. It was done. Time to retrieve the corpses and put them on display in nearby towns and villages – an essential practice to break the spirit of locals who still supported the Democratic Army. But there was a snag: none of the soldiers dared step into the gorge, the fear of the women partisans greater than the threat of court martial. Thankfully, it was getting dark. So, the lieutenant in command decided to play it safe. Tents were pitched, and fires lit. 'Tomorrow, first thing, we shall pick up their bodies,' the lieutenant warned.

At the crack of dawn, Nikos and eleven other soldiers were ordered to go down the gorge to give the all-clear before the retrieval of the corpses could commence. Except there were none! The soil was soaked with the women's blood but, despite their thorough search, not a single body was found. 'Clearly,' Nikos surmised, 'while we were nicely tucked in during the freezing-cold night, a handful of surviving women must have carried the bodies of more than forty of their comrades through our lines and sentries to God knows where.' With an expression of ample admiration that clashed with his choice of words, he concluded: 'I can't get those demonic women out of my mind.'

Margarita listened in utter silence. Hearing Nikos' words mingle with the sounds of children playing and barbecues roaring over his garden fence was surreal, almost ridiculous. Yet it helped the civil war in Earlwood to subside.

50. Endless requiem

A couple of years later, in 1997, following a night out at a local taverna, Georgia was sitting beside me in the passenger seat, Margarita in the back, as we drove back to the farmhouse. It was a special night as, for the first time, Georgia had agreed to drink a little red wine with us. As we left the streetlights of Kyparissia behind, entering the pitch-black country road, there was a lull in the conversation. Suddenly, illuminated only by the reflection of the car's headlights, Georgia began to sing in a faint but melodic voice. But it was her choice of Shostakovich's haunting tune, one which Eisenstein had used in his *Battleship Potemkin* soundtrack, that shattered the silence with a significance amplified by the Greek lyrics:

> You fell victims, brothers, you did,
> In an unequal battle and fight.
> Looking out for the life, liberty and honour of the many,
> You found a grave too early.

Trying to contain my disbelief, I noticed that as she sang, she threw meaningful glances in my direction. 'What are you singing, *Yaya*?' I asked, pretending not to know. Instead of an answer, she sang some more.

> Languishing in damp, dark cells,
> Bitter days you endured.
> And with the hangman's mere nod
> You were brought in front of the noose.

My heart beating fast, I pressed on. 'Are you pulling my leg, *Yaya*?' Again, her answer took the form of another verse:

> The tyrants rejoice and seek oblivion
> In a drunken stupor.
> But their days are numbered
> And a terrible end will be their final suitor.

The last thing I wanted was for us to arrive and Kapnias to spoil the moment. So I pulled over. Margarita suggested that perhaps it was time for her grandmother to let the light in. 'I don't know what you're talking about,' Georgia protested before doing exactly as Margarita had asked. 'Every April, I find some excuse to make my way to Alvena where I meet up with his mates and we sing this song at his grave.' The song was the Greek communists' requiem for fallen brothers and sisters. Singing it was Georgia's way of coming clean. In the stopped car, on the side of a country road, Georgia finally told her story.

Xenos was not the only Resistance fighter in their household. She too was connected to EPON, maintaining close links to the local communist party cell. During the Occupation, unbeknownst to her father, she joined in several operations along with Xenos against Italian troops stationed in Kalo Nero. She ran errands. She delivered messages. And she kept an eye out within her privileged home on how committed the British officers and her dad, Dimitroulas, were to their alliance.

When the war ended, Xenos and Georgia moved into their own dwelling. Georgia was pregnant with Maria and desperate for a peaceful life, but the dark clouds were gathering, ready to rain down a terrible civil war. Xenos, like most partisans, abhorred the idea of another war. The Communist Party too was sending them missives to stay put, to avoid any provocation, to desist from digging their rifles out of the holes where they had buried them following the December 1944 armistice. But it was impossible to resist fate's plans for them for long.

Emboldened by the British authorities' decision not only to get the Greek government to grant them amnesty, but also to hand them the keys to the gendarmerie, the Nazi collaborators delighted in ritually seeking out former Resistance fighters. Every day, some former partisan's body was discovered, often mutilated and bearing evidence of torture. Georgia recalled meetings upon meetings where partisans cried out that, the way things were going, the paramilitaries would pick them off one by one until they were all dead. Others, including Xenos, tried to keep their heads, toeing the party line of no escalation. Only when two close friends were lynched in the middle of the day did Xenos change his counsel in the next meeting: 'They crossed the Rubicon. It is now abundantly clear they will stop at nothing. Let's dig them out.' The heavily pregnant Georgia backed her husband: 'We can't go about our business as usual; we need to protect our community, together. I wish we could let them rust in the ground but we now need these rifles.' So, without the permission of the party, the impromptu committee of local ex-partisans decided they ought to rearm themselves.

Their intention was to act in self-defence, to protect their families and their villages – not to fight further afield. Soon, other local groups followed their lead. It was the collaborators' cue to attack them *en masse*. Within weeks, under immense pressure, the Communist Party issued the call to arms across the land. The civil war was now officially underway. I asked Georgia how she felt when she heard the news. Numb, she explained sullenly:

> When we rose up during the Occupation, we knew we would, one day, prevail over the Nazis and the Fascists. That every one of our sacrifices was a chink in their armour, helping us

win. But, in a civil war, there is no victory, my boy. I knew that my defeat was guaranteed, no matter who won. Every time one of theirs would die, I would be burying one of mine. If we won, I would be burying my father, who I knew would never cross the British to join us. If they won, I would be digging the dirt to bury my husband. What I didn't know was that I would be weeping over both their graves within a week.

With a heart of lead, I restarted the car. Kapnias was at the front door to greet us with his usual sarcastic grin and, with his sixth sense intact, to ask: 'Had a good chat, did we now?' Georgia almost passed through him, as if he were a ghost, heading for her bedroom from which he had been kicked out some time ago – proof, I liked to think, of Georgia's small measure of empowerment in having people just a phone call away who were on her side of the civil war still quietly ablaze in her home.

Feminists who heard Georgia's story, including Eleni, were appalled by her disinclination to run a mile from Kapnias. To them, her choice smacked of sheer subjugation. The Marquis de Condorcet, an enlightened eighteenth-century French aristocrat, once wrote that the greatest secret is 'that real power lies not with the oppressors but with the oppressed'. Yes, the 'mind-forg'd manacles', as the English poet and painter William Blake called them, are as real as the ones forged by skilled ironsmiths, but, no, Georgia was her own woman capable of forging her own chains.

Besides not wanting to give up a farm that she had created with her hard labour and sharp wits, there were two reasons that were hers and hers alone. One was Dimitri, her younger son and Kapnias' only child. A kind soul who lived in nearby Kyparissia and worked as an electrician at the local hospital, he lived under a double burden. There was the burden of growing up under the constant threat of Kapnias' thrashings. And there was the much heavier burden of knowing that Kapnias' genotype was swarming in his, unlike his siblings who – once the truth was out – could take pride in the thought that their father Xenos was a good man, a hero even. By staying on the farm, with Kapnias, Georgia enabled Dimitri to look after her, to have a virtuous purpose of protecting her from his father.

Her other reason for not escaping was difficult to bear. Georgia cared for Kapnias! When she said this, my hair stood on end, a deep revulsion rising in my gut. 'How can you possibly care for a thug who hurt you, who drove your children to the four corners of the planet, who traumatised his own son, who is an unreconstructed Nazi for goodness' sake?' I exploded. Mollifying me with a wave of her hand, her soft words revealed a rich emotional matrix that shifted my perspective.

When she saw Kapnias, she said, of course she saw the timeless brute. But that's not all she could see. After testicular cancer had diminished him physically, she saw in him the sad little boy who once worked on her family's estate. The Resistance had taught her one thing well: the Nazis brought out of the occupied what their society had connived to inject into their soul before the Wehrmacht rolled in. Occupation breeds civil war and, together, they beget monsters on every side. 'Kapnias is the monster fate assigned me,' she concluded: 'I hate him and I nurture him. And I shall let no one tell me I am doing wrong.'

Just before the new millennium arrived, my marriage to Margarita began to unravel – me staying in Greece permanently, teaching at the University of Athens, Margarita spending more and more time in Sydney where she completed her doctorate on the Greek women who had raised arms.* Throughout our

---

* Her thesis was published as a book in 2009. See Margaret Poulos, *Arms and the Woman: Just Warriors and Greek Feminist Identity*, New York: Columbia University Press.

separation, Georgia stood by me without ever taking sides. As fate would have it, a child – a baby girl – came into the world just as Margarita and I were splitting up. When we told Georgia we would name her Xenia, after her Xenos, but also because it is a name reminiscent of the ancient concept of 'kindness to strangers', Georgia only said five words: 'He would have liked it.'

When the cancer in his testicles finally killed Kapnias, it was rumoured that several impromptu celebrations broke out spontaneously. In a final act of malice, Kapnias had bequeathed everything to Dimitri – his best shot at ensuring that neither Georgia nor her children with Xenos would inherit anything. Overnight, Dimitri had not only been spared his father's malice but had also inherited Georgia's estate – with which to enact, contrary to Kapnias' will, his own virtuous plan. Georgia would be restored to her rightful throne, he told me merrily, while he laid the groundwork for a Great Reunion with his siblings. In essence, the estate would be divided into three plots: one for his own family, now that he was married and had a baby girl too; one for his brother, whom he hoped to lure back from up north; and one for Maria, who he hoped would retire there rather than in Sydney.

The noughties were unfolding and the feeling that life was, at last, getting easier was not confined to Georgia's small world. To Georgia's puzzlement, her small pension was no longer delivered by the postman in drachmas, but by an ATM in Kyparissia churning out euros. Greeks were told we were now part of Europe's hard core. Her neighbours were borrowing euros as if there was no tomorrow: to buy new appliances, giant off-roaders and far-flung holidays. The world seemed to Georgia to have lost its marbles but, on television, the talking heads insisted that 'this time it is different'. Of course it wasn't.

The fact that the whole of the Western world had lost its

mind did not shield the Greeks from the fallout. Indeed, quite the opposite. As soon as Wall Street went pear-shaped in 2008, and the banks of Germany and France came down like houses of cards, Greece – undoubtedly Europe's flimsiest economy – fell into a black hole that made the stony years of the 1950s look like a golden age, at least financially.

History had its fun, once more, by subjecting Georgia to a fresh personal tragedy wrapped up in the latest global crisis. Her son Dimitri, a keen and able free diver whose happiest moments were spent descending to considerable depths in the middle of the night to retrieve the odd giant red mullet, to be cooked and devoured the next day with great fanfare, one night failed to surface – his corpse washed up on the rocky beach just down the road from Georgia's farmhouse.

Even before Dimitri's body was cleansed and prepared for the funeral, his wife's father, a man conspicuously reminiscent of Kapnias, engaged a lawyer with a simple brief: to evict Georgia from her estate, now that his daughter was the legal owner. The courts concurred. Dimitri had drowned before the documents were finalised.

At the well-attended funeral, Georgia was front and centre, but inattentive. When the moment came to open the casket to give the mourners a last glimpse of the deceased, just before he was laid in the freshly dug grave, a well-meaning but clumsy friend catapulted Dimitri's favourite underwater torch into the coffin so that it would accompany him in the afterlife. As the heavy object hit her dead son's face with a sickening thud, Georgia winced. A moment later, our eyes locked. She stared into mine for a few seconds. Only she wasn't there anymore. Just as fate pretended to smile at her for the first time since her years with Xenos, its invisible fist had struck her with all its might – for the last time.

It didn't take long for her daughter-in-law's family to evict her from her home, from their lives. Moved to a run-down old folks' home nearby, its corridors reeking of boiled cabbage and chlorine, she watched in silence for clues of the world that she and Xenos had lost. When those empty, staring eyes shut for good, it was not tragedy but deliverance that came knocking.

51. From Kyparissia to Kabul

As a boy, I witnessed uniformed versions of Kapnias slapping Eleni at Hotel Pefkakia. I observed the creative ways underprivileged women, like Trisevgeni, resisted authoritarianism. And I had my head filled, by Yorgo, with stories of Anna's feminist resistance to the patriarchy and to colonialism. However, by the time I met Georgia and Kapnias, his ilk was seemingly emasculated by social democracy and its feminist allies. For a brief moment, the illusion descended upon my generation that those battles had been mostly won.

Even before Georgia's passing, fascism was, nevertheless, in the air again. The oeuvre of the fresh global financial crisis conspired to turn Greece into Europe's ground zero. And, as in the interwar period, the heat of the crisis was soon to warm up the serpent's eggs. Before we knew it, its hatchlings were running amok. Not just in Greece, where a fully fledged Nazi organisation, Golden Dawn, became the third-largest party in our parliament, but globally. In India, Hungary, Germany, France, Brexit Britain, Spain, Italy, across the Atlantic to Argentina and the United States, a wave of fascistic authoritarianism would have warmed Kapnias' stone-cold heart.

In the summer of 2021, amid chaotic scenes reminiscent of the American retreat from Saigon, US and British troops evacuated Kabul as the Taliban closed in. With Georgia firmly on my mind, I instinctively tweeted a message of solidarity to the women of Afghanistan who were facing the spectre of gender apartheid under the Taliban: 'On the day liberal-neocon imperialism was defeated,' I wrote, 'our thoughts are with the women of Afghanistan. Hang in there sisters!' On that same day, Nandini Naira Archer, a British feminist, was writing along the same lines:

> After two decades of failed Western intervention, don't be fooled again. As was the case with Tony Blair's illegal invasion of Iraq and David Cameron's catastrophic intervention in Libya, when the UK sends troops, it spells destruction for women and girls – and today would be no exception.

Suddenly, Twitter (now X) erupted with angry accusations from liberal feminists, who had supported America's occupation, that I was a Taliban supporter; an enabler of misogynistic fundamentalists; a fool sacrificing Afghan women on the altar of my anti-Western agenda. I was not too distressed, for two reasons. One was their sheer hypocrisy. The other was Georgia's legacy, which pointed to a universal truth: muscular liberal feminism is bunk!

Yes, Georgia loathed and resisted Kapnias. But she knew that only women could liberate themselves. No deliverance could come from bombs unleashed from the sky. That a handful of women might get jobs in some Green Zone run by American brigadiers was no compensation for the carnage that every occupation brings. Georgia knew that you can't just send in ironclad men to liberate women from their men. Or, as Chakravorty Spivak put it, the very idea of 'white men saving brown women from brown men' is facile, not to mention offensive to the Georgias of this world.*

---

* Chakravorty Spivak (1994), 'Can the Subaltern Speak?', in *Colonial Discourse and Post-Colonial Theory: A Reader*, edited and introduced by Patrick Williams and Laura Chrisman, New York: Columbia University Press.

Authentic feminism, as Anna would have warned, is never condescending, nor didactic. It recognises that different women suffer patriarchy differently, just as different people experience racism differently. And it is never concerned with the preservation of the privileges privileged women secure through extracting wealth from people of colour – a power afforded by their class and their capital.

Today's clash between the radical centre and fascists, between neocon feminists who see NATO as a peace project, and the Trumpists who reject it in favour of US isolationism and an all-out war on 'wokeism', brings to mind the juxtaposition of two men from Georgia's chequered life: Dimitroulas and Kapnias – two men who, as different as they were, had one thing in common. They were fighting over the spoils of a system in which, in their very different ways, they were both fully invested.

In the lap of the luxurious circumstances in which I write these lines, in comparison to the conditions under which Georgia lived and died, I sometimes imagine conversations with her and Xenos in a different timeline – one in which our civil war had been avoided. I strongly suspect that the two of them would understand better than most what is happening today: how the culture wars, which allow both liberals and fascists to ignore underlying systematic exploitation, make a free and dignified life impossible for most, especially for women.

PART FIVE
Danaë

52. Into the wind

Danaë smiled as the locals shook their heads in disbelief when she said she could make the old wooden boat sail against the wind along the Niger. They had never seen anyone do that, they claimed. Gasps of surprise and some applause broke out as she reconfigured the sail, vigorously tacked back and forth and succeeded in getting the boat to beat the wind. Her journey from Bamako to Timbuktu could now resume without delay. Time was of the essence.

Convinced that rivers are the Earth's arteries, and that humanity was hurrying them into a planetary-scale arteriosclerosis, Danaë decided to alert the world the only way she knew how. The Niger was one of seven grand rivers that she had planned to sail that year. She had already sailed the Nile, the Ganges and the Danube. The Yangtze, the Mississippi and, of course, the Amazon were next in line. On each river, as her boat glided gently upon the water for weeks on end, she filmed the left bank with a port-side-mounted camera, keeping the shoreline in the lower third of her frame.

Once the seven long films were complete, Danaë planned to bring them together in one art space. There, she would project edited samples of each on seven large screens evenly spaced within the interior walls of a specially built circular room, the video installation encircling the viewer with the sights and sounds of the great rivers, the projections timed so that you experience the sun rising over the Yangtze before, thirty minutes later, it sets down over the Amazon and the Mississippi.

The early years of the new millennium felt soulless. Life was stuck in a losing battle with lifestyle. Financiers peddled the dangerous fantasy of riskless risk, conjured up reckless debts and encouraged conspicuous consumption. Even in peripheral Greece, we were told that we, too, had . . . arrived – that we had finally escaped our orientalist plight, our Near East niche, and were now smack at the epicentre of Europe's hard core, as evidenced by the odd new euro notes that spouted out of Athenian ATMs.

As Danaë was traversing her rivers, a childhood friend invited me to an exhibition she had organised in Athens. The cutesy nineteenth- and early-twentieth-century portraits and landscapes on display bored me senseless. Noticing my listlessness, my friend suggested I follow her into another room to see something quite different. Even before I stepped inside, the soundscape pouring out of the large room flooded my senses.

As I pushed through the black velvet curtain, my foot sank into thick red earth that covered the floor from wall to wall. It was as if Australia's Simpson Desert had invaded the building. In the middle of the dimly lit floor, a bright spotlight illuminated a circular centre where, aided by a concealed mechanism, the red soil moved up and down as if it were breathing in and out, slowly, painfully, continuously. Meanwhile a dynamic, granular, bass-heavy, all-encompassing soundscape sounded exactly as I imagined Mother Earth would sound as she struggled to breathe, weighed down by humanity's hubris.

I hardly knew how long I stayed in that red desert room, stunned, engulfed by the gloriously austere depiction of our collective assault on our planet. I made a mental note of the label posted on the wall: *Breathe*, by Danaë Stratou.*

Six years before Al Gore's *An Inconvenient Truth*, eight years before the collapse of Lehman Brothers, *Breathe* dared to depict a barren Earth struggling to catch its breath. No rational analysis, no well-constructed argument could expose as effectively the folly of the new millennium. As I walked out, I felt humbled. Humbled as a member of a species wrecking its habitat. And humbled as an economist whose pseudo-scientific language stood no chance of sounding the alarm as resoundingly as *Breathe* had.

A few years later, I heard of another exhibition featuring Danaë Stratou. Naturally, having been so impressed by *Breathe*, I went to see it. The centrepiece was a circular projection room, a cocoon in which the viewer was mesmerised. No matter how many times I entered it, each time I saw something different. As I watched life unfold on the bank of one of the seven majestic rivers, at a tempo dictated by the water's natural flow, I saw what Danaë wanted us all to see: *The River of Life*,† whose graceful waters over the aeons had nurtured an ungrateful, increasingly self-destructive humanity.

---

* The exhibition was organised at the National Institute for Research in central Athens in the context of Christie's '10th Greek Auction', – which took place on 7 March 2001. *Breathe*, which had been shown for the first time in 2000 in another space, was later donated to the National Museum of Contemporary Art (EMST) by the collector who purchased it at that auction.

† *The River of Life* was exhibited in Athens as part of 'Transcultures', an international contemporary art exhibition organised by EMST in the context of the 2004 Olympic Games. Since then it has belonged to the EMST permanent collection.

53. Define her in one word

In mid-November 2005, serendipity sat me next to Danaë at an Athenian restaurant, invited by the same friend who had introduced me to *Breathe* four years earlier. Danaë talked passionately about what she wanted to do next.

After *The River of Life*, she explained, the self-deluded West could not contain her. She had to get out there again. She ached to traverse once more lines that, like her seven rivers, ran across the planet's face. This time the lines she chose were not watery, tranquil, life-giving. This time, they would be harsh, malignant, vicious. Lines consisting of barbed wire, concrete, landmines, watchtowers, army outposts, sandbags. Lines built by humans to divide. Lines that scar the Earth. Her next installation, she confided, would go by the title *CUT – 7 dividing lines*.

It was joyfully disconcerting to connect the work with the artist. As she spoke, my mind wandered to Trisevgeni, to Georgia. Unlike them, Danaë was able to travel two continents away, climb the highest mountain, cross the widest river, go deep into the most desolate desert. It hit me that this Greek woman did not fit the 'blacks of Europe' category that I had deployed to good political effect in my Essex university debates twenty-six years earlier. Had we, Greeks, become white enough? I interrupted her to ask: What was it like, for her, to walk the thin line between power and precarity, crossing the no man's land between a Westerner's privilege and a woman's vulnerability? Could she relate to the feeling my Irish comrades and I shared in the late 1970s as the 'blacks of

Europe'? 'When I studied sculpture in London in the mid-1980s,' she replied without a second thought, 'I was treated neither as a legitimate white girl nor as a brown one. Instead, I was treated as a bird of paradise. It was ever so easy to be flattered by this treatment when in fact it was a most insidious way of putting me in my place and keeping me there.'

Having dispensed with my question, Danaë went straight back to her plans. First, she would travel to each division, physically straddle it, and capture in two photographic stills what her camera saw on each side, representing her urge to reunite that which should never have been cut in two.

Then, once safely back home, she would create an eighth line. She would print the seven pairs of photographs on large transparent sheets of Perspex and display both sides facing each other in a visual dialogue. By placing the seven pairs on either side of a single line, a corridor would emerge, which the viewer would tread symbolically to heal the seven open wounds it was made of. Looking left to right to see what lies on either side, the viewer would be accompanied by a soundscape from sounds recorded *in situ*, at the very spots the stills were taken.

Whisked away in the slipstream of her excitement, I felt a little embarrassed. Danaë had a power I coveted: the power to unveil reality in ways that neither words nor mathematical operators can. Her installations spoke vividly to everyone.

'Which seven divisions would you pick?' she asked once she had finished describing her considerable research effort. Certain that she had already posed that question to many others, I weighed my answer carefully. After I don't know how many hours of intense discussion, a list emerged: Palestine; the Green Line through Nicosia, the last divided city in the European Union; Mitrovica, a town in northern Kosovo cut in two; Belfast, with its so-called Peace Walls; Badme, a tiny hamlet in the shifting war zone between Ethiopia and Eritrea; the Line of Control dividing Kashmir; and the US–Mexican border fence.

It was already six in the morning when our list of seven was complete. Intoxicated by our synergy, buoyed by furtive glances, surrendering to the possibility, I heard myself speak the outrageous question: 'Would you like us to grow old together?' Equally recklessly, Danaë replied: 'Yes.' We have been doing so ever since.

When I broke the news to Eleni and Yorgo, they bombarded me with myriad questions. I did not know where to begin, so Eleni instructed: 'Define her in one word.' 'Mutation' was the weird reply I came up with. Eleni looked at me askance.

What I had meant was that I am nothing but an adaptation, an extrapolation, a variation of Anna, Eleni, Trisevgeni, Georgia, Yorgo, Panayis and Yango too. Not Danaë! The more I learned about her family and background the harder it was to see how she could have turned out the way she did: a dissident willing to die rather than end up compromised; an insider ready to be cast out into the wilderness; in short, a class traitor and therefore a particular threat to the established disorder, far greater than a rebel springing from the lower classes. Only a mutation can explain how an offspring can deviate so drastically from its ancestors.

My choice of word was too harsh for Eleni's liking, but at least she warmed to my explanation. She said that an insider-dissident reminded her of Anna. Soon, mother and new partner had formed a solid alliance on everything, including Danaë's inexorable push to get me to escape my academic bubble and re-engage with the world.

54. Stepping out

A few months later, Danaë rang me on my university office line. 'I've secured the funding,' she said, explaining how earlier that day she had presold a copy of *CUT – 7 dividing lines* to a collector. 'Coming?' she asked, specifying that 'it shouldn't take more than a year'. Overflowing with unease, I managed a half-hearted 'yes'. She replied sternly that nothing short of an emphatic 'yes' would do – a rebuke that forced me to confront that, until then, I had been an armchair activist, snug in my university office with old radiators hissing their approval as I pontificated on capitalism, clinging to a safe Archimedean perspective, my hands clean.

Danaë's invitation had burst a dam of phoney self-righteousness. In the long shadow of the globalisation that I took pleasure in savaging in my articles and lectures, countless people – the desperate, the daring – braved the most treacherous of frontiers, crossing seas on splintered boats, sleeping in ditches, kissing the boots of men who spat at them. I had every visa and passport I needed, yet I had been staying put in my comfort zone, sipping my diet Coke while chastising the world on paper.

Ashamed, I repeated my 'yes', this time with feeling. Thus began a year of learning what it truly meant to dread the glint of barbed wire at dawn.

Whether it was the corrugated iron walls south of Nogales in Arizona, or the tall railings along the Shankill Road in Belfast, or the grisly concrete wall on the outskirts of Ramallah in the West Bank, what I saw crystallised a perception that had been growing in me since my arrival in Britain in 1978: in literature, in popular culture, in philosophy and in law, fences and boundaries were key to the mindset underpinning the former empire – a mindset given another lease of life by the United States once the Truman Doctrine was in place.

It goes without saying that the anglosphere did not invent fences or walls. Emperor Hadrian had already built renowned walls from Greece to Scotland, not to mention the stupendous Great Wall constructed by successive dynasties in China. However, these ancient walls were always intended to be porous. What the British pioneered were fences designed to be impenetrable, permanent, exclusionary, forbidding – fences whose purpose was to annul the rights of native peoples to the commons of their ancestors.

Surreptitiously, these fences went on to beget a new economic system, capitalism, and its overseas simulacrum, white-settler colonialism. Moreover, they came endowed with a philosophical justification: their erection was tantamount to the rise of personal freedom, fair play, enhanced productivity and civilisation. From where I stood, Danaë was proposing to visit and subvert not just electrified fences, barbed wire, concrete watchtowers, landmines and machine-gun posts, but our era's moral justification of enclosure.

55. The fence, the mirror, the river

Danaë's instinctive revulsion at fences contravened the West's self-aggrandising narrative. Is it right to erect a fence around land that is not yours and then call it yours? Yes, answered John Locke, the English philosopher and father of liberalism, in 1689. It's fine, as long as the privatised land was previously *terra nullius* (a land empty of people) and the fence builders proceeded to mix their labour with it to produce wheat, meat, wool or anything of value to humans. For Locke, enterprising privateers have a right, indeed a duty, to call such land 'theirs', to turn it into a 'land of milk and honey', and thereafter to fight tooth and nail to protect their title deeds.

Never before had a philosophical argument had such an outsized effect on the world. Intentionally or not, Locke had provided the ethical justification for white settlers, like those who travelled with Captain Cook in 1770 to Australia, to appropriate faraway lands by erecting fences around large estates that they had declared *terra nullius*. The declaration, of course, meant that the natives who lived there were not people, a sinister prelude to genocide.

Meanwhile, at around Locke's time, fences were also going up across Britain. It is no exaggeration to say that they are the reason capitalism sprouted in the British Isles, rather than in France or Germany. Facilitated by the king's army, the landed gentry evicted peasants, fenced them off from the lands of their forebears and replaced them with sheep, whose backs produced the international commodity – wool – that brought in the cash which fuelled capitalism long before the steam engine, textiles, railways and bankers.

In one of history's most ironic twists, the fence had 'liberated' the peasants from the land, rendering them free to sell their labour, time, body and spirit to whomever. And equally free to starve, to enter into desperate contracts with strangers, to become dehumanised cogs in some productive machine owned by faceless shareholders.

Meanwhile, as Britain's peasants were being fenced out, enslaved Africans were being fenced in – in ships that transported them to newly fenced-off lands in the Caribbean and North America, where they were forced to work, producing the massive surpluses that funded the Industrial Revolution.

Once the American Revolution had rid the eastern colonies of British rule, the US Constitution revelled in the light of reason and liberty, while erecting all sorts of constitutional fences whose purpose was to cast in legal stone, as 'universal rights of man', the property rights of white men over stolen land, over women and, of course, over their enslaved Africans. These constitutional barriers kept the riff-raff out and the state at bay, marking the sacred political realm of the land-owning, slave-owning, male entrepreneur.

In the wake of the American Revolution, creole elites spread the idea of nationhood to the rest of the Americas. Continental Europe subsequently pirated New World models and embraced the nation-state too. German philosopher Georg Hegel captured its oeuvre when he said that history will forget any ethnic community that fails to erect a border fence around a territory ruled over by its very own nation-state. Thus the world we take for granted today was born: the fenced-off sovereign nation, the internment camps for immigrants, the gated community, the idea that the enemy of autonomy is the 'other' – from other people to the tax office.

Before the Age of Capital, the European imagination was dominated by the ideology of the ancient Greek *polis*, whose inhabitants dreamt of demolishing its walls or, at least, of never having to keep its gates closed. Danaë's gut antipathy to fences and her rejection of the logic of dividing lines, whether in Kashmir or El Paso, harked back to the ancient tradition which saw locked gates as symbols of failure. Case in point was her fascination with what the city elders would do after a son of theirs won an event at the Olympics: demolish part of the city walls as a gesture with which to demonstrate their citizens' boosted confidence. Only at times of crisis were the walls rebuilt.

It is no accident that the English language – unlike Greek, Latin, French or German – is full of metaphors and verses eulogising the fence, such as denouncing procrastinators as those 'sitting on the fence' or celebrating courage as that which 'draws the boundary between the ordinary and the extraordinary'. Robert Frost did not summon 'good fences make good neighbours' from thin air. H. H. Brackenridge waxed lyrical about how 'good fences restrain fence-breaking beasts and preserve good neighbourhoods', enabling British barons and their colonial brethren in Australia, America, the Indian subcontinent, Rhodesia and South Africa to classify indigenous populations as irrational beasts whose trespassing caused chaos and threatened liberty.

And I remember my astonishment when, as a first-year undergraduate at Essex, I opened the prescribed economics text to find, on page one, the author's definition of what it means to be rational:

> Rational people act as if to maximise the extent to which their preferences are satisfied within their means. The rest are deemed irrational and, therefore, their behaviour falls outside the scope of economic theory.

In two short sentences my economics textbook had tossed out two and a half thousand years of philosophical debate. Gone was the subtle interrogation of Socrates, Aristotle, Ibn Khaldun, Thomas Aquinas, Descartes, Kant and Hegel. Instead, the economists had erected an impenetrable boundary separating the rational from the irrational. And they did so by making choice the only criterion, forgetting John Stuart Mill's warning:

> It is better to be a human being dissatisfied than a pig satisfied, better to be Socrates dissatisfied than a fool satisfied. And if the fool, or the pig, are of a different opinion, that is because they know only their side of the story.

In a social order where power stemmed from privatised land, which necessitated the expulsion and expropriation of inconvenient 'others', the fence was everything. The enclosures fenced more than land. They penned women in. Fields became property. Work became wage-bound, and hearths became cages. The domestic ideal bloomed like brambles, while men claimed the world beyond the fence.

Having demarcated private property, and secured it from trespassers, it was only natural that economists used the idea of the fence to demarcate reason from unreason, freedom from unfreedom. With the rational economic actor, Homo economicus, economists had now prepared the ground for two centuries of thinking in which women featured, at best, as honorary men. Homo economicus ruled out any criticism of the motives of any settler, mogul, banker or tech bro.

It was not, of course, that so many smart people in the best universities had erred into espousing a false theory. No, this economics came with a great utility: it was to the new ruling class what the Bible had been to feudal lords – a source of legitimacy and a language with which to lend it moral authority.

THE FENCE, THE MIRROR, THE RIVER

'Is there a better allegory for understanding ourselves than the fence?' Danaë asked me during our rough bus ride from Amritsar to Srinagar, the capital city of the Indian-controlled part of Kashmir. I replied that I had two alternatives to the fence in mind. The first was the mirror.

The ancient Athenian philosophers thought we can only experience deep joy, *eudaimonia* they called it, in the context of a successful life, a life well lived. The problem was that only others can truly judge whether we have lived such a life, and only once we are dead. This is why, to get a sense of how rational or free we are, the best we can do is to catch glimpses of ourselves, of our reflection, in the eyes of others.

Hegel took this further when he condemned slavery: even masters can never be truly content since it is impossible to catch in their slaves' eyes a glimpse of themselves as worthy or good.

Nevertheless, there was something about the mirror that left me cold, I admitted: a mirror may reflect but, unlike another person's eyes, a mirror is a thing in stasis, an object impervious to change. That's why, I told Danaë, I preferred my second alternative to the fence: the river – an idea I sourced from the title of one of Anna's poems in her tiny red notebook.

Echoing Heraclitus' line 'everything is in flux and nothing remains constant' (τὰ πάντα ῥεῖ καὶ οὐδὲν μένει), Anna's 'The River' contemplated the surface of the Nile – the 'river of constant change', as she called it. Fences divide callously, mirrors reflect passively, but the river – oh, the river – the river reflects us dynamically as it forces us also to flow, to rhyme with the changes in our personality, our society, our times.

'Something in me', I said as our bus entered Srinagar, 'refuses to accept that your previous work was the *River of Life* by sheer coincidence.' Danaë smiled and took my hand.

56. In the fences' long shadow

Rising before dawn, our days were spent with Danaë photographing relentlessly while I distracted army officers, UN personnel, irregular gunmen and local spies – men who were doing their best to turn us back, to disorient us, to make us see only what they wanted us to see. Occasionally they went further, like that undernourished, AK-47-wielding Eritrean renegade, working for the Ethiopian army, who tried to abduct Danaë at gunpoint and drag her behind a makeshift outpost near Zalambessa.

More often than not, my resolve buckled under the threats and the obstacles. But not Danaë's. Capable of disarming the fiercest strongman, she would enter a brigadier's tent, an elder's hut or a paramilitary command post as if she were straddling a cyclone. When we failed to reach one point on the dividing line, she sought the path of least resistance, as she called it, to another point on the 'cut'.

One night, after two frustrating days of being prevented by the Indian army from going anywhere near the sole open crossing on the Line of Control in Kashmir, despite our official permits from the national and regional governments, we held a mini-conference with Kashmir's minister of tourism on a magnificent maharajah boat floating serenely on Lake Srinagar. The minister was embarrassed. We were the only foreigners around at a time of border tensions and bomb explosions, and thus he deemed our satisfaction important – hoping for some helpful publicity from Danaë's work against the background of a decimated tourist sector.

Speaking in old colonial English with a delightful Kashmiri accent, the minister did his best to persuade Danaë that it was out of his hands: 'My lady, the army has trumped my best efforts to help you reach the LoC. I have failed in my endeavour to assist your ladyship to take your photographs.' Burying his face theatrically in both his hands to demonstrate his shame, he then spread out a large map of Kashmir on the dining table. 'But, my lady, Kashmir has so many beauty spots for you to visit and to photograph.'

Danaë studied the map carefully. She then placed her finger on a point of the LoC near the map's top-right corner, where no roads, no villages appeared, just an empty area marked in white. 'Is the army stationed there too?' she asked dourly. 'No, my lady,' whispered the heartbroken minister. 'So, why don't I go there?' she demanded to know. 'But that's the Himalayas, ma'am,' the minister said in desperation: 'it's five thousand metres high! You will perish there.' Seeing her mischievous smile, the poor man gave up.

Two days later, we were up there, Danaë capturing her two stills on the two sides of the LoC. The dividing line turned out to be nothing more than a pile of plinths overlooking a majestic lake fed by a glacier, which has since been annihilated by our climate catastrophe.

As we descended the treacherous mountain, every step came with a non-trivial probability of falling into some kilometre-deep void. Only then did I appreciate fully Danaë's insistence that putting herself in physical danger, experiencing the bodily hardship of the division, was an integral part of *CUT – 7 dividing lines*.

During our travels, the people we chanced upon gave us an unusual perspective on the globalising world that grew out of the collapse of the Soviet Union. One of Danaë's photographs was a vision of hope: two boys, one Turkish-Cypriot, the other Greek-Cypriot, playing football on an abandoned pitch within the no man's land formed by the divided island's Green Line. Juxtaposed against this photograph was the artist Andreas, a Greek-Cypriot friend whose family had been uprooted by the advancing Turkish army when he was a child in the summer of 1974.

Andreas had never been back to his family home since that dreadful day three decades earlier. Reluctantly, he accompanied us in a rented car over Mount Pentadaktilos and into the heart of the Turkish-occupied zone. As we approached, we could feel his trepidation. Its Turkish occupants welcomed him. Politely. But the air was thick with caution. As we left, Andreas revealed that under the UN peace plan that the Greek side had rejected in a referendum the year beforehand, in 2004, his home would have been returned to him. Startled, I heard him say that he, too, had voted against it: 'Division is better than an unjust settlement,' he said. Under the UN plan, he would be getting his house back but not his grandmother's nearby olive grove.

A couple of months later, we were sitting in the back of an ageing Toyota Land Cruiser hoping to get to Badme, a hamlet that had changed hands several times as the front line of the Ethiopian–Eritrean war shifted. Zinabu was at the wheel, a local Tigrayan man eking out a living by driving UN and NGO officials around. Next to him sat Yassu, a dreary figure who claimed to be working for a humanitarian NGO that wanted to help Danaë get to Badme so she could communicate the plight of its inhabitants to the world. During a tea stop, with Yassu out of sight, Zinabu told us that Yassu worked for Ethiopia's hated military intelligence. That his mission was to prevent us from photographing military installations and personnel: 'Make Yassu fear you more than he fears disobeying his orders,' he advised us.

Over the next two days, Danaë photographed as many military personnel and installations as she could, and as conspicuously as possible, in direct defiance of Yassu's screaming protestations.

Zinabu's tactic worked: Yassu now had to pretend to the army officers watching that it was *his* idea that Danaë take those photographs – a pretence that broke his spirit enough for him to acquiesce to our entering the war zone. Just outside Badme, as an excited Zinabu snuck behind a UN armoured vehicle specially equipped to drive over landmines, Danaë audaciously captured the image she was seeking from the Toyota's back seat.

Two weeks later, just before we entered the Chinese-built terminal at Mekele Airport, Zinabu's parting words to Danaë were: 'My wife is Eritrean. If it weren't for you, I would never have seen the line that divides our people. Thank you!'

During one of the most dangerous legs, travelling along the entire length of the US–Mexican border, we saw the absurdity of globalisation baked into the fences, bridges and freeways that, at crossings like Laredo, Juárez, Nogales or Mexicali, worked together to dam a sea of humanity. Lurking in those fences' shadows during the day, biding their time under bridges and freeways, people waited for the night's cover to break into the promised land. Meanwhile, trains and trucks loaded to the brim with cars, chemicals and vegetables were crossing freely into the United States. However, the irony peaked where the border fence enters the Pacific, north of Tijuana, in San Diego's line of sight. There, unable to build solid structures on the white sand, the fence builders planted pieces of railway lines vertically, extending well into the ocean. Iron forged to connect people and places was cut up, turned upright and used to divide humanity on a pristine beach that, in a rational world, would have been left to vacationers.

57. The Globalising Wall

In Kosovo, Danaë found her visual representation of the line dividing Albanian from Serbian Kosovars on the banks of the River Ibar. It comprised two stills she took of a narrow, snow-covered footbridge, in sharp contrast to the much larger steel and concrete crossing nearby – hilariously named 'Peace and Friendship Bridge' – which was weighed down by barbed wire and snipers from three different armies. However, it was not until we travelled seventy kilometres further south-west that the connection with the other divisions began to register.

Just outside the city of Pec, or Peja, very close to Kosovo's border with Albania, an ancient Serbian monastery continued to defy the onslaught of ethnic cleansing. Inside the cloistered walls, surrounded by NATO troops protecting them, fourteen nuns were left to keep alive the flame of what used to be the Serbs' spiritual home. The Italian sergeant in charge of the NATO unit guarding the nuns told us that Albanian paramilitaries had repeatedly tried to 'wipe the nuns out', pointing out the bullet holes on their vehicles and sentry cubicles. The nuns welcomed us like liberators. Their joy at having visitors from a Christian Orthodox country was so great that they barely shrugged when we confessed our atheism. After lovingly serving us coffee, they took us into the monastery's inner garden. There stood an old oak tree. In perfect Greek, they told us its story.

Centuries ago, after their defeat by the invading Ottomans – which gave the Serb nation its creation myth – retreating Serbian fighters warned the priests they must flee. Before fleeing, the priests stopped to pray under the great oak's shadow.

The year was 1690. The very same year of the Battle of the Boyne in Ireland, when Protestant King William of Orange defeated Catholic King James. A battle that is, to this day, commemorated in Ulster's Orange Order marching season – marches that reinforce tensions between Protestants and Catholics which keep Belfast's so-called Peace Walls standing. As chance would have it, those walls were our next destination.

At first, it seemed like a coincidence. However, the coincidences piled up. In Belfast, on the Catholic side of the Peace Walls, our eyes caught a glimpse of a 'Victory to Palestine' message and, a few metres further, a mural depicting the wall that Ariel Sharon had built in Palestine – our next destination.

A month later, in the West Bank, the plot thickened when we spotted graffiti on the Palestinian side of Sharon's wall, promising that 'Palestine supports Kashmir' – again, our next destination. A day later I learned that parts of the US–Mexican border fence were being replaced by concrete walls built by the same Israeli companies that had erected the wall in Palestine – a joint venture that grew stronger after Donald Trump's election in 2016.

What was going on? Could Danaë's seven dividing lines be joining up? And it was not just the writing on the wall. As we moved from one division to the next, I could feel it in the air. Rather than getting brittler, and readier for dismantling, as the prophets of globalisation had promised, those fences and walls were growing taller and stronger by the day. They even began to resemble each other. As did the outlook of the people who lived close to them.

A Mitrovica Serb seemed more at home by the Green Line in Nicosia than in Belgrade. Despite the colder climate, an Eritrean in Tsorona could relate better with alpine Kashmiris along the Line of Control than with Nairobi city-dwellers. An Ulster Unionist empathised with Cypriots obsessed with the ghost town of Famagusta, but felt a stranger in London. A Palestinian in Qalqilya discovered strange bonds with a resident of Juárez that would have been unavailable to her in Cairo.

After the Cold War's end, in the wake of financialisation and globalising trade, walls erected long ago in the name of security were now breeding unprecedented insecurity on both sides. What used to be mere fences were becoming the focal points for resurgent cross-class chauvinism.

As Jim, a Belfast taxi driver, put it to us, after the Northern Irish shipyards closed, at around the same time the Troubles ended, the young paramilitaries in his Protestant neighbourhood were left with only two things: gangs and walls. 'The young lads used to get guns to get Paddy,' he lamented. 'Now they ship drugs to get dough. The walls are their thing. They will kill Paddies to keep these walls sky-high. They will kill their brothers if they have to.'

The fault lines were being reinvented in front of our eyes. New walls of fear were being erected on the streets of Bradford, the northern beaches of Australia and the ports of Sicily and Calais. New electrified fences atop cement walls popped up in Spain's Moroccan enclaves. A similar monstrosity was built next to the divine River Evros marking the Greek–Turkish border. As were walls in Bulgaria, Hungary, Austria. And then, as if to mock Roger Waters and Pink Floyd, who in the 1980s had huge crowds singing 'bring down the wall', 'build the wall' has become the new creed – adopted first by Donald Trump but quickly espoused by cowardly social democrats across Europe.

Almost no aspect of Western society was left unaffected. Instead of the promised global village or the horizontal playing field, globalisation turned the recently crestfallen into aspiring

THE GLOBALISING WALL

wall builders, huddling like sheep in a storm: lumpen nationalists and dithering bourgeois; disenchanted blue-collar workers and edgy stockbrokers; former cold warriors and disheartened youths.

When we finally returned home, and *CUT – 7 dividing lines* was exhibited,* Danaë used thousands of the stills that never found their way into her original installation, to put together an animated film to be projected onto a specially constructed, free-standing wall, with my short text below carved into the other side. The new work was entitled *The Globalising Wall*:

> Walls have a longstanding relation both with liberty from fear and subjugation to another's will. After 1945, walls acquired an unprecedented determination to divide. They spread like a bushfire from Berlin to Palestine, from the tablelands of Kashmir to the villages of Cyprus, from the Korean peninsula to the streets of Belfast. When the Cold War ended, we were told to expect their dismantling. Instead, they are growing taller, more impenetrable, longer. They leap from one continent onto the next. They are globalising. From the West Bank to Kosovo, from the gated communities of Egypt to those of California, from the killing fields of old Ethiopia to the US–Mexico border, a seamless wall is meandering its way, both physically and emotionally, on the planet's surface. Its spectre is upon us.†

---

* *CUT – 7 dividing lines* was first exhibited in Zoumboulakis Galleries, Athens, Greece, 2007. Since then it has been shown around the world. Today, it belongs to the permanent collections of Greece's National Museum of Contemporary Art (EMST), the Emfietzoglou Art Collection and the State Museum of Contemporary Art, Thessaloniki, Greece.

† This text featured as an integral part of Danaë Stratou's installation *The Globalising Wall*, first shown in 2012 at the Adelaide Festival, Adelaide, Australia.

58. Art as politics by other means

Danaë's method left no doubt that, to her, art is politics-by-other-means. Iris Murdoch once wrote that good art requires the artist to transcend her sense of self, to surpass her own desires, to create something good for no reason at all – for the hell of it. Is that not an antinomy? Can art be both political and an end-in-itself? I believe it can. In a state of repose, the artist gives form to the autonomous, sovereign good – she makes it visible in our mind's eye. Can anything be more political than this aspiration?

Picasso was right, I once heard Danaë tell her students, that art is not for decoration but to be used as a weapon with which to wage war against the enemy. Asked by one of them who the enemy was, she replied: The fence builders eager to divide and rule. First they put fences up in distant places, then closer to home, and finally in our backyards, in our communities, in our very souls.

For Danaë, her art was a struggle to unite the divided, to win the freedom we yearn for but have not yet won. With such an attitude, it was only a matter of time before Danaë would incur the fury of certain powerful people: as far as they were concerned, she was one of their own, a prodigal daughter who had betrayed her class, her tribe, her family. She was, in short, a major threat to their authority: she didn't care if she stayed on the desirable side of the fence.

Danaë, to this day, refuses to acknowledge that we come from different sides of the class divide. At one level, I get it. Even though she did not remember me, nor I her, we both attended the same posh school, Moraitis. We were taught by the same teachers and had scores of common acquaintances. We both went on to study in England, she at Central Saint Martin's College of Art and Design, me at the University of Essex. Our musical tastes were alike. We liked the same movies. Her parents had read more or less the same books as Yorgo and Eleni. Her maternal grandmother hailed from the Peloponnese, like Trisevgeni. So, why do I insist, to her consternation, that she and I hail from different worlds?

Because, to me, social class is defined in terms of one's relationship to the machines, to capital. Phaedon, Danaë's father, like Yorgo, worked in heavy industry. But that's where the similarity ends. Phaedon was a scion of the family that founded and owned the largest textile manufacturer in Greece. When Danaë and I were growing up, she was the boss's daughter and I the son of a man who lived in constant dread that his boss, Angelopoulos, could humiliate him at the drop of a hat. Having grown up seeing this fear consume my father's face every time the phone rang to summon him to the boss's office, I find it hard properly to convey its impact to one who had never witnessed it.

Danaë's family's textile empire had gone bankrupt in 1983, which rapidly shrank the income differential between our families, and reinforced her determination to deny our different class origins. However, one only needs to look at the crowds attending her exhibition openings to see a who's who of polite society, the wealthy who buy art, and who continue to treat her like one of their own. That Danaë intended her works as weapons against ingrained privilege was either beyond their comprehension or a jejune curiosity that increased her art's market value.

When I arrived on the scene, her circle accepted me readily – at first. They could pass me off as a tenured academic but also, due to a bizarre development, almost as one of them. In 2001,

Yorgo's boss, Angelopoulos, had died, leaving behind two feuding sons in typical *Succession* style. The two things the heirs had in common were a fear of their deceased father and an affection for mine – the reason being that, over the fifty-odd years Yorgo had worked for their dad, he was probably the only person his two young sons could turn to for assistance in getting him to give them a break. So, as the man the two brothers could both trust, and who also knew the factory inside out after fifty-odd years, Yorgo was offered Angelopoulos' position: Chairman of the Board of Directors of Chalyvourgiki – a mostly symbolic position which, nevertheless, had an impressive ring to it.

Upon hearing the news, Eleni laughed and laughed until she almost ruptured a hernia: 'The revenge of the nerd,' she cried out. But Yorgo was not offended, his heart scarcely able to believe that for the first time he was able not only to walk into Angelopoulos' office without fear, but also to claim it as his own.

During our first six or seven years together, Danaë continued to be the prominent one, basking in the life of an accomplished artist whose work was celebrated by art lovers, respected by critics and bought at handsome prices by collectors. Neither of us wanted or planned for this to change. But, around 2006, after hearing my prognosis that the world as we had known it was about to come crashing down on us, Danaë urged me to step out of academia to warn the public. 'Even if what I have to say crosses your people?' I asked. 'Especially then,' she countered.

59. Eleni's verdict

On 15 September 2008, Lehman Brothers collapsed, triggering our generation's 1929 moment, which I had been writing and speaking about for two years. That same day, Yorgo called with a tremolo in his voice I had not heard before. Eleni was undergoing emergency surgery to remove a massive, recently diagnosed cancer. After the operation, she went straight from anaesthesia to a coma. Taking turns to sit with her in the intensive care unit, an hour at a time, our hazmat suits amplified the sensation that events were taking an apocalyptic turn.

In between our stints, sitting on the worn orange plastic chairs lined up against the flaking wall of the corridor outside, my mind travelled back twenty-five years to that other waiting room where, as we waited for Trisevgeni to regain consciousness, Panayis, Eleni and Yorgo recounted and reassessed the end of another era of frustrated hopes – the 1980s.

This time, no one was talking much. Instead, Yorgo, my sister Trisevgeni, Danaë and I were silently willing Eleni to wake up. In that silence, I could not help but wonder whether the people outside the hospital were concerned about what had just gone down in New York City. Did they appreciate the magnitude of the shockwave that was about to hit us thousands of miles away? Or were they looking the other way, hoping that the tsunami would run out of steam before it reached our sun-drenched shores?

Caught up in these thoughts, I found myself feeling peeved with Eleni for being in a coma! 'Have I ever told you that, during my quarter of a century abroad, I used to call Eleni almost daily to discuss politics?' I asked Danaë. 'Yes, yes, you have told me a thousand times,' she replied with a smile, adding: 'You are worse than your dad and that mother of his, Anna.' 'That's why I am pissed off,' I continued: 'the world is being flushed down the toilet and I can't tell her about it – how dare she be in a coma!'

A few days later, Eleni woke up. While still groggy, I asked her what it was like to be in a coma. 'It was a hell I would not wish upon my worst enemy,' she replied: 'a constant torture of heightened consciousness, acute pain and no capacity to communicate with you that I was locked in there.' 'Could you hear us?' I asked in disbelief. 'Every word,' she confirmed.

A few hours later, she erupted like a geyser of emotions, edicts and enlightenment. The doctors blamed the opioids they had pumped into her but I knew it was more than that. Knowing her, she was driven by the urgency to tie up all her loose ends before the dark curtain came down again. A few hours later, when she felt her strength abandoning her, she asked to see us separately.

First, she summoned Yorgo to the dimly lit second-floor hospital room where she had been taken after the intensive care unit. As we waited outside, I noticed a strange smell and an overwhelming silence coming from the room next door. Overcome by curiosity, I entered. It was like stepping through a wormhole. Clearly no longer in use, that hospital room had been turned into a shrine, overladen with offerings, Byzantine icons, candles and burning incense sticks – the bed dressed as you might expect baby Jesus' cradle to have been adorned had it ever been discovered by Christian pilgrims. A helpful nurse, who saw me enter, explained that, on that same bed a priest of some note had died in 1920. Later, he became the last saint to be beatified by the Orthodox Christian Church. 'At least your mother is in divine company,' she volunteered in good faith. 'Sure, just don't tell my mother that,' I retorted knowingly.

As Yorgo left her room, I asked him what she had said. 'She instructed me to live on and look after myself,' he whispered, his eyes pinned to the floor. 'Plus a long list of what to do for, and what to say on her behalf to, her friends, comrades and selected adversaries.' Then it was my sister's turn. Finally it was our turn.

Ignoring me, Eleni showered Danaë with overwhelming gratitude and heartfelt wishes. When she, eventually, looked at me, borrowing Yaya Trisevgeni's favourite expression when something poignant was at stake, she said: 'My prayer and my curse is that you treat this woman as you would a saviour.' Later, when I was alone with her, Eleni dropped her epic tone and talked to me plainly, as she had always done since I was a kid: 'I have made it my life's work to study women. I have looked into many a female soul. But this one, no, I have encountered nobody like her – she must be a mutation, you were right. She can raise any soul that needs raising.' When her hand loosened its grip of mine, it felt more like a relay than a passing.

Eleni lived long enough truly to know Danaë, but not long enough to see us enter the eye of the storm. Maybe that was a blessing, maybe not.

60. Midnight missive

Soon after Eleni's passing, Danaë read a heavy-going, seven-hundred-page analysis I had written on the causes of the Wall Street crash and how it would, in all probability, send not just Greece but the whole of Europe into a catastrophic tailspin. Her verdict was that my text was as great as it was useless. 'If you can't communicate your warning to a wider, non-academic audience,' she said, 'what's the point?' I heard her and so I sat down to pen *The Global Minotaur*, a relatively slim book aimed at a wider audience eager to know why a new version of the 1930s was descending upon us.

By April 2009 Wall Street's collapse had triggered the bankruptcy of Germany's and France's banks, Greece's largest lenders. With its creditors bankrupt and unable to roll over its enormous public debt, the state was on the brink of bankruptcy too, dragging down with it into the pits of insolvency Greece's private banks, whose assets were invested in Greek government debt. In no time, the unhinged German, French and Greek bankers blackmailed politicians – chiefly those whose campaigns they had shadily financed – to impose on taxpayers vast new loans with which to bail out the bankrupt bankers while they, the bankrupt bankers, retained full control of the banks.

One thing led to another and soon I started appearing regularly on the BBC, CNN, CBS, Deutsche Welle and a host of Greek media, challenging the dominant narrative and infuriating the powers-that-be with the notion that TINA – Margaret

MIDNIGHT MISSIVE

Thatcher's famous dictum that There Is No Alternative – ought to be replaced with TATIANA – That, Astonishingly, There Is AN Alternative.

I also talked to politicians in a futile bid to convince them that the basic needs of the many were incompatible with the outrageous demands of the bankers and the oligarchs. One evening, upon returning home to recount the spinelessness of the leading politician I had just met, Danaë startled me: 'If they won't do it, you will need to get yourself elected – someone has to do something, it might as well be you.' 'But', I protested, 'any party that stands a chance of winning office will chew me up and spew me out.' She continued undaunted: 'Then start your own party.' I thought she was joking and laughed heartily. In retrospect, she was dead serious.

Unwilling to consider the possible repercussions on us, I embarked on a lone campaign to expose the mafia-style tactics of the Greek bankers. A Reuters exposé, to which I had contributed, revealed how two of the most powerful yet insolvent bankers lent each other monies their banks did not have – a revelation that would have guaranteed them long prison sentences in the United States or Britain. But this was Greece, a country where ten or twenty families ruled with impunity.

Proof of their impunity hit home in the early hours of 13 November 2011. Nikola, Danaë's seventeen-year-old son, had been out on the town with friends. Athens is the safest city I know, but still, as we lay in bed, our cue to fall asleep was the reassuring clang of our front door closing behind him as he returned home. But on that Saturday night someone had other plans.

Soon after Nikola's return, I let myself drift off into Morpheus' arms, Danaë already fast asleep beside me. But then the landline rang. Anxiously, I ran to get the phone before it woke her. An uncannily soft male voice asked: 'Mr Varoufakis?' Tentatively, I said: 'Yes, who is this?' 'We are very glad to see that your boy has returned,' continued the voice. 'He had a great time, it seemed to us, in Psyrri. He then made his way back along Metropolis Street, taking a detour along Hadrian Road, arriving home via Byron Street.'

Ignoring the chill running down my spine, I shouted into the phone: 'Who the hell are you? What do you want?' His answer, more of a missive in fact, was icy cool: if I wanted Nikola to continue to return home, I had better stop talking about the banks and, in particular, about one of the two, which he mentioned by name, in that Reuters article. My passage from armchair theorist to something quite different was now complete. Nonetheless, it was one thing to risk our lives in Ethiopian minefields or on Kashmiri mountains, and quite another to endanger Danaë's teenage son in Athens.

That Sunday morning, as Danaë sipped her morning coffee on the veranda overlooking our courtyard, I agonised over how to tell her what had happened in the middle of the night. And like a sandcastle that the tide makes swift work of, the momentary fantasy that I could have kept it from her, handling it on my own, was swept away. So, I told her matter-of-factly. And then I waited as she mulled it over. When she was ready, Danaë confined herself to an ultimatum: 'Either you get into politics, to protect us, or we leave the country.' Within weeks, we were moving to Austin, Texas.

61. In the eye of the storm

Life in Austin was easy, perhaps too easy. Barack Obama had just won his second term, but, from our apartment overlooking the Colorado River, Danaë sensed the gathering clouds on the Atlantic's other side, which impeded her innate creative process. As she watched me spend our balmy Texan nights either appearing on European television networks via Skype or scribbling articles like a madman, she sensed it would not be long before we were drawn back into the storm.

In late November 2014, I was due to travel to Firenze to address yet another conference on Europe's appalling mess. On my way there, I received a call from Athens. The young man who would, according to the latest polls, become Greece's next prime minister wanted to talk to me urgently, and in private. Could I make a detour on my way back to Austin? Assuming he needed clarification on one of the many policy recommendations I had issued over the last four years, I agreed.

From Athens Airport I went to his apartment, where he waited with two of his closest associates. Over several hours I explained in detail the coup d'état that the European Union's financial and political personnel were preparing against him, were he to win office on behalf of Syriza, the radical-left party. Then, in a second instalment, I outlined a plan for deterring that coup d'état. If he and his team needed me to offer a helping hand with advice, analysis or speech-writing, I would make myself available. Grinning, the young prime minister-in-waiting shocked me with his next sentence: 'Because we agree with your analysis and plan, but do not feel confident to implement it,' he said, 'we want *you* to implement it. As my finance minister.'

My head was ringing with alarm bells. Being the finance minister of a bankrupt government is bad enough. Being the finance minister of a bankrupt country using the euro currency was worse by many orders of magnitude. For, in the so-called eurozone, the only person who can sign a loan agreement is not the prime minister, not the president, not God herself – but the hapless finance minister! And given that I would accept the position only on condition that I never take out another unpayable loan, I would be loathed and pressurised, harassed and bullied, by every bankster, oligarch, media magnate – the whole established order that expected little Greece to keep taking one toxic credit card after the next. It was, literally, an electric chair and a rifle range target wrapped up into one ministerial position.

To stall, I presented them with a litany of reasons why I was the wrong person for the job. When that didn't stick, I added a series of tough conditions, ranging from what defensive weapons we would use against the European Central Bank to my winning a parliamentary seat in the highly competitive Athenian constituency which included Naiadon Street. They agreed with every one of them. It was already four in the morning, and I had a plane to catch back to Austin. But they needed an answer. I stepped outside to ring Danaë. After pausing to think, she gave me her verdict.

The risks of accepting were tremendous, she concurred. I was exploitable because I was expendable. If I were to bring a decent deal back from Brussels, she predicted, they would claim the credit. If not, I would get the blame. 'I know this,' I said. 'So, what do I tell them?' 'This is an offer you *can* refuse,' Danaë prefaced her counsel. 'But is this an offer Eleni would want you to refuse?'

'It is an offer that Trisevgeni would have wanted me to run a mile from,' I interjected. Ignoring me she cut to the chase: 'Look, it's your decision. But, from where I am standing, even though they most probably want you as their sacrificial lamb, their scapegoat, I don't want you, when we are in our nineties, to be weighed down by the unanswerable question: "What if I had had a go?"'

Having seen me so livid for so long with the response to 2008 – a lethal combination of socialism for bankers and harsh austerity for their victims – Danaë knew that if there was even a tiny probability I could terminate these policies in any country, I would forever regret not trying to. Besides, Greece was not *any* country. It was a special case – and not just because we hailed from there. For some strange reason, Greece was ground zero both for the Cold War, which began in Athens in December 1944, and now for the European financial disaster. Just as Truman had decided to hone his famous doctrine on the battlefields of our civil war, European and American authorities had turned Greece into the guinea pig on which they tried out their nasty experiments, turning a small country that should be insignificant in the larger scheme of things into a globally significant calamity.

And then there was the spectre of fascism. If we could stop the rot in Greece, by breaking the vicious cycle of debt-austerity-depression-poverty-debt that warmed up the serpent's eggs, we might inspire others to break it across the West. Danaë second-guessed my instinct that it was worth a shot.

We hid behind the consolation that we had a year and a half to prepare before the scheduled Greek elections. Except that we did not. A month later a snap general election caught us unawares in Sydney, where we were visiting Xenia for the New Year holiday. In a panic, we flew to wintry Athens in our summer clothes to join in a frantic three-week election campaign leading to 25 January 2015. The morning after our emphatic election victory,

DANAË

Danaë flew back to Austin to pack up our life and return to join me in Athens. At the same time, on a different plane, having been anointed finance minister of the most bankrupt country, I was heading for Paris, London, Brussels, Frankfurt and Berlin to fight my first battles. Our six-month immersion in a soul-shattering maelstrom had begun.

62. Holding on

How our story of these six months is told is a feminist issue. There is the male finance minister clashing with the Goliaths of the German Treasury, the European Central Bank, the International Monetary Fund, the European Commission and, of course, the banksters. And there is Danaë, the artist-activist who never took a back seat in her life, never conceded primacy to father, husband or lover, but whom the media were determined to reduce to a glamorous, blonde, haute bourgeoise trophy wife of a controversial motorcycle-riding minister. Her reaction was pure gold.

She ignored the media. Instead, she sought to reclaim her agency as a practising artist. When I would arrive home in the early hours desperate for sleep, Danaë would keep me awake and insist that I recount what had happened that day while she filmed me on her phone. Those recordings were her secret project, her art as politics-by-other-means, her bulwark against the countless hours of trashy television programs distorting who she was. Months later, watching her dozens of clips helped me grasp, for the first time, what had really happened. No written diary, no Netflix or BBC documentary could have done it better.

At the beginning of my six months in office, from day one, the pressure to sign on the dotted line was phenomenal. As was the speculation – by the press, enemies, colleagues and even close friends – as to whether I would withstand it or cave. Danaë knew, of course. She knew that the pressure I was under felt like a summer's breeze compared to the pressure Yorgo had resisted when, time and again, he refused to sign – not even when a distraught Anna begged him all night in that hotel room, with a naval ship waiting on the quayside ready to take him to Makronisos.

The question that was truly exercising Danaë was a different one: would the prime minister support me to the bitter end? If he would, we stood a chance. It was around April that Danaë knew the answer: no, he would not. The prime minister, it became clear to her, was trying to surrender – which meant he had to get rid of me. His problem, however, was that my uncompromising stance towards the country's hated creditors lent *him* enormous popularity. Getting rid of me, while I remained popular, would be an act of political self-harm. Thus, his team embarked on a character assassination of a thousand leaks which, of course, the international media lapped up and reinforced, also taking potshots at Danaë for good measure.

Entire political science and media studies courses should be dedicated to the dexterity with which the Greek media covered the tracks of their owners, who needed someone, anyone, to replace me as finance minister, to take more loans on their behalf and charge them to the 'little' people. Exactly as Donald Trump mobilised disgruntled blue-collar workers against Wall Street, before appointing the CEO of Goldman Sachs or some hedge fund raider as US Treasury Secretary, so did the Greek oligarchs even try to mobilise the left against me. They portrayed me as the US-backed stooge with an ultra-rich industrialist wife – a turncoat who talked the talk but whose real mission was to sign the loan agreement and sell the Greek people down the river.

One evening, we were dining at a favourite off-beat restaurant. As we were finishing our meal, seated with my back to the entrance, I heard them before I saw them. Three hooded men, with two dozen more waiting outside, burst into the restaurant shouting abuse and smashing beer bottles on the floor. Ordering the other patrons to leave, the attackers approached our table, brandishing broken bottles and shouting: 'You won't leave here alive tonight, you fucking bankers' lackey.' As they moved to strike me, Danaë came between us and jumped on me, her back towards them, her hands protecting the top of my head. She had literally turned herself into a human shield. I tried to push her away but her hold was too strong. The assailants couldn't hit me without hitting her too. After several blows that landed on Danaë, they were embarrassed enough to relent.

Back in our apartment, I asked Danaë the question that would consume us every day and night for another two months: 'When should I resign? Today? Tomorrow?' My resignation would trigger a sudden collapse of the majority's morale. As long as there was a chance that the prime minister would not surrender, Danaë was adamant I lacked the moral right to resign. So, I stayed on until the night of 5 July 2015, the day of the glorious referendum in which 62 per cent of the electorate instructed us to fight on – the very same night the prime minister told me he was surrendering.

That night, walking out of the prime minister's residence, Danaë and I found ourselves in a scene that would have given the ancient Athenian tragedians a run for their money. It was well after midnight but the streets were jam-packed with crowds wildly celebrating the referendum result. Dignity had been restored to a humiliated people. Recognising us, they hugged us, lifted us up and demanded that we celebrate with them.

How could we tell them the truth, that a palace coup to overthrow them, the people, was under way behind closed doors, orchestrated by their prime minister? That at dawn their brave 'no' would morph into an unseemly 'yes'? That Danaë and I were rushing back to our apartment so that I could compose my letter of resignation? That shortly we would be battening down the hatches, waiting for the wrath of the bankers and the oligarchs to come crashing down on us like a ton of bricks – especially now that we no longer enjoyed ministerial protection? That soon our own comrades in government – just as Danaë had predicted – would blame me for their capitulation, and throw us both to the wolves?

Holding hands, we entered our apartment. After my resignation letter had been emailed, and Danaë's last video interview of me was completed, we vowed to keep on holding on.

63. The incomplete purge

Growing up at 102 Naiadon Street, I had fallen into the presumption that time was on women's side. Anna convinced me that women's steady empowerment could not be denied. Eleni and Trisevgeni reinforced it: having begun life in a state of virtual gender apartheid, they won freedoms their mothers could never have imagined. Georgia, on the other hand, demonstrated that the path to women's liberation was neither linear nor safe.

Like Anna, everyone who looked at Danaë saw a privileged woman upon whom society was bestowing more opportunities. But anyone who cared to look more carefully would have noticed something else: a deepening loneliness caused by the realisation that privileges were bought at the expense of the majority of women. Yorgo had felt the double burden of being the only man who knew this about Anna, and of contributing to her isolation through his politics. It was the same with me. I was the only man who knew of Danaë's isolation from her privileged social milieu, and I was contributing to it through my political choices.

As expected, my resignation caused an immediate backlash. The art collectors abruptly disappeared. The socialites who once couldn't get enough of her now recoiled. Funding bodies that had supported projects such as *Breathe*, *The River of Life* and *CUT – 7 dividing lines* closed their doors. Stalin would have been proud of those who silently and efficiently attempted to purge her. Through gritted teeth, Danaë carried on.

Purges are never complete, of course, until they reach the very core of the dissident's family. Although Danaë's parents remained supportive, many of her circle denounced us in McCarthyite fashion – in other words, mostly out of fear that if they failed to denounce us, they might be denounced themselves. Again, Danaë was unperturbed – except when the purge affected her children. Torn between us and the rest of their circle, her children were forced to pick sides against their will – a situation that no child should have to face. It was as if, through them, her circle was forcing Danaë to pick a side: her children's or mine. Painfully, methodically, she succeeded in remaining loyal to her children without giving in to the blackmail.

Intriguingly, it wasn't just the opposite side that was prone to belittling Danaë. Six months after my resignation, the two of us, together with thousands of activists across Europe, embarked on a crazy project to keep alive the idea of progressive internationalism by meeting in Berlin, at the symbolic Volksbühne theatre, to launch DiEM25 – a transnational, pan-European movement. It was all inspiring, uplifting stuff. Except for one thing: the shocking ease with which too many radical progressives treated Danaë as my appendage.

In June 2019, at the Venice Film Festival, we attended the premiere of *Adults in the Room*, a film based on my published memoir of those six months in government directed by Costa-Gavras – our dear friend, the brilliant Oscar-winning director of *Z* and *Missing*. Deeply grateful that our childhood idol had chosen our story as the basis for his latest film, it was impossible not to notice how Danaë's character – played by Valeria Golino – was underdeveloped. Anna's and Eleni's work was nowhere near done.

Danaë allowed none of this to keep her down. She travelled to South Africa, where she transformed a lake's waters into an elegiac artwork;* to Western Australia, where she created a poignant land artwork tracing underground streams of water that only the Wardandi women continued to dream of;† to Elefsis, where she turned a decaying factory into a massive installation in honour of Persephone and the refugees who had been arriving there since the 1920s.‡

In the summer of 2019, when DiEM25 decided to field candidates in national elections, Danaë stood in a constituency where she had no chance of winning a seat. However, by helping to attract votes to our party nationwide, we won nine other parliamentary seats. Thus I re-entered Greece's parliament to continue where I had left off: naming and shaming the oligarchs who had, in the meantime, fully regained their exorbitant powers to plunder an utterly exhausted population.

---

* *Concentric* (Nirox Sculpture Park, South Africa, 2019), a kinetic water installation. It turns a lake in the Kkatlhamphi region into a moving sculpture by utilising an underwater device generating perpetual concentric ripples.

† *Water Traces – Making the Invisible Visible*, a land art installation on the land of the Wardandi people, supported and produced by 'The Farm Margaret River', Margaret River, Western Australia, 2023.

‡ *Upon the Earth Under the Clouds* (Elefsis, 2017).

64. Hypatia's daughters

Yorgo passed in September 2021. It was a beautiful death at the ripe age of ninety-six, free of anguish and only a couple of hours after he had communicated to us everything he needed to. A few days later Danaë showed me something a stranger, a taxi driver, had posted on Facebook, tagging me:

> When I heard of your father's passing, I felt the need to tell you what he once did. It was a Sunday morning when he hailed my cab and asked me to take him to the Paleo Phaliro cemetery. On the way, he asked me to stop at a florist's where he bought two bouquets of roses. Outside the cemetery he asked me politely to wait a few minutes while he visited his wife, Eleni. 'Of course,' I answered. He took one bouquet and disappeared into the cemetery, leaving the second bouquet on my cab's back seat. Fifteen minutes later he returned and asked me to take him to 102 Naiadon Street. When we got there, he paid me the fare but also gave me the second bouquet of roses, saying: 'These are to give to your partner. Respect and love her, always.' As he walked away, I was lost for words.

One evening, in March 2023, after a long day in parliament, we found ourselves in the same restaurant where Danaë had shielded me in 2015. As if in a nightmarish déjà vu, seven assailants burst in with bad intent. Only these were professional thugs who surgically shattered my nose and eye socket in front of Danaë, who this time had no opportunity to leap in front of me. The day before,

I had addressed parliament to expose how two public children's hospitals had been handed over, for free, to the foundation of a prominent oligarch whose clan had a reputation for thuggery. Then again, our parliamentary team had exposed other oligarchs equally capable of wanting to teach me a lesson. It didn't matter who was behind the brutes. What mattered was that Danaë was left to wrestle with the memory of her helplessness – and I with the vulnerability in her eyes.

Several months beforehand, I had been contacted by BBC Radio 4 to lead an episode of their *Great Lives* program, a favourite of mine. Would I kindly choose the historical figure to whose life would be dedicated that week's episode? Without a second thought, I picked Hypatia.

Like Anna, Hypatia was a Greek woman living in Egypt, striving against the patriarchy and determined to bring people of different creeds and ethnicities together. Of all the thinkers Anna could have introduced Yorgo to, Hypatia was the only one she chose. Eleni had done the same to me when I was a kid – her way of honouring her resolve to complete her degree in the School of Chemistry. Danaë's own Egyptian legacy was the monumental *Desert Breath* installation she created in 1997 in the eastern Sahara between the Nile and the Red Sea as part of an art team of three young women.*

Land art is the domain of mostly male, white artists who treat the land, the deserts in particular, like blank canvases, reflecting

---

* *Desert Breath* was conceived and constructed in the eastern Sahara Desert bordering the Red Sea in El Gouna, Egypt, by the D.A.ST. Arteam, comprising Danaë Stratou, Alexandra Stratou and Stella Konstantinidis. Having shifted eight thousand cubic metres of sand, it consists of conical volumes which form two interlocking spirals that move out of their common centre with a phase difference of 180 degrees. The centre is a thirty-metre-diameter vessel formed with a W-shaped cross-section and filled with water to its rim. The work was completed in 1997.

the settler tendency to declare every distant land they desire *terra nullius*, devoid of people or culture. Not so Danaë. To her, the desert she and her two collaborators chose was the opposite of a blank canvas. It was her place but also the place that belonged to the nearby Bedouin tribe who took the three young women under their wing, blessing their creation every step of the way. It was as if Danaë and her two collaborators, unknowingly, were treating that soil with the respect, the love, that Hypatia would have expected. The result was a land artwork situated in an indigenous history that gave birth to a shared, intercontinental breath.

One of Hypatia's major scientific achievements was to work out the algebraic formulae that define the surface area and volume of cones. *Desert Breath* consisted of more than one hundred and eighty cones, arranged along two interlocking spirals and ranging in height from a few centimetres to three metres. It was as if the spirit of Hypatia lay behind *Desert Breath*.

Of course, neither Anna nor Danaë was dragged out of the Great Library of Alexandria to be torn to pieces by scores of misogynist fanatics. But they came as close to that fate as the modern era allowed. Not unlike Hypatia, their peers saw them as unruly. They were scorned for betraying their class and not knowing their station as women. Anna was hounded for siding with the victims of her own community, and Danaë for turning against her own class as she pursued art-as-politics.

Eleni once told me that, in their respective battles, she had a secret power that Anna lacked: Yorgo. Anna's boy, Eleni's staunchest ally. Danaë never needed a male ally. Still, I'd like to think that, before we met, she longed for one, one who could draw upon the legacy of Eleni, Anna, Trisevgeni and Georgia to say to her: 'Come on, raise your soul, my girl.'

Epilogue

On the eve of Yorgo's funeral I began writing my previous book, *Technofeudalism*, as an imagined dialogue with him. When I finished it, I felt a void. Where was Eleni? Was she not the person I would call every day, from wherever I happened to be in the world, to debate politics? Eleni was my political mentor. And Anna had been Yorgo's mentor. Why were they absent?

So, no sooner had I finished *Technofeudalism* than I decided to try to make amends. I wanted it to be different from *Talking to My Daughter*, my 2017 book addressed to the then twelve-year-old Xenia. Her one question may have inspired that brief history of capitalism, but she was largely absent from the book. This time, I wanted to recover the voices of the women who taught me the most important lessons for the here and now: how to resist fascism, authoritarianism and the male chauvinist within.

However, did I have the *right* to write up their lives? Should a man appropriate a woman's voice? I was the last person who remembered Eleni's, Anna's and Trisevgeni's lives fully enough to attempt a reconstruction. The choice I faced was between abandoning them to oblivion or trying to revive their voices as best I could. I chose the latter – not only to salvage *herstory*, their story, but to tell *our* story, *my* story too.

There is no question that feminism needs to be embodied in a woman's body – to be experienced through womanhood. But attempting to put myself in the position of the women who shaped me felt not only legitimate, but actually important. So

EPILOGUE

I began to write with a zeal underpinned by the conviction that how a man tells a woman's story, while sincerely trying not to appropriate it, is a feminist, indeed a humanist issue. It also helps, I would like to think, detoxify the way we men communicate.

Anna was both the hardest and the easiest to write. It was the hardest because it was about a woman I had never met in a country, Egypt, I do not know. But it was also the easiest, because Yorgo's incessant reminiscing made it feel as if I had been a fly on the wall during his formative two decades in Cairo. I also had access to Anna's photographs, diaries and notebooks. Additionally, after Yorgo died, my sister and I discovered on the hard drive of his laptop an eighty-six-page document entitled 'My Life' – largely devoted to his life with Anna.

By then, it was already 2024 – a little over a century since Anna had stepped out of her boarding school, braving the khamsin and its whirling dust as she made her way to Ramses Railway Station and into adulthood. Back then, fascism was already beginning to sweep everything in its path. A century later, an eerily similar tsunami was gathering pace worldwide. That's when I knew I needed Georgia, a cipher for the manosphere's dark entanglement with fascism.

Unlike *Anna*, *Eleni* and *Trisevgeni*, stories that would have been lost forever if I did not write them down, Georgia was different. She was the grandmother of Margarita, the mother of our daughter Xenia. I hope Margarita also writes her grandmother's story one day, not least because she is an accomplished academic historian. Nevertheless, Georgia's story, and how we unearthed it, is also mine – one that left an ineradicable mark on my own grasp of our present moment in history.

By this point, I realised that, in a way, I was assembling not only an intimate memoir of five women but also a history of a

EPILOGUE

displaced twentieth century. To close that history's circle, and show how it paved the ground to today's discontents, prospects and hopes, I needed Danaë.

Writing *Danaë* also showed me how hard it is to describe the world through the eyes of a partner. Danaë was on hand to correct and discipline me, and when she read my first draft, she frowned at my interpretations of her art, her intentions, even her actions refracted through my gaze. It was a gift, that friction – a reflection of the wild beauty of different perspectives on shared experiences, a reminder that no two hearts beat the same history.

Besides Danaë, our great friend artist and activist Jonas Staal also read my original manuscript and offered meticulous, nuanced, touching and hugely helpful comments and ideas. Wendy Strothman and Lauren MacLeod, my literary agents, helped me knock the early draft into shape while Will Hammond and Alice Skinner, my editors at Penguin, shepherded the manuscript home with love and delicate care. I thank them all for their copious tenderness and critical support. I thank them also for it was with their help that the preceding pages may – I hope and pray – appeal, as part of their ongoing story, to my sister Trisevgeni, my daughter Xenia, her mother Margarita, her mother Maria, to all the women who read this book.

❆ ❆ ❆ ❆

At the very end, I sat back and reflected on the wider significance of Eleni, Anna, Trisevgeni, Georgia and Danaë. Not so much for me, but for younger people making their way against the grain of an authoritarian surge which encourages them to the paths of least resistance terminating in various versions of dystopia. The five women in this book, I concluded, shared one rare virtue: an unwillingness to be deterred by personal hardship from following the paths of most resistance, the paths along which hope springs for a world lacking empirical grounds for optimism.